# Women Leaders
and the Church

D1627193

## 3 Crucial Questions
Grant R. Osborne and Richard J. Jones, Jr., editors

# Women Leaders and the Church

## 3 Crucial Questions

# Linda L. Belleville

Baker Books

A Division of Baker Book House Co
Grand Rapids, Michigan 49516

© 2000 by Linda L. Belleville

Published by Baker Books
a division of Baker Book House Company
P.O. Box 6287, Grand Rapids, MI 49516-6287

Printed in the United States of America

**Library of Congress Cataloging-in-Publication Data**

Belleville, Linda L.
    Women leaders and the church : 3 crucial questions / Linda L. Belleville.
        p.        cm. — (3 crucial questions)
    Includes bibliographical references and index.
    ISBN 0-8010-5351-X (pbk.)
    1. Women clergy—Biblical teaching. 2. Women—Biblical teaching.
3. Leadership—Biblical teaching. 4. Women in Christianity—History—Early
church, ca. 30–600. I. Title. II. Series.
BV676.B37        1999
262'.1'082—dc21                                                            99-051608

For information about academic books, resources for Christian leaders, and all new
releases available from Baker Book House, visit our web site:

http://www.bakerbooks.com

In memory of my mother
Sophie Mae Stipek (1912–1999)

# *Contents*

# Editors' Preface

The books in the 3 Crucial Questions series are the published form of the 3 Crucial Questions Seminars, which are sponsored by Bridge Ministries of Detroit, Michigan. The seminars and books are designed to greatly enhance your Christian walk. The following comments will help you appreciate the unique features of the book series.

The 3 Crucial Questions series is based on two fundamental observations. First, there are crucial questions related to the Christian faith for which imperfect Christians seem to have no final answers. Christians living in eternal glory may know fully even as they are known by God, but now we know only in part (1 Cor. 13:12). Therefore, we must ever return to such questions with the prayer that God the Holy Spirit will continue to lead us nearer to "the truth, the whole truth, and nothing but the truth." While recognizing their own frailty, the authors contributing to this series pray that they are thus led.

Second, each Christian generation partly affirms its solidarity with the Christian past by reaffirming "the faith which was once delivered unto the saints" (Jude 3 KJV). Such an affirmation is usually attempted by religious scholars who are notorious for talking only to themselves or by nonexperts whose grasp of the faith lacks depth of insight. Both situations are unfortunate, but we feel that our team of contributing authors is well prepared to avoid them. Each author is a competent, Christian scholar able to share tremendous learning in down-to-earth language both laity and experts can appreciate. In a word, you have in hand a book that is part of a rare series—one that is neither pedantic nor pediatric.

The topics addressed in the series have been chosen for their timelessness, interest level, and importance to Christians everywhere, and the contributing authors are committed to discussing them in a manner that promotes Christian unity. Thus, the authors discuss not only areas of disagreement among Christians but significant areas of agreement as well. Seeking peace and pursuing it as the Bible commands (1 Peter 3:11), they stress common ground on which Christians with different views may meet for wholesome dialogue and reconciliation.

The books in the series consist not merely of printed words; they consist of words by which to live. Their pages are filled not only with good information but with sound instruction in successful Christian living. For study is truly Christian only when, in addition to helping us understand our faith, it helps us to live our faith. We pray, therefore, that you will allow God to use the 3 Crucial Questions series to augment your growth in the grace and knowledge of our Lord and Savior Jesus Christ.

Grant R. Osborne
Richard J. Jones, Jr.

# *Author's Preface*

I am grateful to Richard Jones and Baker Book House for the invitation to write a volume on a topic that I have spent many years researching, teaching, thinking about, and reflecting on.

This book would not have materialized without the generous input of a number of people. I am beholden to my tutorial assistants, Ery Prasadja and Sarah Bergstrom, and to my husband, Brian, for a careful reading and cheerful correcting of various portions of the first draft. A special note of thanks is due Grant Osborne who read the manuscript with a keen eye to its strengths and weaknesses. I also wish to thank my colleagues and students at North Park Theological Seminary for their unfailing support and constant challenge to be academically rigorous and yet pastorally sensitive.

Finally, I would be remiss not to mention the Evangelical Covenant Church, who made the completion of this volume possible through a quarter's sabbatical leave.

*Soli Deo sit gloria*

# *Abbreviations*

BAGD   *A Greek-English Lexicon of the New Testament and Other Early Christian Literature,* by W. Bauer, W. F. Arndt, F. W. Gingrich, and F. W. Danker, 2d ed. (Chicago: University of Chicago Press, 1979)

BGU   *Ägyptische Urkunden aus den königlichen Museen zu Berlin: Griechische Urkunden,* 4 vols. (Berlin: Weidmann, 1895–1912)

CIG   *Corpus Inscriptionum Graecarum,* edited by August Böckh, 4 vols. (Berlin: G. Reimer, 1828–77)

CII   *Corpus Inscriptionum Iudaicarum,* edited by J. B. Frey (Rome: Pontificio istituto di archeologia cristiana, 1936)

CIJ   *Corpus of Jewish Inscriptions,* edited by J. B. Frey (New York: KTAV, 1975)

CIL   *Corpus Inscriptionum Latinarum* (Berlin: De Gruyter, 1862–1975)

CPJ   *Corpus Papyrorum Judaicarum,* 3 vols. (Cambridge, Mass.: Harvard University Press, 1957–64)

HSCP   Harvard Studies in Classical Philology

IG   *Inscriptiones Graecae* (Berlin: G. Reimer, 1873–)

IGR   *Inscriptiones Graecae ad res Romanas pertinentes,* edited by R. Cagnat et al. (Paris: E. Leroux, 1911–27)

ILS   *Inscriptiones Latinae Selectae,* edited and translated by Marcel Durry (Paris: Société d'Edition, 1950)

LSJ   *A Greek-English Lexicon,* by H. G. Liddell, R. Scott, and H. S. Jones (Oxford: Clarendon Press, 1968)

LXX   Septuagint

MM   *The Vocabulary of the Greek New Testament: Illustrated from the Papyri and other Non-Literary Sources,* by James Moulton and George Milligan (repr., Grand Rapids: Eerdmans, 1982)

MT   Masoretic Text

P. Oxy.   *The Oxyrhynchus Papyri,* edited by B. P. Grenfell, A. S. Hunt, et al., 42 vols. (London: Egypt Exploration Fund, 1898–1974)

Pleket   H. W. Pleket, *Epigraphica II: Texts on the Social History of the Greek World* (Leiden: E. J. Brill, 1969)

SEG   *Supplementum Epigraphicum Graecum,* edited by J. J. E. Hondius. Lugduni Batavorum, apud A. W. Sijthoff, 1923.

s.v.   under the word

13

The abbreviations below are used for the names of tractates in the Babylonian Talmud (indicated by a prefixed b.), Palestinian or Jerusalem Talmud (y.), Mishnah (m.), and Tosepta (t.).

| | |
|---|---|
| B. Meṣ. | Baba Meṣiʿa |
| B. Qam. | Baba Qamma |
| Ber. | Berakot |
| Giṭ. | Giṭṭin |
| Ḥag. | Ḥagiga |
| Hor. | Horayot |
| Ker. | Keritot |
| Ketub. | Ketubot |
| Meg. | Megilla |
| Menaḥ. | Menaḥot |
| Ned. | Nedarim |
| Pesaḥ. | Pesaḥim |
| Qidd. | Qiddus̆in |
| S̆ebu. | S̆ebuʿot |
| Soṭa | Soṭa |
| Sukk. | Sukka |
| Yebam. | Yebamot |
| Yoma | Yoma |

Bible translations and versions used in this manuscript include:

| | |
|---|---|
| AT | Author's Translation |
| CEV | Contemporary English Version |
| KJV | King James Version |
| JB | Jerusalem Bible |
| NAB | New American Bible |
| NASB | New American Standard Bible |
| NEB | New English Bible |
| NIV | New International Version |
| NJB | New Jerusalem Bible |
| NKJV | New King James Version |
| NLT | New Living Translation |
| Phillips | The New Testament in Modern English (J. B. Phillips) |
| REB | Revised Standard Version |
| TEV | Today's English Version |
| TLB | The Living Bible |

# *Introduction*

T hank God that I am not a woman, a slave, or a pagan." So said second-century Rabbi Judah ben Ilai (*b. Menah.* 43b; *y. Ber.* 9.1; *t. Ber.* 7[6].18). Down through the centuries, many have breathed the same sigh of relief. Good reasons existed for a rabbi to be thankful he was a man and not a woman. It was not uncommon to find Jewish theologians talking about a woman's flawed nature and limited religious capacities that prevented her from responding to a call to ministry, pursuing theological training, or taking up a leadership position in the family.

There are some within evangelicalism today who think much the same way. They feel this is the reason Jesus chose twelve men to be the future leaders of the church. It is also why Paul tells Timothy he is not permitting women "to teach or to have authority over a man" (1 Tim. 2:12). There are others, however, who believe Christ has set women free to pursue their God-given gifts in whatever leadership role or ministry capacity they desire. Jesus is lauded as a liberator of women, and Galatians 3:28 is hailed as the Magna Carta of women everywhere: "There is neither Jew nor Greek, slave nor free, male nor female, for you are all one in Christ Jesus."

The debate on the role of women in the church and in society rages fast and furiously today. It is the rare church or denomination that has not waded into the fray. Some have even split over it. In part, this is because the debate lacks any middle ground. The issues and terms are defined in such a way that one must choose either for or against women in leadership. All too often the debaters begin (and end) with contested passages such as 1 Corinthians 14:34–35 and 1 Timothy 2:11–15. Or they start with a thesis securely in hand and the biblical texts come into play only insofar as they support the central thesis.

Inevitably the debate comes down to three crucial questions:

1. In which ministries can women be involved?
2. What roles can women assume in the family and in society?
3. What, if any, positions of authority can women hold in the church?

The first question often elicits a bewildering range of opinions. Some suppose women can be involved in the whole gamut of church ministries. Others think any role labeled as *ministry* is forbidden to women. Still others believe women can be included in the ministries of the church as long as men are not involved. To begin to answer this question, we will look at the ministries of women in the pages of Scripture and at the religious roles of women in the culture at large. The latter is especially important, for while the biblical references are plentiful, they are often so brief and matter-of-factly stated that it takes a closer look at the ministry roles of women in antiquity to make sense of them.

The social impact of the feminist movement over the last few decades and the increased presence of women in the workplace make the second question a particularly vital one. Is there a place for the working mother in God's plan, or is the stay-at-home mother God's desire? Can a woman give spiritual direction to her children, or is this the father's prerogative? Can a woman provide leadership in the marriage, or is this the husband's responsibility? To start to answer such questions, we will look at the roles women played in the society of biblical times and determine the ways in which the women of the early church departed from or fell in line with them. We will also explore which of these roles are rooted in the creation order and which are tied to the conventions of a particular time and place.

The last of the three questions is the one that ultimately divides. The debate over women's roles today is in the final analysis a debate over authority. Can a woman preach God's Word? Can she teach an adult Sunday school class? Can she serve as an elder or chair a church board? Can she serve communion, baptize, usher, or lead in worship? These are the questions that end up dividing churches, friends, and even families today.

A lot depends on how we define the term *authority* and whom we believe rightfully holds it. So we will start there. Then we will examine the character of leadership in the New Testament period and determine its authoritative contours. Finally, we will explore the ways in which 1 Corinthians 14:34–35 and 1 Timothy 2:11–15 seem to limit the roles women can play in the church.

We need to begin by recognizing the limitations of the task. There is no systematic teaching in Scripture on these topics. Where teaching does occur, it is only a small piece of a larger discussion that is focused on the needs of a particular church at a particular point in time. Still, there are numerous references to women in the pages of Scripture, and these references provide a good picture of the range—if not the extent—of women's roles. There is also a good amount of material on the roles of women in the culture at large, so we are rarely left in the dark as to what is being affirmed in Scripture. While biblical teaching on these topics might have been prompted by the needs and circumstances of that day, it is easy to grasp the principles that undergird it. The challenge is how to apply them to our day and age.

# In Which Ministries Can Women Be Involved?

**I** am a woman. I have committed my life to Christ. What place of service exists for me in the church of Jesus Christ?" Many women are asking this question today, and depending on whose doors you walk through on a given Sunday morning, the answers can be as varied and bewildering as the numbers of denominations and congregations that dot the American landscape.

A woman can teach astrophysics at a Christian university, but she cannot teach an adult Sunday school class on the biblical doctrine of creation. She can work as a certified public accountant for a Christian company, but she cannot keep the church's books. A woman can be a trustee of a Christian liberal arts college, but she cannot serve on the church deacon board. She can be a chief administrator at a Christian hospital, but she cannot serve on the church council or board of elders. A woman can lead children's worship, but she cannot conduct congregational worship. She can preach the children's sermon, but she cannot preach the congregational sermon.[1] What is a woman to do? Does the Bible truly exclude women from serving the church in these and other capacities?

It is the rare denomination that has not struggled with this issue. Some have even split over it. The Christian Reformed Church is a good example. It has debated the issue for decades, and the results have not been encouraging. In June of 1995 the Synod of the Christian Reformed Church permitted women in the denomination to serve as pastors, elders, and evangelists. Many hailed this decision as a major victory for evangelical women. Yet only the previous year, the denomination had resolved that the clear teaching of Scripture prohibits women from serving in these capacities.[2] Which decision was truly biblically based and Spirit led? How is a person to respond to such mixed signals? The impact on the Christian Reformed Church has been devastating. Families and friends have divided over the issue, prominent members have voiced their opinions in the local newspaper, and entire congregations have left the denomination.

One of the main difficulties with controversial topics such as this one is that what may be clear biblical teaching to one person is quite the opposite to another. Another difficulty is the starting point. Debated passages such as 1 Corinthians 14:34–35 and 1 Timothy 2:11–15 are typically where the discussion begins and ends. In addition, most come with an already determined position and marshall only those biblical texts that support it.

A more profitable approach is to start with the objective data. What ministry roles *did* women assume in the first century? Once we answer this question, then we will have a framework within which to tackle the more difficult passages.

## *The Ministries of Women in Antiquity*

Looking at the ministries of women in antiquity is especially important. Biblical references to women are numerous, but they are typically brief and to the point. Jewish and Greco-Roman society serves then to shed much light on some otherwise terse texts. This is especially true of Judaism, so we will start by looking at the religious roles of women in the culture of the day.

### *Religious Roles in Judaism*

It is fair to say that religious involvement of Jewish women was more limited than that of Greek (with the exclusion of Athens) or Roman women. This was partly due to the fact that the formal education of Jewish girls stopped at the marriageable age of twelve—the age when Jewish boys began to pursue serious theological training and education. It also has to do with the fact that it was in the domestic, rather than the public, realm that Jewish women were expected to excel.

Even so, where a Jewish woman lived pretty much determined her ministry opportunities. For Jewish women living in Palestine, these opportunities were limited. But for women living outside of Palestine, the ministry options were greater. In fact, synagogue records, burial markers, inscriptions, and works of art show that a surprising number of Jewish women played significant roles in their local congregation.[3]

This had to do to a great extent with the standing of women in the eyes of Mosaic law. Although Jewish women did not receive the covenant sign of circumcision, women and men were considered equal members of the covenant people of Israel. Women were subject to all the prohibitions and obligations of the law and fully bore the consequences of disobedience, including the death penalty. (See, for example, Lev. 19:2—"Speak to the entire assembly of Israel"; compare Deut. 27:1–28.) The Sabbath laws, tithing, and celebrating the three annual festivals were the duty of both women and men (e.g., Exod. 22–23; Deut. 14–16; 1 Sam. 1:1–8).[4]

It was actually not until the late first century A.D. that legislation restricting women's societal roles (e.g., bearing witness in a court of law, Josephus, *Jewish Antiquities* 4.8.15 §219;[5] oath taking, *m. Shebu.* 4.1) and limiting their religious duties (e.g., *m. Ber.* 3.3; *Hag.* 1.1; *Sukk.* 2.8) began to appear.[6] This undoubtedly was a reaction to the rapidly developing freedoms of women in Hellenistic and Roman times.[7] Yet sweeping generalizations are commonly made about women that have no basis in first-century realities. For example, it is not uncommon to hear modern scholars state categorically that Jewish women were forbidden to teach. Yet one is hard-pressed to find first-century texts that support such a claim.

Even among rabbis after the first century, attitudes toward women varied. One rabbi, for example, states that any man who would give his daughter a knowledge of the Law teaches her lechery (*m. Sota* 3.4), while another rabbi credits the redemption of God's people from Egypt to the righteousness of the women of Israel (*b. Sota* 11b).[8]

The same variation is reflected among first-century Jewish authors. For instance, Philo (a Jewish theologian and contemporary of Jesus) claimed that a woman is more accustomed to be deceived than a man. Her mind is more effeminate, so that through her softness she easily yields and is readily caught by the persuasions of falsehood (*Questions and Answers on Genesis* 1.33). On the other hand, the slightly earlier author of the Book of Judith lifted up a woman as the model of scrupulous devotion to the Mosaic law.

Attitudes, however, do not automatically equate with actual roles. Nor do the attitudes of one author necessarily reflect the attitudes of society as a whole. So it is important to keep the two separate.

### WOMEN AND WORSHIP

Corporate worship and instruction in the law were incumbent on all Israelites. Women were no exception. Moses commanded, "Assemble the people—men, women and children, and the aliens living in your towns—so that they can listen and learn to fear the LORD your God and follow carefully all the words of this law" (Deut. 31:12; compare Josephus, *Jewish Antiquities* 14.10.24 §260).

In Jesus' day, women were faithful synagogue attenders. Their presence is frequently noted by the New Testament authors. It was the custom of Jesus' mother and sisters to attend (Matt. 13:55–56; Mark 6:3). There were also many women who heard Paul preach in their local synagogue and responded favorably to the gospel message (Acts 16:13–15; 17:4). Before his conversion, Paul even went to the synagogues in Damascus expecting to extradite women who had fled there after Stephen was stoned (Acts 7:60–8:3; 9:2).

It is sometimes said that women were segregated from the men during the worship service (either in a women's gallery or behind a screen) and, therefore, could play no active role in the worship service.[9] Surprisingly, there is no evidence for this. Archaeological digs have uncovered side rooms in some of the synagogues, but there is no indication that these rooms were used to segregate the women.[10] Nor are there any rabbinic passages that mandate or refer to separate seating as a regular practice.

Luke notes that there were Jewish women of high standing among those who heard Paul preach in the synagogues of Asia Minor and Greece (Acts 16:13–14; 17:4; 18:2). What roles did they play? Technically, women were qualified to function in virtually every way men functioned. This applied as well in post–New Testament times. *T. Meg.* 3.11 states: "All are qualified to be among the seven [who read the Torah in the synagogue on sabbath mornings], even a woman or a minor." Qualified and encouraged, however, can often be two different things. This is as true today as it was in the A.D. first century. The same rabbi goes on to express his personal opinion that a woman should not be allowed to come forward to read the Scripture in public.

In general, one can say that the farther removed from Jerusalem, the more Jewish women were encouraged to assume leadership roles. Yet even in the most conservative Jewish circles, there were exceptions. While the rabbis exempted women from various religious obligations—in part out of consideration for duties in the home—there were some women who outdid their male counterparts in observing the law and others who were acknowledged for their piety. Hannah's prayer in 1 Samuel 1:11, for example, is lifted up as one from which many important laws concerning prayer can be derived (*b. Ber.* 31a–b). Beruriah's (daughter of Rabbi Hananiah ben Tardion) knowledge of the Torah is said to have exceeded that of the most learned rabbis of her time.[11] These and other examples show that women could and did explode gender stereotypes and gain peer recognition from their male counterparts regardless of their geographical location.

## WOMEN AND THEIR RELIGIOUS ROLES

A close look at the ancient sources shows the wide-ranging leadership roles Jewish women played in their local communities and synagogues. Synagogue inscriptions and burial markers are the most helpful sources of information on women's religious roles that we have. Five formal roles are routinely noted, all of which belie the notion that Jewish women were not involved in the public arena. Jewish women are singled out for their roles as donors, heads of synagogues, elders, priestesses, and mothers of the synagogue.

### Donors

Tation . . . having erected the assembly hall and the enclosure of an open courtyard with her own funds. . . . The synagogue of the Jews honored Tation . . . with a golden crown and the privilege of sitting in the seat of honor. (*CII* 738)

Jewish women took an active financial interest in their local synagogue. This was especially the case in Asia Minor. The woman mentioned above underwrote the building of a synagogue and the enclosure of its courtyard (Phocea, Ionia; *CII* 738). Another woman called Theopempte funded a chancel screen post (Myndos, Caria; *CII* 756). A third woman named Julia Severa donated a number of the murals, reinforced the windows, and made some of the ornamentation (Akmonia, Phrygia; *CII* 766). Still another woman named Capitolina paid for the entire dais and stone facing of the stairs in her synagogue (Tralles, Caria; *CII* 756).

Jewish women were financially active in other parts of the Roman Empire. Juliana paved her synagogue with mosaic in Hammam Lif, Africa (Erwin Goodenough, *Jewish Symbols in the Greco-Roman Period,* 13 vols. Bollingen Series 37. Princeton, N.J.: Princeton University Press, 1953–68.). Anatolia donated a day's wages for the honor of her synagogue in Hammat Gader, Palestine (*CII* 858). Alexandra, Ambrosia, Domnina, Eupithis, Diogenis, Saprikia, and Colonis all contributed toward the mosaic floor of their synagogue in Apamea, Syria (about one hundred miles north of Damascus; *CII* 806–11; 816). In fact, nine of nineteen recorded donations at Apamea, Syria, were from women.[12]

The geography of these inscriptions is to be noted. It shows that there were Jewish women of independent means in a wide range of locations

who handled their finances and disposed of their properties as they saw
fit.[13] These materials also demonstrate that women contributed funds in
ways that made them pillars of their communities. A number of these
women were recognized in the highest possible way for their financial
contributions. Tation was honored with a golden crown and the privilege of sitting in the seat of honor. Julia Severa received a gilded shield.
The rest were memorialized in one way or another.

Given this background, it is not at all surprising to find women in the
New Testament recognized in similar fashion (e.g., Acts 12:12; 16:14–15;
Rom. 16:1–2; Col. 4:15). What is surprising is that *only* women are mentioned as the financial backers of the two key movers and shakers of
Christianity—Jesus and Paul. In the case of Jesus, Luke notes that as
Jesus and the Twelve traveled from place to place preaching the gospel,
a group of women accompanied them "helping to support them out of
their own means" (Luke 8:3). The inclusion of women among Jesus'
traveling coterie shows they were permitted to make the same radical
commitment in following Jesus as the Twelve and others did.

Women are also singled out in equal numbers to men for their contribution of personal resources to local congregations (Acts 4:34–5:1;
Rom. 16:3–5, 23; Philem. 1–2). Two women, Mary in Jerusalem (Acts
12:12) and Nympha in Colossae (Col. 4:15), are mentioned as having
sufficient financial means to own their own homes, which they in turn
offered as meeting places for the local body of believers. A third woman,
Lydia—a businesswoman from Thyatira—opened her home in Philippi
to Paul as a base of operations (Acts 16:14–15). This gesture becomes
especially significant when it is remembered that the Philippian church
is the only one from which Paul says he accepted financial support (Phil.
4:10–19; cf. 1 Cor. 9:15–18 and 1 Thess. 2:9).

### Heads of Synagogues

Rufina, a Jewess synagogue ruler *[archesynagōgos]*, built this tomb for her
freed slaves and the slaves raised in her household. No one else has a
right to bury anyone here. ([2d century, Smyrna, Asia Minor]; *CII* 741;
*IGR* IV.1452)

Four Jewish women (that we know of) served as the chief executive
officer of their synagogue: Rufina of Smyrna in Asia Minor (above), Peri-
steria of Thebes in Thessaly (a city in Greece; *CII* 696b), Theopempte
of Myndos in Asia Minor (a little distance from Ephesus; *CII* 756), and
Sophia of Gortyn in south-central Crete (*CII* 731C). To be named the
head of a synagogue was, of course, a distinct privilege. *B. Pesah.* 49b

ranks the leadership positions in the synagogue as first scholars, second "great ones of the congregation," and third synagogue ruler.

The synagogue ruler, among other things, was responsible for the building and its upkeep.[14] This required a fair amount of capital. So it is not surprising that synagogue ruler and donor are frequently linked in the inscriptions of the day. In all probability, synagogue rulers were the heads of the monied families in the congregation. Mention in Acts 18:8 of "the entire household" of Crispus the Corinthian synagogue ruler is suggestive of the same.

The synagogue ruler planned and led the worship service (including who would do what and when).[15] At Pisidian Antioch it was they (apparently large synagogues had more than one) who invited Paul to give the sermon. Luke reports, "After the reading from the Law and the Prophets, the synagogue rulers sent word to them [Paul and Barnabas], saying, 'Brothers, if you have a message of encouragement for the people, please speak'" (Acts 13:15).

From Luke 13:10–17 it would appear that the synagogue ruler was also responsible for keeping the congregation faithful to the law. Indignant because Jesus had healed on the Sabbath, the head of one of the Galilean synagogues said to his congregation, "There are six days for work. So come and be healed on those days, not on the Sabbath" (v. 14).

Some have suggested that *synagogue ruler* was merely a title of honor given to women whose husbands functioned in this capacity (rather than designating an actual ministry). There is no evidence, however, that any of the leadership titles were honorific in the early centuries. Moreover, none of the women so named in these inscriptions carries the standard surname for a married woman (such as, "Deborah, . . . the wife of Lappidoth," Judg. 4:4).

### Elders

The tomb of the blessed Mazauzala, elder. She lived . . . years. Rest. God is with the holy and the righteous ones. (*SEG* 27 [1977] no. 1201)

Seven tomb inscriptions have been identified to date in which women bear the title *elder.* The geographical locations include Crete, Malta, Thrace, North Africa, and Italy.[16] The term *elder* is difficult to nail down because it can designate age and leadership capacity. But the two quite often went hand in hand, because the Jewish community was (and continues to be) one that values the wisdom and leadership skills of its elderly.

In both biblical and extrabiblical materials, the title *elder* typically appears in the plural and designates a group within the Jewish community with particular leadership functions. Elders as a distinct grouping can be traced back as far as the wilderness generation, when Moses appointed seventy "leaders and officials among the people" to assist him (Num. 11:16; cf. Exod. 24:1). Individually, they represented their tribe and acted on its behalf (Deut. 31:28; 1 Sam. 30:26; 2 Kings 23:1). Collectively, they ruled on legal matters pertaining to the welfare of the community as a whole (1 Sam. 8:4; 2 Sam. 3:17) and so were expected to have a good knowledge of Jewish law (e.g., Deut. 22:15; Josh. 20:4). Within their community they functioned as the town council and carried out their business at the city gates (e.g., Ruth 4:1–13).

In New Testament times elders formed a group in the Sanhedrin, the highest judicial and legislative body in Israel (e.g., Matt. 16:21; Mark 8:31; 14:53). It was the elders, along with the chief priests and the scribes, who questioned Jesus regarding the source of his authority (Mark 11:27). The elders were also the official representatives of the Jews to the Romans. A case in point is Luke 7:3–5 in which it is recorded that they negotiated with the Romans to build a synagogue in Capernaum.

Elders were so highly regarded in the Essene communities that they were given special seats: "This is the rule for an assembly of the congregation. . . . The priests shall sit first, and then the elders second, and all the rest of the people according to their rank" (*Rule of the Community* 6.8–9). For a woman to carry the title *elder*, then, was quite an achievement.

The primary function of an elder was that of community leader—not synagogue officer. This is not to say that the elders were not involved in their local synagogues. In fact, they were often invited to lead the congregation in prayer or read from the Scriptures, but they held no official status like that of synagogue ruler.[17] This is quite different from Christian elders, who (as we will see in chapter 3) did have official standing in the early church.

It is obvious from the surrounding language that the term *elder* does in fact designate a leadership capacity for the Jewish women so named (rather than merely age). Sophia of Gortyn is called "an elder and head of the synagogue of Kisamos on the island of Crete" (*CII* 731C), and Mannine of Venosa, Italy, held this title at the age of thirty-eight (*CII* 590).

Could it be that *elder* was an honorary title given to the wives of male elders? All the evidence to date indicates otherwise. First, there is no ascribed family connection apart from that of daughter. Also, none of the wives (or daughters) of elders known to us are said to have possessed the title *elder.* "The memory of the righteous one" (tomb inscription of Sophia of Gortyn) and "God is with the holy and the righteous one" (tomb inscription of Mazauzala of Oea, North Africa) indicate that these women gained the status of *elder* in the same way that men did, namely, through maturity, proven leadership ability, and known piety.

### Priestesses

Here lies Gaudentia, priestess *(hierisa)* [aged] 24 years. In peace be her sleep. (A.D. 3rd/4th centuries; *CII* 315)

O Marin, priestess *(hierisa)*, good and a friend to all. (28 B.C.E.; *CII* 1514)

Sara, daughter of Naimia and mother of the priestess *(hierisa)* Lady Maria, lies here. (A.D. 3rd/4th centuries; *CII* 1007)

Three Jewish inscriptions hailing from Rome, Egypt, and Galilee mention a woman *priestess.* Female priestesses were not at all unusual; in fact they were commonplace in Egyptian, Greek, and Roman religious circles. Mosaic law, however, limited the Jewish priestly line not only to males but to males in the line of Aaron. From Mosaic times down to the destruction of the temple in A.D. 70 there is only one recorded exception (Menelaus in 171 B.C., and that by Greek appointment). What then are we to make of the title *priestess* in each of these inscriptions?

At a minimum these women were named *priestess* as a way of recognizing their privileged status as a wife or daughter of a priest. One of the main privileges stipulated by Mosaic law was the right of the priest's family members to eat the priestly sacrifices. The daughter normally forfeited that right if she married outside the priestly line. If she married a priest, she could continue to eat of the priestly offering. Or if at some point she returned to her father's house, she could once again claim her due (Lev. 22:12–13). Even in the case of marriage outside the priestly line, there are recorded instances where the daughter retained the rights of her family connection and even passed these rights along to her daughters. This may be the case with the Lady Maria (above)—although the fact that her grandfather Naimia is not called a priest does pose a problem.

Could it be, though, that the title *priestess* carries with it some sort of ministry function short of that normally associated with the Mosaic priesthood? Miriam exercised a recognized liturgical role when she led the women in dance and song (Exod. 15:20–21). Exodus 38:8 and 1 Samuel 2:22 both refer to "the women who ministered at the door of the tent of meeting" (AT). Also, after the death of her husband, Anna committed her remaining years to ministry in the temple (Luke 2:36–37). Although none of these women are specifically called *priestess,* their connection to the Jewish cultus raises intriguing possibilities.[18]

It is also possible these women are singled out because of their liturgical contributions. Although priests had no official status in the synagogue, they were often invited to read a passage of Scripture during the worship service. In some cases, they not only read the biblical text but also preached a sermon on it. In fact, according to the rabbis, a priest was preferable to an elder in carrying out this liturgical function. *M. Giṭ.* 5.8 states that "a priest is the first to read (from the Torah) and after him a Levite, and after him a common Israelite."

That this was an A.D. first-century practice is confirmed by Philo's statement that "some priest who is present or one of the elders reads the sacred laws to them [the congregation] and interprets each of them separately until eventide" (*Hypothetica* 7.13). While it is unlikely a woman would give the sermon, it is possible that she was invited to read from the Scriptures out of respect for her priestly lineage.[19] The importance of lineage in antiquity is underscored by Luke's tracing the priestly line of Jesus through his biological mother, Mary (Luke 3:23–38).

### Mothers of the Synagogue

Veturia Paulla . . . mother of the synagogues of Campus and Volumnius (date unknown; *CII* 523)

Marcella, mother of the synagogue of the Augustesians (2d/3d centuries; *CII* 496)

Simplicia, mother of the synagogue, who loved her husband (1st–3d centuries; *CII* 166)

Six women from Italy have the title *mother of the synagogue*. While donor, elder, priestess, and synagogue ruler are familiar roles, *mother of the synagogue* is quite unfamiliar to the modern ear. Yet, synagogue mothers and fathers are the most commonly found titles in the inscriptions and literature of the early centuries. In Venosan (a city in Italy) inscriptions alone, the title occurs twelve times.

That *mother* and *father* were terms of leadership is clear from the *Theodosian Code* (fourth century), which exempts priests, heads of the synagogues, fathers of the synagogues, and all other officers from compulsory public service (16.8.4). Jesus also recognized such a leadership capacity when he told his disciples not to call anyone rabbi, *father*, or master (Matt. 23:8–10 RSV).

The functions of a mother or father of the synagogue are not spelled out anywhere—probably because they were so well-known. We do, however, catch a glimpse here and there of what was involved. A number of times, family ties played a part. So it is likely that some mothers and fathers of the synagogue were members of the leading families. In some cases, age seems to be a factor. One mother of the synagogue was eighty-six when she died and one father of the synagogue was one hundred ten (*CII* 509). In one inscription free access to the community's funds is assumed: "I Claudius Tiberius Plycharomos . . . father of the synagogue at Stobi . . . erected the buildings for the holy place . . . with my own means without in the least touching the sacred [funds]" (third century; *CII* 694). If one had to hazard an educated guess, chair of the deacon board or chair of the board of trustees come immediately to mind as modern parallels.

The importance of a mother or father of the synagogue can be gauged from the fact that an early second-century inscription from Italy ranks *father of the synagogue* before *gerousiarch* (a high-ranking official of the local Jewish ruling council).[20]

Could the title be an honorary one in the case of Jewish women? Some have suggested women were given the title mother of the synagogue by virtue of their marriage to a father of the synagogue. The difficulty is that no husbands are mentioned in any of the relevant inscriptions. Moreover, prestige was attached to being a relative of such a person, as the following tomb inscriptions show: "Here lies Annanios, infant archon, son of Julinus, father of the synagogue of the Campesians, aged 8 years, 2 months" (*CII* 88). "Here lies Eirene, wife of Clodios, brother of Quintus Claudius Synesios, father of the synagogue of the Campesians of Rome" (*CII* 319). It seems highly unlikely that a tombstone inscription would emphasize a relative's relationship to someone who held only an honorary title. It is much more plausible to imagine that women were granted what would appear to be one of the highest titles among the Italian Jewish communities because of their distinguished leadership.

That women of the leading families were honored in this fashion should not be a strange notion to us. Not a few women today receive honorary doctorates in recognition of their leadership contributions. We also sometimes overlook the fact that down through history women have functioned in top positions of leadership—even in the most conservative religious circles. Under Lucy Wright's leadership, for example, the Shaker communities experienced twenty-five years of unprecedented growth in the early 1800s, and Frances Willard in the 1900s was perhaps the best known leader of the Women's Christian Temperance Union.

### Other Roles

Certain roles are noticeably absent from the materials we have looked at so far. There is no explicit mention of women preaching, leading the congregation in prayer, or reading from the Scriptures. This is not to say that women did not function in these roles. Men are not singled out in these capacities either. Two explanations come to mind.

First, these are not the prestigious type of roles honored in inscriptions, lauded in burial epitaphs, or highlighted in the literature of the day. While important parts of the synagogue liturgy, they nonetheless were considered routine ministries. Nor do we commemorate them today. (When was the last time a prayer leader or Scripture reader was publicly recognized?)

Second, these roles were not performed by those with official standing in the synagogue. Average laypeople as well as temple priests and community elders were invited to serve in this fashion. So it is not surprising they were not publicly recognized.

What about ministry roles in the family context? Were Jewish women active contributors? The familial ministries of first-century Jewish women are difficult to determine. Our only sources of information are the rabbis, and they had very little interest in such matters. It is fair to say, though, that the leadership responsibilities of the mother were more limited than those of the father.

One responsibility of Jewish women was welcoming the Sabbath at the Friday meal. Another duty was the lighting of the lights for the feast of dedication (Hanukkah)—a recognition that women were equal beneficiaries of the cleansing of the temple in 164 B.C. A third obligation was the religious instruction of children from infancy on up. Teachers told their pupils, "Keep your father's commands and do not forsake your mother's teaching" (Prov. 6:20; see also vv. 21–23). Paul, in fact, reminds Timothy of the sincere faith that was passed along from his grandmother Lois to his mother Eunice and then to Timothy himself (2 Tim. 1:5). A fourth responsibility was to make sure the family's meals were kosher.

As one reads the rabbis, one is struck by the number of religious exemptions that are granted to women. They include reciting the Shema, wearing of phylacteries, making pilgrimages to Jerusalem three times a year, and dwelling in tents during the Feast of Tabernacles (*m. Ber.* 3.3; *b. Qidd.* 34a).

While a woman who was pregnant, breast-feeding, or managing an unruly household of children might well have appreciated these exemptions, it is important to note that these practices go to the heart of what it means to be an observant Jew. The Shema is as close as we come to a Jewish creed, defining a person as monotheistic: "Hear, O Israel: the LORD our God, the LORD is one" (Deut. 6:4). The exemption from the wearing of phylacteries is also critical, since it is tied to study of the Torah. Deuteronomy 6:6–8 commands the people of Israel to talk about what God commands when they sit at home and when they walk along the road, when they lie down and when they get up. They are to tie the commandments as symbols on their hands and bind them on their foreheads. One rabbi goes so far as to say that a woman's merit does not arise from her own formal study of the Torah but from making sure her children go to the synagogue to learn Scripture and her husband goes to the Beth Hamidrash (the house of midrash) to learn Mishnah (*b. Ber.* 17a).

## The Religious Roles of Women in Greek and Roman Society

It can be said generally that a far greater number of women in the Greco-Roman world of the A.D. first century were religiously involved at home and in public than were their Jewish counterparts. This was due in large part to the fact that Romans (regardless of their status, age, or gender) were expected to play an active role in their community and to participate in both state and municipal cults. It was also due to the greater freedom Roman society afforded women and to the wider range of leadership roles open to them. Unlike the Jewish community, where domestic and public spheres were fairly well defined, the lack of such a distinction in Roman society enabled women to move outside the domestic sphere into the broader world of public life and politics. This movement was facilitated by increasing numbers of wealthy women, the greater public face that religion took in the Roman Empire, and the growing popularity of nonstate religious cults where women were on equal footing with men.[21]

This is not to say that all Greco-Roman women jumped at the available opportunities. The percentage of female involvement in fact varied from place to place. The cult of Isis, which attracted more women followers than any other gender-inclusive cult, is a good example. Inscriptions from Athens and Rome show a high percentage of female involvement (48.6 percent and 37.1 percent), while those from Rhodes (0 percent), Delos (11.3 percent), and Pompeii (14.3 percent) are significantly lower.[22] The high percentages for Athens and Rome are not surprising since both cities were major cult centers. In fact, Athens was so religiously oriented that it had even built an altar "to an unknown god" (Acts 17:22–23).

Yet, whether you were in the metropolis of Rome or the village of Pompeii, female involvement reached to the highest levels in the hierarchy of the local cults. A case in point is a woman by the name of Agrippinilla (wife of a Roman consul and member of a noble family), who served as head of the cult of Dionysus (located just outside the city of Rome). The cult of Diana at Philippi reserved its leadership roles entirely for women. Even within the male-dominated cult of Silvanus, two women named Sempronia Salsula and Valeria Pauline held high-ranking positions (*matres sacrorum* or "mothers of the sacred ones"; either patrons of the cult or cultic leaders of some sort).[23]

### RELIGION IN THE ROMAN EMPIRE

Religion in the Roman Empire was basically of two sorts: native and imported. The native, state-supported cults—such as the cult of Jupiter (god of the sky and weather) and the cult of Vesta (goddess of the hearth)—were highly ritualistic and perfunctory in their observances. Rituals had to be performed just right; formulas were detailed and exact (not unlike praying a rosary). If a mistake was made, the ceremony had to be done over from the beginning.

Roman religion was not interior by nature. It did not involve personal communion with the god or goddess. No Greek or Roman would have thought of keeping a spiritual diary or talking about a personal walk with Zeus or Jupiter. Piety was a matter of respect and obligation, not love. It involved observing accepted social norms rather than practicing any sort of personal piety. In fact, much of the religious activity was done by others. The family head sacrificed and sought the god's goodwill for the household, and the magistrates and priests did the same for the community.

This is not to say that Roman religion did not impact a person's daily life. Every formal grouping was also a religious grouping—from the smallest (the household) to the largest (the nation). There was no separation of religion and state back then. Each city had its patron deities, sacrifice and prayer accompanied civic meetings, and tax dollars supported the cults. The civic calendar was a religious calendar that went far beyond our seasonal celebrations of Easter and Christmas. Even clubs and philosophical schools were dedicated to one of the gods.

The alternative form of religion was the imported, oriental variety—such as Isis, the supreme Egyptian goddess, Cybele, the Phrygian goddess of the earth, and Mithras, the Persian god of light. The oriental cults differed from the native cults in that they made a direct appeal to the individual, offering him or her the chance of redemption through personal communion with the deity. Unlike the native cults, the oriental cults involved ceremonies of initiation, uninhibited worship, ecstatic experiences, and the revelation of mysteries known only to a select and privileged group (hence the name "the mystery religions").

### LEADERSHIP ROLES IN THE CULTS

Irrespective of whether one is looking at native or imported cults, the top-ranking religious office in every case was that of priest or priestess. Priests and priestesses generally served a particular sanctuary (in most cases, a complex of buildings), where they were responsible for its main-tenance, its rituals and ceremonies, and the protection of its treasures and gifts. Liturgical functions included ritual sacrifice, pronouncing the prayer or invocation, and presiding at the festivals of the deity. In pay-ment for their services, priests and priestesses received a modest com-pensation and a share of the sacrifices.[24]

In some cults, priests and priestesses served for a fixed period of time—the most common period being one year. In other cults they served for life. The tomb inscription of Alcmeonis, a priestess of Diony-sus reads: "Bacchae of the City, say 'Farewell you holy priestess.' This is what a good woman deserves. She led you to the mountain and carried all the sacred objects and implements, marching in procession before the whole city" (*H SCP* 82 [1978] 148. Tr. A. Henrichs; Miletis, third/sec-ond century B.C.).

The priesthood in Roman times was basically a part-time activity, requiring few qualifications and no training. In this way it was quite dif-ferent from professional clergy today. One did have to have some know-how with respect to approaching the gods and, as a general rule, had to be free of any physical defect or infirmity. For the civic cults, one also had to be a Roman citizen.

In most cases, women officiated in the cults of female deities and men in the cults of male deities. Even so, virtually every cult had its excep-tions. As early as classical times, inscriptions testify to priestesses in ser-vice to gods such as Apollo, Dionysus, and Helios. By the second cen-tury B.C., priests and priestesses served side by side in exactly the same capacities.

Of particular note are the women who served as high priestess of the imperial cult in Asia. Inscriptions dating from the first century until the mid-third century place these women in Ephesus, Thyatira, Aphrodisias, Magnesia, and elsewhere.[25] Since there was only one high priest at a time in any single city, the naming of women in this capacity is especially note-worthy. The fact that the majority of these women are named without any reference to a husband shows the title was truly given and not merely honorary.

Like many churches today, pagan congregations distinguished between clergy and laity. The clerical offices of the larger cults were quite com-plex in their diversity and responsibilities. A distinction was even made between high and low priestly offices.

The high priestly offices were tightly ordered, with the foremost rank-ing official being that of the chief priest or prophet. Next in line came the stolists, who were responsible for clothing and adorning the statues of the gods (hence our English word *stole*). Then in third, fourth, and fifth places were the scribes, astrologers, and singers.

Ranking among the lower priestly offices is more difficult to determine. The only thing we know for sure is that pastophors (or "shrine carriers") were the highest ranking among the lower officials. They were responsible for carrying the statues of the gods in  processions. Other priests in the lower offices included hieraphors (or neocorus/neokoros), who were responsible for the temple's upkeep, and canephors, who carried the holy baskets in the processions and performed other less significant temple duties. One also runs across references to light bearers, crown bearers, and dream interpreters (of which we know very little).

If we look at women's leadership roles in the pagan cults through a more traditional lens, these roles fall largely into three familiar categories:

> administrative—supervising offerings, managing the finances, overseeing matters of internal order, executing resolutions
> benefactory—underwriting various building projects
> ministerial—ritual sacrifice, prayers, invocations

Women serving in all these capacities are well attested. Yet, not all women who served in the cults had auspicious roles to play. There were those who served as prostitutes, and their fee was undoubtedly pocketed by the cult *(hiereiai).* There were also sacred slaves, who were forced to serve rather than serving by personal choice *(hierodoula).* To them fell all the menial tasks of taking care of the sanctuary.

### Women and Wealth

It is clear that wealth and office often went hand in hand. We have numerous inscriptions attesting the financial contributions of those who held office. Indeed, it was expected that those in the top priestly offices had the financial resources to underwrite civic and religious events (no separation of the religious and the secular here). For example, in her capacity as priestess of the imperial cult, Tata of Aphrodisias supplied oil for athletes who were competing in the public games, offered sacrifices throughout the year for the health of the imperial family, held banquets for the general public, and imported the foremost performers in Asia for dances and plays in her native city (Pleket, #18). Menodora, as imperial high priestess, distributed money and corn to the inhabitants of Sillyon (a city in Pamphylia), gave three hundred thousand denarii to the orphans and widows (one denarius is commonly figured to be a day's wage), and financed the building of a temple (*IGR* III, 800–902).

The connection between wealth and office should come as no surprise. Even today municipal life depends to a certain extent on the charitable contributions of wealthy members of the community. What is noteworthy is that women in the empire were not excused from civic involvement. In fact, women rendered the same social, political, and financial services as their male counterparts, and they were honored in the same ways. For example, Chrysis, a priestess of Athena in the second century B.C., was crowned by the Delphians with the god's crown and granted, among other things, freedom from taxes and the right to own land and a house (*IGR* 1136). Bernice, priestess of the goddesses Demeter and Kore, was crowned by the people of Syros with a gold crown in recognition of her virtue and goodwill toward them (Pleket 25; 2d c). Flavia Vibia Sabina, high priestess of Thasos, was granted honors equal to those of the senators (Pleket 29, date unknown).

The significance of this connection is not to be overlooked. Wealthy women were in a position to be power brokers in the Roman world. Although their numbers were not as great as male benefactors, female benefactors were still numerous enough to wield great influence and power—especially if they held their position for life.[26]

There were some cults in which wealth did not play a role. The most notable exceptions were the Delphic priestesses. At Delphi the priestess under trance was believed to speak the very words of the god Apollo. Legend has it that Apollo killed the sacred female serpent known as the Python and became the spokesperson for Zeus. His priestesses, in turn, were imbued with the Pythian spirit and proclaimed oracles. Luke describes this very thing in Acts 16:16–17, in which a slave girl possessed by a Pythian spirit followed Paul and Silas around proclaiming: "These men are servants of the Most High God, who are telling you the way to be saved" (v. 17).

Although the method by which the Delphic priestesses were chosen is lost to us, one thing is clear: Rank did not play a role. Those chosen were just average women. The only qualification was that they had to be at least fifty years of age. Their influence can be gauged by the numerous times they were sought out by high-ranking officials regarding matters of state.[27]

The vestal virgins, one of the most celebrated of the Roman priesthoods, were quite a different story. Here rank and youth were the determining factors. Unlike the Delphic priestesses, vestal virgins came from upper-class Roman families. They entered the priesthood as mere children between the ages of six and ten and served for thirty years.

The primary duty of vestal virgins was to tend the fire in the temple of Vesta (or Hestia), the goddess of the hearth—the symbol of the Roman people. In exchange for their services, vestal virgins were granted sweeping freedoms, including freedom from male guardianship, the right to make a will without male authorization, and the right to bequeath property during the lifetime of their fathers.

There was, however, a catch. They had to take a vow of chastity, the breaking of which was punishable by scourging and even death. (They were buried alive!) In fact, the virtue of the vestal virgins and the welfare of Rome were so intimately connected that whenever Rome experienced defeat at the hands of an enemy or calamity of one kind or another, the vestal virgins (and their vows) immediately came under suspicion.[28]

### THE CULT OF ISIS AND WOMEN'S LIBERATION

The cult that perhaps did the most to advance the role of women in the Greco-Roman world was that of Isis—an ancient Egyptian cult that migrated to Europe in the second century B.C. One source goes so far as to credit Isis with putting women on the same plane as men: "I invoke thee, who . . . didst make the power of women equal to that of men" (P. Oxy. 1380; about A.D. 100). There is no denying that women and men participated on equal footing in this cult; inscriptions bear this out. Of the twenty-six inscriptions in hand (all that have been discovered) that mention ministry roles within the cult, six name women as priests of the highest rank.

There are other striking features of the cult of Isis. Compared to the official cults that catered to the upper classes, Isis was no respecter of birth or status. Of the six women designated as high priestess, one was of senatorial rank and one was the daughter of a former slave. Even prostitutes found a home in this cult. The cult of Isis was also unusual in that it spread from the slaves and lower classes to the upper echelons of society. This is saying something in a society where the head of the household ruled supreme in religious matters.

The appeal of the cult of Isis was enormous in the A.D. first century. Worshipers of Isis were everywhere. There were no social boundaries, which was rather phenomenal since Roman society was so compartmentalized. Slaves and nonslaves did not mix; nobility and commoners went their separate ways; prostitutes and reputable women did not cross paths. This was also the case in the sphere of religion. Slaves celebrated the Nonae Caprotinae (somewhat like the matronal festival), commoners celebrated Plebeian Chastity (begun, according to legend, after a patrician had been expelled from the cult of her equals for marrying a commoner), and prostitutes participated in the cult of Fortuna Virilis (which took place in the men's baths).[29]

The cult of Isis, on the other hand, saw an intermingling of people who would never have crossed paths in the average social setting. This contributed greatly to the goddess's appeal. The only segment of society where her popularity fell short was the Roman army, where the macho, oriental god Mithras was the favorite.

As a goddess, Isis also had much to attract followers. Her attributes were vast yet personal. She was the creator, dividing earth from heaven, assigning languages to nations, and inventing alphabets and astronomy. She was also the sustainer, governing all things by her providence (inanimate and animate alike; Apuleius, *Metamorphoses* 11). Isis was, further, the supreme goddess. The other goddesses were pale reflections by comparison. She was all powerful, though in a loving and merciful, rather than threatening, way. What Isis offered to her followers was not unlike what people saw in Jesus. It was said that she could heal the sick, perform miracles, and resurrect her followers after death.[30]

The cult of Isis is a critical backdrop for understanding the role of women in the New Testament. Much like the rapidly increasing popularity of the New Age movement today, this was the cult on the rise during Jesus' earthly ministry and Paul's mission to the Gentiles. Against this backdrop, Jesus is not quite the liberator of women as he is sometimes pictured, and Paul's statement that in Christ "there is neither Jew nor Greek, slave nor free, male nor female" (Gal. 3:28) is not as radical a concept as is sometimes thought. This is not to undercut the uniqueness of Christianity, but it points up the fact that women were not as religiously suppressed in the first century as they are sometimes made out to be. At least the women in the cult of Isis knew equality and liberty—albeit within the religious realm.

The potential threat of this cult to the traditional fabric of Roman society was quickly seen by the first-century emperors. Official religion of the Roman variety was closely supervised, and the women who participated were carefully organized and their activities strictly regulated. The unrestrained activity and inclusive nature of oriental cults like Isis made them immediately suspect, if for no other reason than the fear that such openness would adversely affect the family unit and erupt in antisocial behavior. With few exceptions, every attempt was made to limit the cult's activities and, in some cases, to eradicate its presence. Emperor Augustus ordered the demolition of the temple of Isis. Emperor Tiberius crucified her priests, demolished her temple, and had the statue of the goddess thrown into the Tiber.

Why such an extreme response? The close linking of religion and society was largely to blame. What impacted one was bound to impact the other. This, of course, is what scared the religious leaders in Jesus' day. Popular followings such as these could easily lead to popular uprisings against the status quo.

### THE SUM OF THE MATTER

Whereas twentieth-century society has taken the lead in bringing women into the public arena on an equal footing with men, in the first century A.D. the religious cults led the way in modeling male and female parity. This can be seen especially in a major cult center like Athens. In a city that was otherwise very conservative regarding the public roles of women, it is significant that more than forty major cults in Athens had priestesses attached to them. Prominent among these was the priestess of Athena Polias, the city's patron deity, who officiated at the most important state festivals.[31]

Male-female equality could likewise be seen in the oriental cults, which allowed women to break out of their domestic mold and gave them an avenue of self-expression that was normally frowned upon and discouraged by the Roman male population. Indeed, it was not uncommon to blame societal downturns on the liberated women of Greece and Rome. As early as the fourth century B.C., Aristotle blamed Spartan women for the deterioration of Sparta. The first-century B.C. Roman historian Livy stressed the luxuriousness of Etruscan women as a factor aggravating the degeneracy of Etruruia. And the first-century A.D. Roman poet Juvenal harped on the rottenness of Roman women as symptomatic of a sick society.[32]

The official cults also played their part in advancing the public roles of women—especially those in which offices were held for life. Where the top position of leadership was held by a woman, the impact on civil affairs was inevitable given the inseparability of religion and public life. This can be seen, for example, at Eleusis (fourteen miles from Athens), where all the events in the public records were dated by the name of the chief priestess of the cult of Demeter (grain goddess) and the year of her life-tenure in which they occurred.

## *The Ministries of Women in Early Christianity*

In which ministries of the church can women be involved? This is a question that generates a perplexing range of answers. Some contend that all the ministries of the church are open to women. Others believe any role labeled as *ministry* is closed to women. Still others think women can be involved in the ministries of the church as long as no authority attaches to the activity in question: A woman can teach but not with authority. A woman can prophesy, but she cannot judge whether the prophecy is true or false. A woman can give her personal testimony in a congregational setting, but she cannot preach. (The examples can be multiplied ad infinitum.) To a great extent these wide-ranging opinions are the result of a basic disagreement over two fundamental questions: What is the church? and What are its ministries? How one answers these two questions pretty much determines how one answers the question of women's roles in the church.

## The Ministries of the Church

So what *is* the church? One thing is certain—the church is unlike any other religious institution. Even a cursory look at the numerous New Testament passages that deal with the *what* of the church shows this to be the case.

The church is certainly different from the synagogue (the religious institution with which many assume a close affinity). One major difference has to do with leadership roles. In the previous section we saw that ministries in the synagogue were of four kinds. First, there were the official ministry roles. Administrators were appointed to handle planning and implementing the worship service and to manage the facilities. There were also financial officers (the most prestigious being mothers and fathers of the synagogue) and donors, who kept the whole operation afloat. Then there was the scholar, who served as targumist (translator and interpreter of the Hebrew text for the congregation) and schoolteacher. Finally, there were the lay professionals such as the priests, elders, and legal experts, who were invited on an ad hoc basis to assist in the worship service by reading the Scripture, reciting the confessions, leading in prayer, bringing a word of exhortation, or pronouncing the benediction.

The New Testament presents a very different picture of the church's leadership roles and ministry functions. For one, they are charismatically (rather than officially or professionally) driven. Whether it is administration, giving, teaching, or other ministry activity, the New Testament writers are unanimous in their insistence that gift precedes function. Paul's statement in Romans 12:6–8 is representative:

> We have different gifts, according to the grace given us. If it is prophesying, let us use it in proportion to our faith; if it is serving, let us serve;

if it is teaching, let us teach; if it is encouraging, let us encourage; if it is
contributing to the needs of others, let us give generously (AT).

With few exceptions, believers assumed a ministry role in the church not
because they were appointed, nor because they had received professional
training, but because they possessed the appropriate gift(s) to handle the
task.

In the second place, the New Testament presents ministry as something that is done by the whole and not simply the few. Ministry language and titles that had been previously used of the professionals are
now applied to the entire congregation. *The church* is a "royal" and "holy
priesthood" that offers "spiritual sacrifices" (1 Peter 2:5, 9). Apostles,
prophets, evangelists, and pastors-teachers are given to *the church* to prepare God's people "for the work of the ministry" (Eph. 4:9–12 KJV).
*The church* is "God's temple" and where "God's Spirit lives" (1 Cor. 3:16).
"The keys of the kingdom of heaven" are given to *the church* to "bind"
and to "loose" (Matt. 16:19).

The early church also handled worship differently from other first-
century religious institutions. The picture is not that of a church head
planning and supervising the worship service (as one finds in Judaism)
but of a spontaneous yet orderly sharing of *charismata* or "spiritual gifts."
No place is this brought out more clearly than in 1 Corinthians 14:26:
"When you come together, *everyone* has a hymn, or a word of instruction, a revelation, a tongue or an interpretation" (italics added). Worship happened not because official roles were assumed by the few but
because gifts were exercised by the whole.

This is not to say that the traditional elements of prayer, hymns,
instruction, confessions, benedictions, and Scripture reading had no
place in Christian worship. In fact, they were very much present. Paul
was quick to remind Timothy that requests, prayers, intercessions, and
thanksgivings for governing authorities are to be a part of worship—as
are the public reading of Scripture, preaching, and teaching (1 Tim.
2:1–2; 4:13). The members of churches in and around Ephesus were
called to "speak to one another with psalms, hymns and spiritual songs"
(Eph. 5:19). The abundance of confessions, benedictions, and doxolo-
gies in Paul's letters show that they were a familiar part of early Christian worship experience. "Amen" was a typical congregational response
(2 Cor. 1:20). "Maranatha" ("Come, O Lord," 1 Cor. 16:22) was one
of the earliest congregational proclamations. Even worship leaders are
readily found (see for example Timothy's role in 1 Tim. 2:1–2 and 4:13).

The primary difference lay not in the *what* of worship but in the *who*.
Participation in the early church was a participation of the whole, not

the few, and those who participated did so prompted by the Spirit's leading and gifting, not by their official or professional standing among God's
people. Although there is quite a liturgical mix among evangelical
churches today, I suspect we are more indebted to a Jewish than an early
Christian understanding of ministry and worship. Who leads in worship? Who teaches the Sunday school classes? Who handles the finances?
Who chairs the boards and committees? These are the telling questions.

## The Church and Spiritual Gifts

The New Testament writers define the church as a diversity of members with various gifts, whose growth and nurture is dependent on each
member using his or her gift(s) for the mutual edification of the whole
(e.g., Matt. 18:20; Rom. 12:3–8; 1 Cor. 12:1–31; Eph. 4:7–16; 1 Thess.
5:16–22; Heb. 10:25; James 5:13–16; 1 Peter 4:7–11). An accurate
understanding of the church and the place of women within it is thus
dependent on an accurate understanding of the nature and role of spiritual gifts.

The first thing to understand is that when we talk about gifts, we are
talking about something that is imparted by the Spirit and at his complete discretion. The Spirit gives gifts "to each one, just as he determines" (1 Cor. 12:11). Space does not permit an in-depth study of New
Testament teaching on spiritual gifts. Suffice it to say that unlike abilities, which are endowments we possess at birth and are part and parcel
of what it means to be human, spiritual gifts by contrast are supernat-
ural endowments we have by virtue of the Spirit dwelling within us. They
are the *manifestations [-mata] of God's grace [charis]* and are intended for
the upbuilding of Christ's church. "Now to each one," Paul says, "the
manifestation of the Spirit is given for the common good" (1 Cor. 12:7).

Both Paul (Rom. 12:3–8; 1 Cor. 12:1–31; Eph. 4:7–16) and Peter
(1 Peter 4:7–11) stress God's sovereignty in the giving of spiritual gifts.
They also emphasize the responsibility of the recipient to be faithful in
using these gifts. "Each one," Peter says, "should use whatever gift he
[or she] has received to serve others, faithfully administering God's grace
in its various forms" (1 Peter 4:10 NIV). None of the New Testament
passages that deal with spiritual gifts place gender limitations on the giving or the use of these gifts. Men and women are equal recipients of
God's grace; men and women are individually accountable to God for
the exercise thereof. When the question of distinctions is raised, it is
only to categorically affirm that in the church ethnic (Jew/Gentile), social
(slave/free), and sexual (male/female) distinctions do not exist (Gal.
3:28).

God's equal gifting of men and women for service in the church is a foundational truth that should inform any concept of ministry. It is sometimes claimed that while men and women are spiritual equals—that is, equal heirs of salvation—there are nonetheless functional differences. But this is a difficult distinction to maintain in the light of New Testament teaching that women and men alike comprise the priesthood of believers and that gift precedes and gives rise to function.

Others would say passages that affirm gender equality (such as Gal. 3:28) in essence deal with truths about redemption and not truths about the church. This, however, overlooks the fact that to be *in Christ* (a redemptive truth) is to be *in the body of Christ* (a truth about the church). That is why Jesus could confront Paul on the road to Damascus with the claim that to persecute the church is to persecute him (Acts 9:4–5). It is also why Paul could tell the Corinthians that to divide the church is to divide Christ (1 Cor. 1:10–13).

## Models of Charismatic Leadership

Gift- or charisma-based leadership was not a completely new thought back then. While the ministries of the first-century synagogue did not operate this way, precedents were there in Judaism. In fact, official and charismatic types of leadership coexisted throughout much of the history of God's people.

During the period of the judges, for example, leadership was predominantly charismatic in nature. Individuals rose to leadership as the situation demanded and their gifts warranted. Jephthah, for instance, rose to leadership because of his skill as a warrior (Judg. 11:1). Deborah was renowned for her prophetic abilities (Judg. 4:4).

The charismatic leader delivered God's people by means of heroic exploits empowered by the Spirit. Perhaps the most notorious example was Samson who, when the Spirit of the Lord came upon him, struck down one thousand Philistines with the jawbone of a donkey (Judg. 15:14–15). The same thing is said of Othniel, Caleb's younger brother. It was as "the Spirit of the LORD came upon him" that he was able to overpower Israel's arch foe, the king of Aram (Judg. 3:10). Charismatic leadership also inspired a popular following. Even after his stepbrothers drove him away, "a group of adventurers gathered around him [Jephthah] and followed him" (Judg. 11:3).

The epitome of charismatic leadership was the Old Testament prophet. These were women and men empowered by the Spirit to speak a word of correction to God's people. They came from all walks of life. According to Jewish tradition, Isaiah was an official in the royal court. Huldah's husband was a keeper of the royal (perhaps priestly) wardrobe (2 Kings 22:14). Amos was a shepherd (Amos 1:1). Ezekiel (Ezek. 1:3) and Zechariah (Neh. 12:16) were priests. The corrective words of the prophets were often aimed at the failings of the religious leadership of the day. Habakkuk bemoans corruption at the highest levels (Hab. 1:2–4). Micah rails against lies preached by other prophets (Micah 2:6–11). Zephaniah speaks a word of woe to the priests who profaned the sanctuary and did violence to the law (Zeph. 3:4).

Charismatic leadership also existed during Hellenistic and Roman times, although it was external to the religious institutions of the day. The Maccabees (in the centuries before Christ) are a good example. It was Mattathias's zealousness for the Lord's honor in the face of Greek religious oppression that led those seeking righteousness and justice to follow him to the hill country of Judea (1 Maccabees 2). Then came Judas Maccabaeus (Mattathias's son), whose brilliance as a guerrilla-warfare tactician caused Israel to rally around him after his father's death (1 Maccabees 2:65–3:2).

A charismatic figure during Roman times who comes readily to mind is John the Baptist. At his birth, his father, Zechariah, uttered the Spirit-inspired words that John "will be called a prophet of the Most High" for he "will go on before the Lord to prepare the way for him" (Luke 1:76). In line with these prophetic words, John gathered a following in the wilderness regions around the Jordan, preaching a baptism of repentance for the forgiveness of sins. There were also the Zealot leaders (Hezekiah and his family), who were charismatic types after the model of the Maccabees.

Then there were those individuals who gathered a popular following on the claim that they would perform heroic feats like the leaders of old. One individual named Theudas asserted that at his command the Jordan River would part and gain his followers easy passage over it (Josephus, *Jewish Antiquities* 20.5.1 §§97–99). Along similar lines, a self-proclaimed prophet from Egypt avowed that the walls of Jerusalem would fall down at his command and so win his followers entry into the city (Josephus, *Jewish Antiquities* 20.8.6 §§169–70).

Undoubtedly the best-known charismatic leader during Roman times was Jesus himself, whose popular following was so threatening to the official leadership of the day that they constantly plotted and sought his death.

## Women Leaders During Old Testament Times

When a charismatic type of leadership predominated in Israel, the ministries of women were most in evidence. Moses' sister, Miriam, is a case in point. A multitalented individual, she possessed musical, poetic, and prophetic gifts that served Israel well during the wilderness years. After Israel passed through the sea on dry ground, it was she who took a tambourine and led all the women in a rehearsal of God's mighty act of deliverance (Exod. 15:20). It was also she who, as prophetess, was sent by the Lord (along with her two brothers) to lead Israel (Micah 6:4).

Miriam's ministry skills were not only recognized and confirmed, but she was accorded the same respect Aaron and Moses received. In fact, her leadership abilities were held in such high esteem that Israel would not travel until she had been restored to them (Num. 12:1–16).

The range of roles women played during the period of the judges also fits the charismatic orientation of the times. Deborah is called "prophetess" (Judg. 4:4 NIV), judge (Judg. 4:5 NRSV), and "mother in Israel" (Judg. 5:7). She held court in the hill country of Ephraim and all of Israel (men and women alike) came to her to have their disputes settled (Judg. 4:5). So respected was Deborah that the commander of her troops refused to go into battle without her (Judg. 4:8).

Ruth, the Moabite and great-grandmother of David, is also to be noted. Her role as breadwinner of the family (by gleaning in the fields along with the men) earned her the tribute, "better . . . than seven sons" (Ruth 4:15).

Female roles were less evident during the period of the monarchy, when a more official type of leadership prevailed. Even so, there were several notable exceptions—especially among the ranks of the prophets. Perhaps the best-known female prophet is Huldah, who was active during the time of Jeremiah and Zephaniah. It was to her that King Josiah sent a delegation to inquire about the Book of the Law that had been discovered while the temple was being renovated, and it was Huldah's warning to obey everything written in this book that brought about the well-known religious reforms of the seventh century B.C. (2 Kings 22; 2 Chron. 34:14–33).

A less exemplary female prophet was Noadiah, who during the postexilic period was hired (along with other prophets) by Sanballat to forestall Nehemiah's efforts to rebuild the temple walls (Neh. 6). The fact that Noadiah is one of two prophets mentioned by name is indicative of the leadership she gave to this influential group.

There are also references to a number of unnamed women prophets. The prophet Isaiah, for example, was instructed to marry "the prophetess" (Isa. 8:3). And the prophet Ezekiel pronounced judgment against the daughters of Judah, who prophesied "out of their own imagination"

(Ezek. 13:17; see also vv. 18–24). These examples suggest that women were routinely called and readily accepted as prophets of Israel.

There were two additional leadership roles that Israelite women assumed. Scripture from time to time mentions "wise women" who were sent on diplomatic missions. For instance, Joab (David's military commander) sent "a wise woman" from Tekoa to persuade King David to forgive his son Absalom's vengeance against his stepbrother and to facilitate reconciliation with the royal family (2 Sam. 14:1–21). There was also the "wise woman" of Abel Beth Maacah, whose expert counsel saved her city from destruction at the hand of David's troops (2 Sam. 20:14–22). Then there is the figure of Lady Wisdom in the Book of Proverbs and the ideal wise woman of Proverbs 31, whose children call her blessed and whose husband praises her because of her wisdom.

Another ministry that was almost exclusively female was that of mourning. David in his lament for Saul calls on the "daughters of Israel" to weep for the king (2 Sam. 1:24). The prophet Jeremiah refers to professional wailers, who were paid to mourn at funerals and other sorrowful occasions. "Call for the wailing women to come; send for the most skilful of them," he demands (Jer. 9:17). The prophet Ezekiel speaks of the lament the daughters of the nations will chant for Egypt and all her hordes, suggesting that professional mourners were not unique to Israel (Ezek. 32:16).

Professional mourners could also be found in the New Testament period. The Gospel of John notes that women wailers were present even four days after the death of Lazarus (John 11:31, 33). Jesus himself mentions those hired to sing dirges (Matt. 11:16–17).

The extent of female involvement in the tabernacle and temple worship is a matter of debate. The matter-of-fact way that Hannah's sacrifice of bulls, flour, and wine offerings is presented in 1 Samuel 1:24–25 shows that women routinely participated in the sacrificial rituals. They also participated in the building and furnishing of the tabernacle (Exod. 35:22–29). More, women played musical instruments in public processions (Ps. 68:24–25); they danced and sang at communal and national festivals (Judg. 21:19–23) and victory celebrations (1 Sam. 18:6–7); and they sang in the temple choir alongside the men (2 Chron. 35:25; Ezra 2:65; Neh. 7:67).

Women are also said to have served at the entrance of the tabernacle. In Exodus 38:8 the bronze basin and stand in the tabernacle were made from the mirrors of "the women who served at the entrance" (cf. 1 Sam. 2:22). Who these women were and what their work involved is not spelled out. The word for *serve (ṣābā')* is the same word used elsewhere of the work of the Levites in the tabernacle (Num. 4:23; 8:24) and of Israel's warriors (Num. 31:7, 42). While it is impossible to be certain, the women's function was probably to guard the entrance to the tabernacle. This is not all that far-fetched when we recall that when Jesus was brought before Annas (the patriarch of the high priestly family) for questioning, the guard on duty was a woman (John 18:16).

Three observations can be made by way of summary: First, the most commonly mentioned leadership role for women throughout Israel's history was that of prophet. This should come as no surprise given the charismatic nature of the role. Repeated and matter-of-fact references to women prophets show that theirs was a ministry both accepted and affirmed by God's people.

Second, apart from prophetess, few women are mentioned as occupying high-profile positions in Israel. This is undoubtedly because the official religious roles within Judaism (priests and Levites) were exclusively male ones. There were exceptions in the political arena. Athaliah, for example, reigned over Israel from 842 to 836 B.C. and Salome Alexandra ruled from 76 to 67 B.C. The women of neighboring nations fared even better. Jezebel, daughter of the priest-king of Tyre and Sidon and wife of Israel's reigning king (Ahab), was infamous for her political maneuvering (1 Kings 21). The queen of Sheba journeyed to Jerusalem to negotiate a trade agreement with Solomon (1 Kings 10:1–10; 2 Chron. 9:1–9). Egypt and Ethiopia throughout history had queens as reigning monarchs. Two of the best known are Cleopatra, the effective ruler in Egypt from 51–31 B.C., and Candace, the queen of Ethiopia in the A.D. first century (see Acts 8:27).

There were also a number of women who, though not publicly recognized as such, were quite clearly power brokers. Rebekah's role in achieving primacy for Jacob (albeit deceptively) comes immediately to mind (Gen. 27:1–40). Bathsheba's efforts to gain the kingship for Solomon matches the best political maneuvering of our day (1 Kings 1:15–21). Queen Esther's word commanded instant obedience (Esther 4:15–17; 9:29–32). Then there were the daughters of Zelophad, whose persuasive appeal for a woman's right to inherit rivals the finest legal argumentation today (Num. 36:1–13).

Third, although women leaders were far fewer than their male counterparts, it was not because of inferiority, unsuitability, or unacceptability. There is no notion in the Old Testament that female leadership is wrong. The reality of the situation was that domestic needs (especially the bearing and raising of children) left little time to pursue public roles.

Those involved in the public arena were generally upper-class women who were able to delegate their domestic tasks to other women in the household.

### Attitudes toward Women in Early Christianity

When we move from women's roles in Israel to those in early Christianity, the playing field expands greatly. This is in large part because of the charismatic versus official nature of the early Christian experience. No one group or groups of individuals in the church carried out the work of ministry. Instead, the responsibility for ministry was shared by the community as a whole.

This state of affairs accounts for Paul's numerous references to women colleagues. Phoebe, for example, is commended for her role as a "deacon" of the church in Cenchrea and "benefactor" *(prostatis)* of many— including Paul himself (Rom. 16:1–2 NRSV). Priscilla is called a "coworker" (v. 3). Junia is hailed as "outstanding among the apostles" and a co-prisoner (v. 7). Tryphena, Tryphosa, and Persis are applauded for their hard work in the Lord (v. 12). Syntyche and Euodia are addressed as co-evangelists (Phil. 4:2–3).

An expanded playing field for women can also be attributed to increased roles for women in Roman society at large. Although Jesus is often hailed as the liberator of women and Paul's statement in Galatians 3:28 is trumpeted as the woman's Magna Carta, Jesus and Paul, in fact, did not affirm any roles for women that weren't already a possibility in Roman society.

The quantum leap is to be found, instead, in the realm of attitudes. This was even the case in Roman circles. Although Roman women were out and about, attitudes toward women remained largely conservative. The stay-at-home mother was still the Roman ideal. A devoted wife who tended house and hearth continued to be extolled by the poets and moralists of the period. Epitaphs lauded the woman who bore her husband sons and remained faithful to him even after an untimely death. Educated women were still looked upon by many with suspicion, and giftedness in the arts, humanities, or sciences was often attributed to the possession of male genes.

The following tombstone inscription is an apt illustration: "Beneath this stone I, once married, lie . . . nor did my departure leave a childless household" (first century B.C.; *Propertius* 4.11.36, 61–62). In fact, Catullus, writing in the first century B.C., once remarked to one of his female friends that "to live content with one man is for wives an honor of honors" (*The Poems of Catullus* 111).

Viewed against these popular attitudes, Jesus and Paul come across as quite countercultural. This was especially the case in Palestine, where the woman's liberation movement never really took hold. The fact that Jesus included women in his group of disciples speaks volumes in a society where the religious training of Jewish girls stopped at the age of twelve. Nor was this instruction of a casual sort. Mary sat at Jesus' feet and learned in traditional rabbinic fashion—an activity that Jesus deemed a higher priority than domestic chores: "Mary has chosen what is better, and it will not be taken away from her" (Luke 10:42).

Jesus was at ease with women in public. Contrary to Jewish practice, he could be found talking with women (John 4:1–26) and traveling with them (Luke 8:1–3; 23:49). He also broke Sabbath conventions to heal women (e.g., Luke 13:10–17) and associated with women society labeled disreputable (e.g., Luke 7:36–50).

Jesus also treated women with dignity. When he healed a woman crippled for eighteen years, rather than treating her as a religious or social misfit, Jesus addressed her as a "daughter of Abraham" (Luke 13:16). He also approached women as persons capable of intelligent conversation. Not only was he found talking to a woman (and a despised foreigner at that), but he engaged her in theological debate (John 4:19–26; cf. Mark 7:24–30).

Women frequently made their way into Jesus' teaching. Women kneading dough, grinding with a hand mill, and sweeping the floor became ready sermon illustrations (Matt. 13:33; 24:41; Luke 15:8–10). Bridesmaids, pregnant women, women in labor, and nursing mothers appear with regularity (e.g., Matt. 24:19–21; 25:1–13; Mark 13:17; Luke 21:23; 23:29; John 16:21). A widow who persists in seeking justice provides an apt lesson on how to pray (Luke 18:1–8). This is in stark contrast to the rabbis of the day. One looks in vain in their teachings for even one story or sermon illustration that mentions women.

Jesus lifted up women as models of outstanding piety. The widow who contributed to the temple fund out of her bare income models genuine self-sacrifice, for all the others "gave out of their wealth, but she, out of her poverty" (Mark 12:41–44). The Syrophoenician woman, despite being in the throes of a family crisis, grasped what the twelve disciples still had not understood about Jesus even after two years of intensive training (Mark 7:17–30). The woman who anointed Jesus with an alabaster jar of expensive perfume is memorialized for her act of devotion, while Jesus' disciples bemoan the wasted funds (Matt. 26:6–13; Mark 14:1–9).

Contrary to what is sometimes said, Paul also had a high view of women. This is quite clear from his language. Women are a cause for thanksgiving (Rom. 16:4) and the object of personal greeting (Rom. 16:3, 6, 7, 12, 13, 15; Col. 4:15; 2 Tim. 4:19). Exactly the same language is employed in praising female colleagues that is used in commending male coworkers. The men are "co-prisoners" (Col. 4:10 [AT]; see also Rom. 16:7), "co-workers" (Rom. 16:3, 9; 1 Cor. 3:9; 2 Cor. 8:23; Phil. 4:3; Col. 4:11), and hard laborers (1 Cor. 4:12; 16:16; 1 Thess. 5:12) who risked their lives for Paul (Rom. 16:3) and contended at his side for the gospel (Phil. 4:3). The women are equally "co-workers" (Rom. 16:3; Phil. 4:3) and hard laborers (Rom. 16:6, 12) who risked their lives for Paul (Rom. 16:3) and contended at his side for the gospel (Phil. 4:2–3).

While it is sometimes said that *hard work (kopiaō)* is a term that could apply to just about any serving capacity in the church, it is instructive to note that the Greek term is one Paul used exclusively of the work of the gospel ministry. In fact, it is the term he typically used to describe his own apostolic labors (1 Cor. 4:12; 15:10; 2 Cor. 6:5; 11:27; Gal. 4:11; Phil. 2:16; Col. 1:29; 1 Thess. 2:9; 3:5; 2 Thess. 3:8; 1 Tim. 4:10).[33] He could do this because he looked at ministry as a cooperative venture, whose success depended on the gifting and empowerment of women and men committed to serving Christ and his church.

Women also figured prominently in Paul's evangelistic efforts. According to Luke's record, the first European convert was a businesswoman named Lydia (Acts 16:11–15). Paul's second stop saw the conversion of "many of the leading women" of the capital city of Thessalonica (Acts 17:4 TEV). Then in Berea "a number of prominent Greek women" received Paul's message with "great eagerness" (Acts 17:11–12). Paul's brief stay in Athens resulted in only a handful of converts, but of the two mentioned, Luke observes that one was a woman named Damaris (Acts 17:34).

While Luke tends to note the conversion of highly positioned women, Paul's letters attest to women converts from all walks of life (e.g., 1 Cor. 1:26). Luke stops counting once Paul gets to Corinth, but Paul's many references to women show that their favorable response continued throughout his ministry.

## Women Leaders in New Testament Times

There is no lack of women leaders in the pages of the New Testament. This is not unexpected given the many women who responded to the gospel message. Luke notes that Mary the mother of Jesus and "the women" were among the 120 whom the Holy Spirit empowered for witness in Jerusalem, Judea, Samaria, and "to the ends of the earth" (Acts 1:8, 14–15; 2:1–4). This, so Peter observes, fulfilled what was spoken by the prophet Joel:

> In the last days, God says,
> I will pour out my Spirit on all people.
> Your sons and daughters will prophesy. . . .
> Even on my servants, both men and women,
>       I will pour out my Spirit in those days.
>                               Acts 2:17–18; Joel 2:28–29

Male leaders were still more numerous, but virtually every ministry role that named a man also named a woman.[34] This was partly a carry-over from the involvement of women in leadership positions in the cults. It also had to do with where women were active and involved. The more Romanized the area, the more visible the leadership of women. Since Paul's missionary efforts focused on the major urban areas of the Roman Empire, it is not at all surprising that most of the women named as leaders in the New Testament surface in the Pauline churches.

Virtually all of the churches planted by Paul were in heavily Romanized cities, where the population was a mix of Latin and Greek speaking people. Thessalonica, Corinth, and Ephesus, for example, were provincial capitals. Philippi was a leading city in the province of Macedonia. Cenchrea housed a Roman naval station. Then there was Rome, the hub of the empire. Is it any wonder that so many of the leaders whom Paul greets in the church at Rome are women (Rom. 16)? That the list should include two married couples (Priscilla/Aquila; Andronicus/Junia) is especially noteworthy. It reflects the move in Roman circles toward viewing marriage as a partnership (see pp. 92–94).

### Women Patrons

There is no better example of the impact of culture on the church than in the area of patronage. As we saw in the previous section, patronage was one of the most visible roles played by women in Greco-Roman society. Women were patrons of organizations and institutions as wide-ranging as the local synagogue, the civic cults, craft guilds, social clubs, burial associations, and professional societies.

Patronage was a good way for a woman to gain status and honor for herself and her family. Many women took advantage of this; so did the men. Where money was concerned, gender rarely was (or, for that matter, ever has been) an issue. Wealthy women were even asked to be patrons of men's clubs.[35]

The ability of married women to serve as patrons increased significantly during Roman times. This was partially due to newly acquired rights to own and manage their dowry and to possess and dispose of land (the primary form of wealth back then). It was also a result of there being simply more women around with more money.[36]

The New Testament reflects this state of affairs. More women are commended for their patronage than for any other ministry role. There are several exceptional features of this patronage. For one, while Luke duly notes that women supported Jesus, the simple fact is that they are the *only* supporters mentioned. Also, they did not merely write a check to cover the expenses but accompanied Jesus and the Twelve as they traveled from place to place (Luke 8:1–3). While this fits with the increased mobility of women in the Roman Empire, such independence in Jewish society was quite unusual—even shocking. Yet it gets little or no mention in the standard reference works. Our attention is usually drawn instead to the fact that none of the Twelve apostles were women. Yet the truly amazing detail is that Jesus welcomed women among his traveling coterie, allowing them to make the same radical commitment in following him that the Twelve did.

Luke provides us with the names of three women in this group of financial backers: Mary Magdalene, Susanna, and Joanna (Luke 8:2–3). Mary Magdalene figures prominently in the Gospel tradition, but we know nothing about Susanna. Joanna is identified as the wife of Herod's steward, a high-ranking individual and hence a person of substance. The naming of these three women could imply they held leadership positions in the early church. At the least, they had to have been well-known personalities.

No other women are named in Luke's account, but Mark provides us with two additional names: Salome, the wife of Zebedee and mother of James and John, and Mary, the mother of James and Joses (Mark 15:40; cf. Matt. 27:56). This brings the total to five, of which two are identified as the wife of someone. That married women would be traveling with Jesus' group is striking indeed.

It is these same women who were at the cross (after all the disciples except John had fled), observed where the body was laid, and made sure that the body received a proper burial (Mark 15:40–41; Luke 23:55–56; John 19:25–27). They were also the first to witness the empty tomb, the ones to whom Jesus initially appeared, and the ones charged with proclaiming Jesus' resurrection to the other disciples (Matt. 28:1–10; Mark 16:1–8; Luke 24:9–12; John 20:1–18). These women are our primary witnesses to what the church from earliest times has confessed, that Christ "was crucified, dead and buried; and on the third day he rose again" (the Apostles' Creed; see 1 Cor. 15:3–5). The importance of their role, especially as witnesses of Jesus' resurrection, can be gauged from the value that the early church placed on this experience (Acts 1:8, 21–22; 1 Cor. 9:1; 15:3–8).

Another common form of patronage in the first century was to provide a meeting place for a local club or religious organization, quite often in the patron's home. It was perfectly natural, therefore, for the early Christians to follow suit. The New Testament writers mention six churches meeting in the home of a certain person, and five of these were the homes of Christian women (or couples) (Acts 12:12; 16:14–15; Rom. 16:3–5; 1 Cor. 16:19; Col. 4:15; Philem. 2). Mary, the mother of John Mark, made her home available for the local body of believers in Jerusalem (Acts 12:12). Nympha's house was where the church of Laodicea met (Col. 4:15). Priscilla and Aquila provided a meeting place for the church, first in Ephesus (1 Cor. 16:19) and then in Rome (Rom. 16:3–5). A fourth woman named Lydia, a businesswoman from Thyatira, opened her home in Philippi to Paul (as his and the church's base of operations; Acts 16:14–15). This last gesture takes on special meaning when it is remembered that the Philippian church was the only church from which Paul felt comfortable accepting financial support (Phil. 4:10–19; cf. 1 Cor. 9:15–18; 1 Thess. 2:9).

Making one's home available as a meeting place involved more than cleaning the house and offering cake and coffee. The patron in those days was in charge of the group, including some legal responsibility.[37] So the fact that Mary, Nympha, Priscilla, and Lydia functioned as patrons indicates they possessed substantial financial resources.

Women were naturals for serving the church in this capacity. The household was their domain, and a large domain it was. Households in the first century included not only the immediate family and relatives but also slaves, freedmen, hired workers, and even tenants and partners in a trade or craft. This required that the woman of the house possess keen administrative and management skills. Paul, for this reason, places great emphasis on leadership capabilities in the family as an important indicator of leadership potential in the church (1 Tim. 3:4–5; 5:14). In fact, the term used for the leadership role of the woman of the house (*oikodespotein,* "to be master of a house," or "head of a family," 5:14) is much stronger than that used of the man (*prostēnai,* "to direct," "guard," "protect," 3:5).[38]

There are two other women patrons who are worthy of mention. Paul refers to Phoebe in Romans 16:1–2 as a *prostatis* of many, including himself. Translations vary in their rendering of this Greek term. They include "succourer" (KJV), "helper" (RSV, NASB, NKJV), "of great assistance" *(Phillips),* "a help to many" (NIV, NAB), "a good friend" (TEV, NEB, REB), "has looked after" (JB), and "a respected leader" (CEV).

In the culture of that day, however, a *prostatis* was a "benefactor" (NRSV, revised NAB)—or as we would say today a "sponsor." Sponsors in the first century welcomed their clients from time to time to their house and table, rendered assistance in time of need, offered legal aid as called for, and gave their clients gifts as the occasion warranted.[39] Jason, for instance, posted bond to ensure the good behavior of his client, Paul (Acts 17:5–9), and it appears that Lydia sent Paul money from time to time (Acts 18:5; Phil. 4:10–19).

Apphia could also legitimately be called a patron. Her name appears in the letterhead of one of Paul's letters: "Paul, a prisoner of Christ Jesus, and Timothy our brother, to Philemon our dear friend and fellow-worker, to Apphia our sister, to Archippus our fellow-soldier and to the church that meets in your home" (Philem. 1–2). The arguments go back and forth on whether Apphia was Philemon's wife, sister, or even slave. But whatever else may be said about her, the fact that she appears in the letterhead indicates she was a leader of the church at Colossae.

There is substantial support for this claim. Although we speak of "the letter to Philemon," it is actually addressed not to one but to three individuals. Also, "the church in *your* house" is plural, including all three individuals within its scope. In addition, Timothy ("our brother") and Apphia ("our sister") are referred to in exactly the same way. Since the letter is a public one (addressed to the church) rather than a private one (addressed to three personal friends), Paul is not merely being courteous in extending a greeting to Philemon's family members. Instead he is recognizing the leaders of the Colossian church.

It was not uncommon for Paul to recognize the leaders of a community in the opening and closing greetings. Philippians is a good example of Paul greeting the leaders at the beginning of his letter: "To all the saints in Christ Jesus at Philippi, together with the overseers and deacons" (Phil. 1:1). Romans (16:1–24) and Colossians (4:7–18) are illustrations of greetings to leaders at the letter's end.

WOMEN APOSTLES

In the church God has appointed first of all apostles.

1 Corinthians 12:28

Apostleship is a gift that Paul places first in two of his four lists of spiritual gifts (1 Cor. 12:28–31; Eph. 4:11). But what does it mean to possess this gift? And who can be included among the ranks of the apostles?

One thing is clear: Being an apostle is not synonymous with being one of the Twelve. Andronicus, Junia,[40] Barnabas, James, Silas, and Timothy are all called apostles (Rom. 16:7; 1 Cor. 9:5–6; Gal. 1:19; 2:9; 1 Thess. 1:1; 2:6), and yet none of them was one of the Twelve. Nor was Paul one of Jesus' chosen few. Yet, he opens almost every one of his letters with the claim that he is "an apostle of Christ Jesus by the will of God" (1 Cor. 1:1; 2 Cor. 1:1; Eph. 1:1; Col. 1:1; 2 Tim. 1:1; see also Rom. 1:1; Gal. 1:1; 1 Tim. 1:1; Titus 1:1).

So what does it mean to be an apostle? Some say you had to have seen the resurrected Christ to be an apostle. Paul himself uses his encounter with the risen Christ on the road to Damascus as a legitimizing mark of his own apostleship (1 Cor. 9:1; cf. 1 Cor. 15:7–8; Gal. 1:15–16). But not all of those whom Paul calls "apostles" were privileged to have had this experience. James certainly was among those who saw the risen Christ (1 Cor. 15:7). Barnabas, Silas, Andronicus, and Junia could well have been among the five hundred to whom Christ appeared (1 Cor. 15:6) or even among "all the apostles"—a group Paul distinguishes from the Twelve (1 Cor. 15:5, 7). Timothy, a Jew who was converted during Paul's first missionary journey, would not have had this opportunity (Acts 16:1–5), yet Paul calls him an apostle (1 Thess. 2:6). So an understanding of apostleship must lie elsewhere.

Paul's broader usage leads us to think that *apostle* was similar in function to a church planter. For one, the term appears in contexts that stress the person's role as a coworker in the church planting process (e.g., 1 Cor. 9:1–6; 1 Thess. 2:6–8). As "apostles of Christ," Paul, Silas, and Timothy could have been a financial burden on the newly founded Thessalonian church but waived this right (1 Thess. 1:1; 2:6–7). It also fits with Paul's understanding of the church as a house that is "built on the foundation of the apostles and prophets" (Eph. 2:20).[41]

If put this way, then apostleship was a role that both men and women could have filled during the New Testament period. But *could* and *did* can be very different things. Were there, in fact, any women named as apostles?

Priscilla and Aquila are spoken of in ways that suggest some evangelistic or church planting activity. Their joint tent-making operation with Paul in Corinth (Acts 18:1–3) and risking their lives for him to the benefit of "all the churches of the Gentiles" (Rom. 16:3–4) are easily understood in this fashion.

Junia, on the other hand, is explicitly named as an apostle. In fact, she is commended by Paul for her outstanding apostolic labors (Rom. 16:7). Paul also states that she had been in prison with him, suggesting a role distinctly comparable to his own.

A word must be said about the translation "Junia." English translations done from the 1950s to the early 1970s do not typically translate the name as feminine. Instead the Greek accusative *Iounian* is taken as a contraction of the masculine name *Iounianus* (rendered in English as "Junias" in the NASB, NAB, NIV, JB, NEB, RSV, and *Phillips*).[42] This is a complicated way of saying that *Junias* was a nickname or shortened form of *Junianus.*

Both older and more recent translations, however, render *Iounian* as the feminine "Junia" (KJV, ASV, TEV, NKJV, NRSV, NLT, revised NAB, NIV Inclusive Language Edition), and rightly so. The masculine name *Junias* (contracted or otherwise) simply does not occur in any inscription, on any tombstone, in any letterhead or letter, or in any literary work contemporary with Paul's writings. Indeed, the nickname does not appear in any existing Greek or Latin document of the Roman period. On the other hand, the feminine *Junia* is quite common and well attested in both Greek and Latin inscriptions. In fact, scholars have found over 250 examples of this name in Rome alone.[43]

None of the early versions of the Greek New Testament considered *Iounian* as anything else but feminine. For example, the Vulgate (the standard Latin translation of the Western church) has "Junia . . . well-known among the apostles." Also, the only variant on this name in the ancient manuscripts is also feminine—"Julia."

The fact of the matter is that no translator or commentator prior to the Middle Ages understood *Iounian* as other than feminine. John Chrysostom (bishop of Constantinople in the fourth century), for example, said: "How great is the devotion of this woman [Junia] that she should be even counted worthy of the appellation of apostle" (*Homilies on Romans* 31 [on Rom. 16:7]). Even Johannes Drusius in 1698 reminded his colleagues that *Junia* is the feminine form of *Junius.*[44]

In short, there is no reason to read *Iounian* as masculine and every reason to read it as feminine. Modern translators and commentators have difficulty with *Junia* because they have difficulty believing that the term *apostle* could be used of a woman. If we understand *apostle* as someone who has been specially commissioned by Christ with an authority parallel to a Peter or a Paul, then the difficulty is justifiable. (With that definition it would also be difficult to apply the word to Timothy.) If we focus on the gift of apostleship and understand it as equivalent to a church planter, however, then we are placing the matter in its proper context (unless, of course, one categorically denies that women can function in any sort of leadership capacity).

There is one other matter to bring up. Junia does not stand alone. The text reads: "Greet Andronicus and Junia my compatriots who were in prison with me; they are outstanding among the apostles and were in Christ before I was" (AT). What we likely have is a husband-wife team. Paul has already greeted Priscilla and Aquila as one such married team. So it is natural to think that he is doing the same here.

### WOMEN PROPHETS

> In the church God has appointed first of all apostles, second prophets.
>
> 1 Corinthians 12:28

Prophecy is placed second in two of Paul's four lists of gifts (1 Cor. 12:28–31; Eph. 4:11) and included in the other two (Rom. 12:6–8; 1 Cor. 12:8–10). Its importance is readily seen from Paul's instructing the church at Corinth to eagerly desire this gift (1 Cor. 14:1).

The role of prophet in the early church was a complex one. Although it included a predictive element (e.g., Acts 21:10–11), the primary task was comparable to the forthtelling role of the Old Testament prophet in reminding God's people of their covenant obligations. Done in the context of public worship, prophecy served to convict of sin (1 Cor. 14:24), to instruct (1 Cor. 14:31), to exhort (v. 31 NASB), to encourage (Acts 15:32), and to guide in the decision-making process (Acts 13:3–4; 16:6–7). How crucial this gift was can be gauged from the fact that it alone warranted examination for falseness or truthfulness by those with the gift of discernment (1 Cor. 14:29). Moreover, the role of prophet (along with that of apostle) is labeled as foundational in establishing and growing the church (Eph. 2:20).

There are numerous examples of women prophets, stretching back to Mosaic times. In fact, if there is one gift women consistently possessed and exercised throughout the history of God's people, it is this one. Miriam (Moses' sister), Deborah (during the period of the judges), Isaiah's wife (during the reigns of Uzziah, Jotham, Ahaz, and Hezekiah), Huldah (during the reign of Josiah), and Noadiah (during the postexilic period) are female prophets we noted in the previous section.

Anna continues this tradition in New Testament times. Luke describes her as a woman of outstanding piety. Instead of remarrying after the death of her husband (while still a young woman), she devoted herself to serving the Lord. "She never left the temple but worshiped night and day, fasting and praying" until she was eighty-four. Luke calls Anna a "prophetess" (NIV), for she "spoke about the [Christ] child to all who were looking forward to the redemption of Jerusalem" (Luke 2:36–38).

Women continued to exercise the gift of prophecy in the church. Philip, one of the leaders of the Hellenistic wing of the Jerusalem church, had four daughters who were prophetesses (Acts 21:9). Luke's brief mention in Acts whets the appetite for more information, but none is forthcoming. This undoubtedly is because women prophets were so well accepted as leaders in the church that no further commentary was necessary.

Postapostolic authors provide a few more details. Papias tells how he heard a wonderful story from the lips of Philip's daughters (Eusebius, *History of the Church* 3.39). Proclus (third-century leader of the Phrygian Montanists) places their prophetic ministry in Hierapolis, Asia. Eusebius ranks them "among the first stage in the apostolic succession" (*History of the Church* 3.37.1).

A Philadelphian woman named Ammia is also said to have prophesied during New Testament times (Eusebius, *History of the Church* 5.17.2–4). In fact, the second-century Montanists, Priscilla and Maximilla, used women like Ammia to justify their own prophetic office (Eusebius, *History of the Church* 5.17.4).

It is important to see that prophecy was not merely an impromptu movement of the Spirit but also a recognized leadership role in the church. Luke makes this clear when he identifies the leadership of the church at Antioch as "prophets and teachers" (Acts 13:1). Nor was prophecy, as some would claim, a less valued activity than other forms of ministry. This is evident from Paul's identification of prophetic speaking with "revelation" (*apokalyphthē;* 1 Cor. 14:29–30). He even goes further and puts the apostles and prophets in a category by themselves. It is to "God's holy apostles and prophets" that "the mystery of Christ . . . has now been revealed by the Spirit" (Eph. 3:4–5). In a very real sense, therefore, the New Testament prophet carries on the "Thus saith the Lord" task of the Old Testament prophet.

This is important to see, because Paul puts the prophetic activity of women on the same plane as the prophetic activity of men. According to 1 Corinthians 11:4–5, both exercise this role in exactly the same fashion. The only distinction is in their attire: Men were to prophesy with heads uncovered, while women were to have their heads covered (vv. 4–5). While scholars debate the exact nature and significance of this head covering, one thing is eminently clear: Women functioned in a highly visible leadership capacity.

## Women Teachers

> In the church God has appointed first of all apostles, second prophets, third teachers.
>
>                                                              1 Corinthians 12:28

Teaching is found in all of the Pauline lists of gifts (Rom. 12:6–8; 1 Cor. 12:28–31; Eph. 4:11). It is ranked third in one of these lists (1 Cor. 12:28), paired with *pastor* in another (pastor-teacher;[45] Eph. 4:11), and most likely to be identified with "a word of knowledge" in still another (1 Cor. 12:8 NASB).

There is probably no gift in the church today that is more valued than that of teaching. But is this good? Perceptions have undergone a substantial shift since New Testament times. It is not uncommon to have New Testament teaching treated as an office and conceived of as a position of authority. Some even go so far as to distinguish unofficial and official, public and private, and authoritative and nonauthoritative types of instruction.

Making such distinctions, however, is a decidedly modern phenomenon. The New Testament knows no such distinctions. Nowhere in the New Testament are teaching and authority *(exousia)* linked in any official sense (except, of course, in Jesus' case; e.g., Mark 1:21–22 and parallels). Nowhere is a distinction made between public and private spheres of instruction.

To make such distinctions is to lose the essentially charismatic nature of the teaching role. Teaching was an integral part of every facet of church life. The whole congregation at Colossae was called to "teach and admonish one another" (Col. 3:16). The writer to the Hebrews rebukes his listeners for still needing someone to teach them, since by this time they ought all to be teachers (Heb. 5:12). When the church at Corinth gathered in worship, it was presumed there would be those with a "word of knowledge" (1 Cor. 12:8) and that each would have "a psalm, a teaching, a revelation, a tongue, or an interpretation" (1 Cor. 14:26 NASB). The church at Antioch chose its missionaries from among the ranks of prophets and teachers (Acts 13:1–2). The older women in the church at Crete were expected to teach the younger women something about Christian character and family values (Titus 2:3–5). Timothy, Paul's stand-in at Ephesus, was instructed to devote himself "to preaching and to teaching" (1 Tim. 4:13). An overseer was expected to be "able to teach" (1 Tim. 3:2), and the work of some elders was that of "preaching and teaching" (1 Tim. 5:17).

When it came to women, however, the culture at large presented quite a different picture. Both women learners and teachers were a rarity. Jewish rabbis typically judged women as unsuitable to be taught the Torah (see p. 21). In Greek society, the education of women beyond the elementary grades was thought to be impractical or unnecessary. The education of Roman women began to be taken more seriously in the centuries before Christ, but even so, there were still relatively few women teachers in the public arena during New Testament times. Within Judaism, especially, women learners and teachers were a rarity. This makes Jesus' instruction of Mary and the inclusion of women disciples particularly striking (Luke 10:38–42). It also set the stage for women to have an instructional role in the church.

While it can be assumed that both men and women exercised the gift of teaching in the early church, no one is specifically named as possessing it. A number are named as doing it, however. Priscilla and Aquila, for example, instructed Apollos in the "way of God" (Acts 18:24–26). Teaching was also a part of what a prophet did. "You can all prophesy in turn," Paul says to the Corinthians, "so that everyone may be instructed and encouraged" (1 Cor. 14:31; cf. 14:19 "to instruct," *katecheō*). Since there were women prophets in Corinth (1 Cor. 11:5), instruction was most definitely part of their role.

It is sometimes said that women may have taught, but their instruction was informal and private rather than formal and public in nature. Priscilla took Apollos aside for some informal words of instruction; teaching was only incidental to the prophetic task (so it is claimed). The difficulty, though, is that exactly the same term is used in all these contexts. The congregation at Colossae is called to "teach" *(didaskō)* one another; Timothy is instructed to "teach" *(didaskō)* the church at Ephesus, and the older women at Crete are to "teach" *(kalodidaskalous)* the younger women. The sole exception is Acts 18:26, where Luke says that Priscilla and Aquila "expounded" *(exethento)* the way of God to Apollos, but this is the same term Luke uses for Paul's teaching. "From morning until evening," Luke reports, "Paul expounded *[exetitheto]* and testified about the kingdom of God" (Acts 28:23 AT). So to draw a distinction between private and public forms of instruction or between informal and formal types at this stage in the church's development is simply anachronistic.[46]

Instructional roles continued into the postapostolic period. Women were especially at the forefront in exposing and condemning heretics. Perhaps the most renowned was Marcella, who was praised by Jerome for her ability to confront heretical error (*Epistles* 127.2–7).[47]

WOMEN EVANGELISTS

It was he who gave some to be apostles, some to be prophets, some to be evangelists.

Ephesians 4:11

There was no lack of evangelists in the early decades of the church's history. This is not surprising since the primary energies of the church's leadership during those years were directed toward outreach. Were any of these evangelists women? The answer to this questions is a definite *yes.*

The women who traveled with Jesus and financially supported him come immediately to mind (Matt. 28:8–10; Luke 24:9–10; John 20:17–18). Mary Magdalene, singled out by John as the leader of the group, was commanded by Jesus to: "Go . . . to my brothers and tell them, 'I am returning to my Father and your Father, to my God and your God'" (John 20:17). She did exactly what Jesus asked and presented herself to the disciples with the news: "I have seen the Lord!" (John 20:18; cf. Matt. 28:8–10).[48]

Yet, although Mary Magdalene and the women were the first commissioned witnesses to Jesus' resurrection, they were not the first women to share the Good News about Jesus. Long before this, John credits the conversion of many in the Samaritan town of Sychar (a small village near Shechem) to the testimony of a woman (John 4:39).

Women were actively engaged in evangelism during the early years of the church. Paul commends Priscilla and Aquila as "co-workers" (Rom. 16:3) and Tryphena, Tryphosa, and Persis as "those who work hard in the Lord" (Rom. 16:12). This is the language of missionary activity. In fact, Paul uses exactly the same language of his own and other male colleagues' missionary labors (see p. 49). Paul's joint imprisonment with Junia and Andronicus indicates they, too, were engaged in some sort of evangelistic activity (Rom. 16:7). Preaching the Good News back then landed people in prison (e.g., Acts 16:19–24; 2 Cor. 11:23).

Euodia and Syntyche are the only women explicitly named as evangelists. They were Paul's co-workers, "who have contended 'by' his side in the cause of the gospel" (Phil. 4:2–3). Some would say these women did nothing more than provide hospitality, but the language does not in the least suggest this. For one, the term Paul uses of their role is a strong one: *synathleō* is the athlete who strains every muscle to achieve victory in the games (Phil. 4:3; LSJ s.v.). Also, Paul says that they labored side by side with him and names them as partners.

There is more. The broader context shows that these women were not only co-evangelists but key leaders of the Philippian church. Why else would Paul publicly appeal to a third party (the enigmatic "yokefellow") to help these women work out their differences? Their role was so important that their disagreement put the unity of the church in jeopardy.

### WOMEN DEACONS

If a person's gift is serving let him or her serve.

Romans 12:7 AT

If you serve, you should do it with the strength God provides, so that in all things God may be praised through Jesus Christ.

1 Peter 4:11

Two of the New Testament lists of spiritual gifts include the gift of serving. What does it mean, though, to possess the gift of serving? Are not all Christians called to serve the church in one capacity or another? The answer is a definite *yes.* Peter tells the churches of Asia Minor that "each one should use whatever gift he [or she] has received to serve others" (1 Peter 4:10 NIV). Yet, there were some whom the church recognized for the leadership they provided in this area. The title that the early church gave to such a person was *deacon.* In the church at Philippi, for instance, one of two primary leadership positions in the church was that of deacon (Phil. 1:1, "together with the overseers and deacons"), and in 1 Timothy the qualifications of a deacon are spelled out in detail (1 Tim. 3:8–13).

Did women serve as deacons in the early church? The answer again is *yes.* Phoebe is one woman who is singled out for this very role. In writing to the church at Rome, Paul commends her as "a *diakonos* of the church at Cenchrea" (Rom. 16:1).

There is a bit of variation among translations in rendering the Greek. The KJV, NKJV, NASB, and NIV translate *diakonos* as "servant," but this misses the official character of Paul's comments. Phoebe is the person designated to deliver Paul's letter to the Roman church. Paul's commands that the church "receive her in the Lord" and "give her any help she may need" make this quite clear (Rom. 16:2). To gain entry into a Christian community back then, it was customary to provide the person's credentials. Paul does this quite consistently with other colleagues (e.g., 2 Cor. 8:16–24; Eph. 6:21–22; Phil. 2:25–30; Col. 4:7–9), but it was especially important in Phoebe's case because Paul himself had never visited Rome.[49]

*Servant,* therefore, would hardly pass muster in this context. Nor would the REB's *minister,* which was not the officially recognized position it is today. The key phrase is "of the church at Cenchrea." "Fellow servant" and "faithful minister in the Lord" are fine for familiar personalities like Tychicus, Titus, and Epaphroditus (2 Cor. 8:16–24; Eph. 6:21–22; Col. 4:7–9; Phil. 2:25–30), but "a deacon of the church at Cenchrea" would have been essential for a virtual unknown (NLT, NRSV; cf. NEB "who holds office in").

The opposite extreme is to translate *diakonos* as "deaconess" (NAS, RSV, JB, NJB, *Phillips*). The difficulty here is that the rendering is anachronistic. It translates a term that was not in use during the apostolic period *(diakonissa).* In fact, the first clear instance is about the time of the Nicean

Council in A.D. 325 (Canon #19). Also, *deaconess* in the postapostolic period defined a role that was distinct and in many ways different from that of the New Testament deacon.[50]

The simple fact is that *diakonos,* like a number of Hellenistic Greek terms, could be used of either a man or a woman. It defined a function, not a person. The person in this case happens to be a woman. This was the way the early church fathers understood it. For example, Origen's commentary on the text of Romans asserts: "This text teaches with the authority of the apostle that even women are instituted deacons in the church" (third century; *Homilies on Romans* [on Romans 16:1]). Later John Chrysostom (fourth century) notes that Paul "added her rank by calling her a deacon" (*diakonon; Homilies on Romans* 30 [on Romans 16:1]).

A second text that treats the role of deacon at some length is 1 Timothy 3:8–13: "[Male] deacons, likewise, are to be worthy of respect, sincere, not indulging in much wine, not greedy for gain. . . . Women [deacons], likewise, are to be worthy of respect, not malicious talkers, but temperate and trustworthy in everything" (AT).

What is important about this passage is that it spells out qualifications for both male and female deacons. This means the church at Ephesus had women in at least one of its key leadership positions. Yet not all translations render the passage in this way. Some assume that Paul shifts at verse 11 to a treatment of the deacon's spouse and translate: "Their wives" (KJV, NKJV, NLT, *Phillips,* NEB, NIV, TEV) rather than "women [deacons]" (JB, RSV, NRSV, CEV, REB, NASB). The problem is that the Greek term *gynē* can mean either *wife* or *woman.* So the context must determine which is meant.

That Paul is setting forth the credentials of a group of women who served the church in some recognized capacity is apparent from the language and the grammar.[51] In the first place, the qualities specified in verse 11 are the exact duplicates of those listed for male deacons in verses 8–10. Also, the Greek word order of verses 8 and 11 is identical:

> verse 8: *diakonous hosautōs semnous mē dilogous*
> deacons likewise must be men worthy of respect, not double-tongued
> verse 11: *gynaikas hosautōs semnas mē diabolous*
> women likewise must be worthy of respect, not slanderers

Is Paul listing qualifications for women deacons or for the wives of deacons? That he is doing the latter is improbable for a number of reasons. First, the grammar does not support it. If Paul were turning to the wives of deacons, he would have written "*their* women likewise" (*gynaikas*

*tas autōn hōsautōs)* or have included some other indication of marital relationship, and he does neither. Second, there is no parallel for the wives
of overseers in the verses immediately preceding this section. Why highlight the wives of one group of leaders and ignore the wives of the other
group? Was the character of a deacon's wife intrinsically more important than that of the overseer's wife?

There is an even more serious difficulty, however. To read, "likewise
their wives must," is to assume that the wives of all deacons possessed the
necessary gifting and leadership skills to fulfill a role parallel to that of
their husbands. The Holy Spirit gives gifts to individuals, not couples, and
it is he, not the church (or a spouse), who determines who gets what gift
(1 Cor. 12:11). This is not to say that a married couple cannot have the
same gifts, but to assume that they do plainly contradicts what we know
about the work of the Spirit (see "The Church and Spiritual Gifts" above).

The postapostolic writers understood the texts both here and in
Romans 16:1 to be talking about women deacons. Clement of Alexandria, for instance, says, "For we know what the honorable Paul in one
of his letters to Timothy prescribed regarding women deacons" (*Stro-
mateis* 3.6.53); and John Chrysostom quite clearly understood Paul to
be speaking of those women who held the rank of deacon in the apostolic church (*Homilies on Timothy* 11 [on 1 Timothy 3:11]).

How, then, is one to explain Paul's return to male deacons in 1 Timothy 3:12? Is verse 11 merely a digression after which he returns to the
topic at hand? The important thing to note is *what* he returns to: "A deacon must be the husband of but one wife and must manage his children
and his household well." A reasonable explanation is that Paul goes on
to add qualifications that simply do not apply to women. It could be that
women deacons were drawn from the ranks of the unmarried (in which
case there would be no need to list qualifications having to do with marital status and family management).[52] An even more likely possibility is
that Paul goes on to list qualifications that apply to heads of households.
In a Greek city like Ephesus, this would invariably be the married male
(not the married female).

The church not only recognized the role of women deacons in the
apostolic period but continued the tradition with enthusiasm—especially in the East. Pliny (the governor of Bithynia in the early years of the
second century) tried to obtain information by torturing two female
deacons (*Letters* 10.96.8). In the third, fourth, and fifth centuries, virtually every Eastern father and church document mentions women deacons with approval.[53] The *Didascalia Apostolorum* (a third-century book
of church order) spells out their duties. The *Apostolic Constitutions* (a

fourth-century work about pastoral and liturgical practice) includes an ordination prayer for them (9.82; 16.134–36). Canon #15 of the Council of Chalcedon (fifth century) details the ordination process for women deacons and places them in the ranks of the clergy.[54]

In many ways female deacons were a very practical development. Women could gain entry into places that were forbidden to the average male and perform activities that would be deemed inappropriate for the opposite sex.[55] The duties of female deacons in the postapostolic period were quite extensive. They taught children and youth. They discipled new female believers. They went to the homes of believers and evangelized unbelieving women of the household. They visited the sick, cared for the ailing, administered communion to the shut-ins, and distributed charitable donations to women in need in the congregation. In the worship service they served as doorkeepers, assisted with the baptism of women, and administered communion in times of need.

### WOMEN WORSHIP LEADERS

> When you come together, everyone has a hymn, or a word of instruction, a revelation, a tongue or an interpretation.
>
> 1 Corinthians 14:26

Worship in the New Testament period was not orchestrated and directed by a single individual; it was much more of a cooperative venture. This cooperative venture included women. Women were actively involved in the worship life of the early church. Luke records that the apostles gathered frequently to pray as a group "along with the women and Mary the mother of Jesus" (Acts 1:14). Paul expects to find both men and women leading in prayer when the Corinthian believers gather for worship ("Every man who prays . . . every woman who prays," 1 Cor. 11:4–5). His only qualification is that women and men attire themselves in socially acceptable ways so they do not give offense to God or to outsiders (1 Cor. 11:13–16).

The women in the church at Ephesus also played an active role in worship. In 1 Timothy 2:9 Paul instructs: "Likewise [I want] women [to pray] . . . with proper clothing, modestly and discreetly" (NASB). Some think this passage is merely concerned with appropriate dress for a worship service. For example, TEV has "I also want the women to be modest and sensible about their clothes." But the grammar of the surrounding verses and the flow of the argument indicate Paul is concerned with fitting attire for women who lead in prayer. Paul opens the chapter with a general discussion of the kinds of prayers that should be a part of the typical worship experience and for whom these prayers should be made

(1 Tim. 2:1–7). He then goes on to discuss inappropriate conduct while praying. The men must "lift up holy hands in prayer, without anger or disputing" (2:8). "I *will* it," Paul states. "Likewise women should dress modestly, with decency and propriety, not with gold braided hair or pearls or expensive clothes (2:9 AT).

Two things should be noted. First, the word *likewise* (1 Tim. 2:9 NASB) refers back to the subject matter at hand, namely, proper demeanor for praying in public. Second, the grammar lacks a subject and a main verb. The NIV ("I also want the women to dress modestly") does not really reflect what is actually there in the Greek. A literal translation would run: "Likewise the women with modest dress." This type of shorthand is common in the New Testament when an author is treating a series of matters related to a general topic (e.g., Eph. 5:21–33; 1 Peter 2:13–17). When this occurs, the missing grammatical pieces are supplied from what precedes. In the case of 1 Timothy 2:9, the missing grammatical pieces can be found in verse 8: "*I want* the men *to pray in every place* with raised hands that are holy and without anger and disputing. Likewise [I want] women [to pray in every place] with modest dress and to attire themselves decently and properly" (AT).

It is important to see that Paul does not contest the appropriateness of women praying either in 1 Timothy or in 1 Corinthians. In fact, he assumes women will be so engaged. The propriety of what they wear while praying in public is Paul's only concern—a concern we can appreciate today. It is equally inappropriate today for a worship leader to flaunt his or her wealth ("gold," "pearls," "expensive clothes"; 1 Tim. 2:9) or to dress in a fashion that can distract from worship of God (i.e., short dresses, low necklines, tight pants).

### MINISTERING WIDOWS

> No widow may be put on the list of widows unless she is over sixty, has had but one husband, and is well known for her good works such as bringing up children, showing hospitality, washing the feet of the saints, helping those in trouble and devoting herself to all kinds of good deeds.
>
> 1 Timothy 5:9–10

There are good reasons for thinking that Paul is talking about a ministry of widows in 1 Timothy 5:9–10. First, he lists requirements that parallel the qualifications for other recognized leadership positions. The widow must have been the wife of one husband and have raised her children well (cf. 1 Tim. 3:2, 12; Titus 1:6). She must also be well-known for her good deeds (cf. Titus 1:8) and have a reputation for offering hospitality (1 Tim. 3:2; Titus 1:8). Second, Paul uses a technical term that has to do with drawing up a list for purposes of enlistment (*katalegō*, v. 9; LSJ s.v.). So it is not just a matter of being "put on a list" (1 Tim. 5:9) but of being officially "enrolled" (RSV, JB, REB, note). The Living Bible's "a widow who wants to become one of the special church workers" catches the basic idea. Third, there is mention of an ongoing ministry. These widows devoted themselves to praying for the church "night and day" (1 Tim. 5:5). Fourth, Paul instructs that they be financially compensated for their time (v. 3 *timaō* means to "reward" or "pay"; LSJ s.v. and BAGD s.v.; cf. 1 Tim. 5:17). Finally, Paul's concern about broken pledges suggests that widows took a vow of widowhood in which they pledged full-time service to Christ (1 Tim. 5:11–12).[56]

The qualifications Paul lists provide an insight into the widow's range of activities. Among the good deeds are washing the feet of the saints and helping those in trouble (1 Tim. 5:10). Foot washing was a common courtesy extended to guests attending a meal at one's home. Since showing hospitality comes right before, it would appear that the ministry role of these widows included providing food and lodging for Christians on the road. "Helping those in trouble" can be more literally translated "helping those persecuted for their faith" (*thlibō* means "to press," "oppress"). What form this help took is difficult to determine. It could have involved visiting and caring for those in prison, providing shelter for those fleeing persecution, or meeting the basic needs of those who had lost family and jobs because of their commitment to Christ.

The duties of these widows may also have included caring for orphans—one of the major challenges faced by the early church (e.g., Hermas, *Mandate* 8; *Apostolic Constitutions* 3.3). This would explain the requirement of being a good parent. Some house-to-house visitation is suggested by Paul's criticism that younger widows (with too much time on their hands) were "going about from house to house . . . saying things they ought not to" (1 Tim. 5:13). They probably did this under the pretext of distributing charitable contributions or of caring for the needy. "Saying things they ought not to say" may indicate a teaching role— somewhat along the lines of what is found in Titus 2:3–4, "The older women . . . can train the younger women to love their husbands and children, to be self-controlled and pure, to be busy at home."[57]

Acts 9 may well give us the first glimpse of a ministerial order of widows outside Jerusalem. Luke mentions a widow in Joppa named Dorcas, "who was always doing good and helping the poor" (Acts 9:36). When she died, all the widows stood around Peter, crying and showing him the robes and other clothing Dorcas had made while she was still with them (Acts 9:39). This sounds very much as if there was a select number of widows who served the needs of the larger group.

It is clear from the nature of Paul's comments in 1 Timothy 5 that he is not instituting a ministry of widows but introducing quality controls over an existing one. "Compensate only widows who are truly in need," he states (v. 3 AT). "Do not enroll widows younger than sixty years of age" (vv. 9, 11 AT). "I counsel younger widows to marry" (v. 14). It would seem from the length of Paul's treatment and the corrective nature of his instruction that this ministry had gotten out of hand in several respects (including perhaps an unexpected growth in numbers of widows) and was in need of clear protocols.[58]

The early church was not unique in recognizing the ministry potential of elderly women. Anna, a widow who fasted and prayed night and day in the temple, is commonly taken to be the prototype for this kind of ministry (Luke 2:36–38). Elderly women (and men) took up leadership roles in the Essene communities ("And she will take a place in the council of the elder men and women," *Ritual of Marriage*).[59]

Ministering widows flourished in the postapostolic period. Polycarp calls them "God's altar" (*To the Philippians* 4.3), and Clement of Alexandria ranks them after elders, bishops, and deacons (*Paidagogos* 3.12.97). By the third century, their ministry was quite extensive. There was some variation from church to church, but recurring responsibilities included praying for the church, teaching the rudiments of the faith, hospitality, caring for the sick, fasting, prophecy, and caring for the needs of destitute widows and orphans.[60] There were some limitations. For example, widows were discouraged from teaching more than basic Christianity and from taking the initiative without a deacon's permission (e.g., *Apostolic Constitutions* 2.26). But by and large what we have here is a distinctly pastoral position.

## Multigifted Women

Just as Miriam and Deborah were multigifted Israelite women who engaged in a range of ministries, so there were multigifted Christian women who served the early church in a variety of ways. Two women in particular come to mind—Priscilla and Phoebe.

Priscilla represents the cosmopolitan, well-traveled Roman businesswoman. She and her husband, Aquila, moved from Rome to Corinth to Ephesus and then back to Rome in the space of only eight years (Acts 18:2; Rom. 16:3–5; 1 Cor. 16:19). They must have had sufficient finances to do so (beyond the income from their trade), since each time they uprooted themselves, they were able to secure living quarters (*oikos* probably means an apartment above their artisan shop). They, in turn, offered their home as a meeting place for the church and a rest stop for missionaries and other traveling Christians (see, for example, Acts 18:26; 1 Cor. 16:19). At the time Paul wrote his second letter to Timothy, Priscilla and Aquila had moved once again to Ephesus, possibly to continue Paul's missionary efforts there (2 Tim. 4:19).

Priscilla was a colaborer with her husband in every way. It was not uncommon in first-century Roman society for the wives of artisans to work side by side with their spouse—much like mom-and-pop businesses today (Acts 18:2–3).[61] What is unusual, however, is that when Luke refers to their occupation as tentmakers, the order is "Aquila and Priscilla" (Acts 18:2; cf. 1 Cor. 16:19), but when Luke and Paul speak from a ministry point of view, the order is always "Priscilla and Aquila." Paul was accompanied by "Priscilla and Aquila" (Acts 18:18). Apollos was instructed by "Priscilla and Aquila" (Acts 18:26). Paul sends greetings to "Priscilla and Aquila" as "co-workers in Christ Jesus" (Rom. 16:3; cf. 2 Tim. 4:19). This would suggest that of the two, it was Priscilla who possessed the dominant ministry and leadership skills.[62]

Priscilla's range of ministry roles included teaching (Acts 18:24–26), patronage (Rom. 16:5; 1 Cor. 16:19), evangelism ("co-worker in Christ," Rom. 16:3 AT), and perhaps overseer ("the church that meets in your home," Rom. 16:5; 1 Cor. 16:19 AT). That her name should surface in a teaching context like Acts 18:26 is significant indeed.

Were Priscilla's activities inappropriate or wrong? There is no hint of disapproval anywhere in the New Testament. On the contrary, Paul commends her as a coworker whose ministry earned her the thanks of "all the churches of the Gentiles" (Rom. 16:4).

Phoebe is another multigifted woman. Unfortunately, this has been obscured in translation (e.g., Rom. 16:2, "a good friend" TEV, REB, "a helper" RSV, NIV). A careful reading of Romans 16:1–2 against the cultural backdrop of that day shows that she served in at least four ministry roles. Her ministry role in her local church was that of deacon—one of several recognized leadership positions in the apostolic period. Paul used her as his letter carrier on at least one occasion ("receive her in the Lord," Rom. 16:2). The role of *prostatis* or patron to the broader Christian community is a third area of ministry (Rom. 16:2). Paul states that he himself was the recipient of her patronage, as were many others.

Finally, Paul instructs the Roman church to welcome and help Phoebe. This kind of language is normally used of itinerant missionaries (e.g., 1 Cor. 16:11; 2 Cor. 7:15) and may indicate that Paul entrusted Phoebe with a ministry task beyond that of delivering his letter to the Roman church. This was certainly the case by the turn of the century. Ignatius, for instance, refers at least twice to a deacon of one church serving as an ambassador to another church (*To the Philadelphians* 10.1; *To the Ephesians* 2.1).

### THE CHALLENGE TODAY

Priscilla and Phoebe challenge us to be accurate about naming the ministries of women. Paul did not hesitate to name these women as colleagues and speak of their ministries in exactly the same terms as their male counterparts.

Apostolic Canon #10 (*Apostolic Constitutions* 8.20) is a fine summary of how the church in the early centuries viewed the ministries of women. It contains a prayer that was traditionally used in ordaining women deacons: "You who filled Deborah, Hannah and Huldah with the Holy Spirit . . . who in the tabernacle and in the temple appointed women to keep the holy doors, look upon your servant chosen for the ministry and give to her the Holy Spirit . . . that she may worthily perform the office committed unto her."

What is noteworthy here is that female leadership was viewed as a continuation of the way God has worked throughout history and not as some new phenomenon or modern development. There is also a recognition that the work of ministry depends on the empowerment of the Holy Spirit, not on the holding of an office. Gift precedes function.

Another thing to see is that this early ordination prayer labels the work of women as *ministry.* How we define this term is essential to having a biblically based understanding of the church. The New Testament knows no other definition than the "work of service" (Eph. 4:12 AT). "Service," the basic definition of the Greek term *diakonia,* is what the early church understood by ministry.

This is not to rule out formal leadership roles, but it is important to understand the proper role of the leader. Paul says that Christ gave leaders to the church, not to govern it or exercise authority over it, but "to prepare God's people for the work of service [*diakonia*]" (Eph. 4:12 AT). The leader's role was to equip the church for ministry, not to replace it (as is all too common today). Only in this way can the church reach God's intended goal, namely, to "be built up until we all reach unity in the faith and in the knowledge of the Son of God and become mature, attaining to the whole measure of the fullness of Christ" (Eph. 4:13). Without this definition of ministry, there can be no real understanding of the church and the role of women within it.

# What Roles Can Women Play in Society?

A second question that needs to be raised is the role of women in the marriage, the family, and society at large. This is a particularly important question given the impact of the feminist movement on societal roles during the past three decades. The number of Christian women in top executive positions in both private and public sectors is telling. To give just three examples: Roberta Hestenes served for nine years as president of Eastern College; Elizabeth Dole acted as secretary of transportation under Ronald Reagan, secretary of labor under George Bush, and president of the American Red Cross; and Margaret Thatcher served as prime minister of England for eleven years. Is this what God would have Christian women do? Are they free to provide leadership in the workplace? Is it acceptable for them to be top executives in the political arena? Or are these roles restricted to men?

Then there is the related question of the legitimacy of women in the workforce. The majority of American families today have two working parents. Many preschool children spend most of their waking hours in day care rather than at home. In some cases, this is dictated by economic necessity. In other cases, it is driven by a woman's desire to use her God-given talents and abilities. Is there a place for the working mother in God's plan?

What about a woman's place in the family circle? Can she provide leadership in the marriage, or is her role to submit to her husband's leadership? Can she instruct and direct her children, or is this uniquely the father's role? Can a woman be the breadwinner of the family, or is this a job reserved for men?

Even more fundamental is the question of whether women are fully human. Are they, like men, created in the image of God? Even though some have denied that this is the case, we have a clear *yes* in Genesis 1:27: "So God created humankind in his image, in the image of God he created him; male and female he created them" (NRSV). Does this mean, then, that women are equal to men in all areas of life?

Perhaps a better question to ask is whether women are fully redeemed, for while most agree that women are fully human, there are some who believe the fall affected the playing out of this full humanity.[1] Simply put, some think Eve's deception and disobedience permanently disqualified women from assuming positions of leadership.[2] Is this the case? If so, what does redemption in and through Christ mean for women?

While it is important not to compartmentalize, it is fair to say that on the question of the place of women in society, evangelicals basically fall into one of two broad camps: traditionalists (or complementarians) and egalitarians. Traditionalists maintain that the role of women is to defer to male leadership in the home, church, and society. Men are to lead, provide for, and protect women. Women are to affirm, receive, and nurture strength and leadership from men.[3] For the traditionalist, leadership is the sole prerogative of men. For a woman to assume a position of leadership over men is to contravene the different masculine and feminine roles ordained by God as part of creation—roles of male headship and female submission.[4]

Egalitarians, on the other hand, believe men and women were created for full and equal partnership. Husbands and wives are bound together in a relationship of mutual submission and responsibility. The husband's function as head is understood as self-giving love and service. Leadership is to be shared, not ordered. It is a gift that men and women are equally to develop and exercise for the good of the church, the family, and society.[5]

What does the Bible have to say about all this? Scripture speaks quite directly to certain aspects of women's roles in society. For example, there is a good bit of information about the creation of humankind as male and female and about the institution of marriage. Regarding other societal roles, however, Scripture provides little information. There are only a handful of passages that speak to the role of women in the family, and virtually all have to do with appropriate behavior for women in a very specific cultural context—such as Sarah calling her husband "lord" (1 Peter 3:6 NASB). Also, there is little teaching about the public roles of women—although there are numerous examples of socially active women (e.g., Acts 16:14; 18:2–3).

Determining biblically acceptable and unacceptable roles for women is, therefore, not as easy as one would wish. One thing is certain, however—to gain any clarity on this question, it is imperative to have a good understanding of the cultural background that informs the relevant biblical passages. What roles did women play in the society of biblical times? Did the women of the early church fall in line with these roles, or did they depart from them in significant ways? This is the first and foremost question. The next question is similar: Which of these roles are rooted in creation and redemption, and which are rooted in the conventions of a particular time and place?

## Women's Roles During New Testament Times

In looking at women's roles in the New Testament era, one must keep several things in mind. First, our sources of information tend to target the accomplishments of the upper classes (those who possessed either earned or inherited wealth). Inscriptions laud the contributions of those with money. Literary works highlight the endeavors of the leisured. Speeches tend to be directed at the power brokers of society.

Tombstone inscriptions are one exception. These are quite helpful in providing a basic idea of the typical occupations of women from all walks of life. Private letters and public documents are another exception. They give us a fairly good idea of the day-to-day activities of women—although not a detailed one.

A second thing to keep in mind is that literary works reflect the point of view of the author, not necessarily the attitudes of society as a whole. Authors often wrote to express an opinion one way or another on a particular subject or issue. The opinions of Jewish rabbis are especially to be handled with care. They not only reflect a particular point of view, but one that often postdates the biblical period.

Writers often took pen in hand in reaction to prevailing trends in society. Greek and Roman satirists and moralists, in particular, are renowned for their biting criticism of anything that challenged the status quo. The role of women in society was no exception. In the centuries before Christ, a gradual liberation of women occurred in the Greco-Roman world. While the gains for women in legal, economic, and educational spheres were striking, the reaction against these gains was often quite strong.

The reason is easy to see. The family unit, which was basic to Roman society, was thought to be threatened by the intrusion of women in the public arena. Some went so far as to blame the high divorce rate on what they saw as the inevitable neglect of wifely and household responsibilities that came with increased public roles.

There is some truth in this perception. Increased public participation did in fact mean that fewer women concentrated their efforts on bearing and raising sons for Rome. So much was this the case that Emperor Augustus introduced legislation that offered attractive incentives for women who bore at least three children and made it illegal for women between the ages of twenty-five and fifty to be unmarried. He also promoted cults that centered on childbearing, fidelity, and familial bonds in an effort to shore up the family unit.

The consequence of all this for women can be summed up by the word *tension.* We all live with tensions; life in the early centuries was no different. For women the tension between public and private roles was especially noteworthy. In the A.D. first century women were out and about in public, functioning in highly visible roles and, with few exceptions, in free exchange with men. Roman society by and large supported this public visibility (although Jewish society did not). Epicureans and Cynics, for instance, both defended expanded roles and accepted women within their ranks. Highly placed women were lauded and honored by the communities in which they served. This, in turn, enhanced the standing of all family members (even members of the extended family). The end result was not unlike Proverbs 31, in which, because of the woman's accomplishments, her husband is respected at the city gate and her children arise and call her blessed.

Yet, despite expanded public roles, the private sphere remained largely traditional. The husband (or father) remained the legal head of the household. The key word is *legal.* At no time during the early centuries was a woman able to act without male representation. No contract could be finalized or business transaction carried out without appropriate male consent. For a daughter, this meant her father; for a wife, her husband (or her father if the marriage was "without power" or *sine manus* [that is, not under the husband's control]); for a widow or divorced woman, her brother or other male guardian. Even during the New Testament period, when male representation decreased in importance, Roman law remained unchanged in this area.

There was a second tension—one between the ideal and real roles of women. The ideal (as mentioned in the previous chapter) was a stay-at-home mother who devoted her time to managing her household, attending to her husband, and caring for her children. Tombstone inscriptions and funeral orations bear out the feminine ideal of domesticity. One such inscription penned by a husband runs: "Here lies Regina . . . your piety, your chaste life, your love for your people, your observance of the Law, your devotion to your wedlock the glory of which was dear to you. For all these deeds your hope of the future is assured" (Rome second century C.E.; *CIJ* 476).

In reality, however, an increasing number of women were desirous of pursuing a different career path (such as gladiator, musician, painter, or doctor). How did the men of that day respond? Some were honestly conflicted. The Stoic philosopher Musonius Rufus is a good example. While he defended the right of a woman to learn philosophy and argued that girls should receive the same education as boys, the primary goal of such an education was not to better prepare women for public service but for managing their households.

### Women in Jewish Society

What about women in Jewish society? It is fair to say that women in Palestine were slower to take advantage of the legal, economic, and educational gains under Roman rule. In part, this was because of male attitudes toward women remaining largely conservative—at least insofar as Jewish writers of the day give us an accurate picture of prevailing male sentiments. Even so, there are some signs of changing attitudes, and there is evidence of modest developments in the public sphere.

Changing attitudes are reflected, for instance, in the bipolar statements made about women in the literary materials. On the one hand, women are the originators of sin and so should be allowed no outlet to bold speech (Joshua ben Sira, *Ecclesiasticus* 25:24–25). This is because they (like Eve) are more susceptible to deception than men and their minds are easily caught by the persuasions of falsehood (Philo, *Questions and Answers on Genesis* 1.33).[6] For this reason a woman is to be obedient to her husband in every way (Josephus, *Against Apion* 2.24 §201; Philo, *Hypothetica* 7.3). Some (especially later rabbis) even go so far as to characterize women as lazy, stupid, garrulous, vain, frivolous, and unteachable.

In other literary materials, however, women are portrayed as the intellectual, moral, and spiritual equals (and in some cases superiors) of men. Job's daughters are said to have received a better inheritance than that of their seven brothers (*Testament of Job* 46–53). Rebecca is pictured as the spiritual leader in her marriage (*Jubilees* 25:11–23). The Book of Judith lifts up Judith as a model of scrupulous devotion to the Mosaic law and as Israel's deliverer. The moral integrity of Asenath equals (and at some points excels) that of Joseph (*Joseph and Asenath*). Writers (including some rabbis) who speak positively of women typically characterize them as hardworking, compassionate, and intelligent.[7]

Negative opinions about women need to be placed in their proper cultural context. Jewish men were reacting to the fast-changing roles of women during Hellenistic and Roman times. For example, the strong statements of Philo (a native of Alexandria, Egypt) come as no surprise when it is remembered that of all women in the Roman Empire, Egyptian women (both native and foreign) exercised the greatest freedom. Nor is Joshua ben Sira's attitude surprising, coming from a Jewish academician fighting the tide of Hellenism that swept Palestine in the second century B.C.

Overall, though, Jewish thinking fell largely in line with traditional and ideal cultural attitudes. For Jewish society to function well, two things needed to happen: Women had to be subordinate to men in every aspect of life, and they had to devote themselves to the domestic sphere. Three reasons were commonly put forward by the theologians of the day. The first was the unclean condition of women. In a theological context where cleanliness was next to godliness, the physical uncleanness of women once a month caused no little difficulty for those of a Pharisaic mindset. The second reason was a woman's supposedly flawed nature. Women were thought to be prone to sin and so in need of male leadership and direction. The third reason was a belief that God had ordained the headship of men and the subordination of women so that the woman's very well-being—and that of her family—depended on her remaining subordinate to male authority.[8]

### The Rights of Jewish Women

One way to measure the status of women in a particular society is by the rights they possess compared with their male counterparts. This kind of comparison has yielded some helpful insights regarding Jewish women and has served to debunk several common misconceptions.

One such misconception is that Jewish women had no rights. They were legally and socially much like beasts of burden to be bought and sold in the marketplace. Certain evangelical scholars say this even today.[9] But this was not so. To be sure, there were then as there are today the denigrating opinions of the disgruntled. For instance, Rabbi Naman (third–fourth century) went so far as to describe Deborah the judge and Huldah the prophetess as "two haughty women" whose "names are hateful" (b. Meg. 14b).[10] But opinions like these are the rare exception rather than the norm.

Mosaic law does not support the misconception that Jewish women had no rights. Although the tenth commandment forbids a man to covet his neighbor's wife (Exod. 20:17), a woman was not her husband's property any more than the language of "my husband" or "my wife" implies such today. A wife could not be sold as an ox or a donkey could. Mosaic law clearly prohibited this—even in the case of captive women (see, for example, Deut. 21:14). Also, a woman's conjugal rights, which were spelled out in the marriage contract, distinguished her from the slave who was truly owned.

It is fair, though, to say that inheritance laws favored men (Num. 27:8; cf. *m. Ketub.* 4.6). It is also true that a father held more authority over his daughters than over his sons and that the husband was viewed as the head of the household (e.g., Num. 5:11–31; 30:10–15).

Yet, in the eyes of Mosaic law, men and women were equal (even in cases of adultery or illicit sexual relations; Lev. 20:10–21). Men and women were joint members of the covenant people of Israel. Women were subject to all the prohibitions and obligations of the law (e.g., Exod. 20:1–2; Lev. 19:2; Deut. 5:6). The ten commandments applied equally to men and women. Children were duty-bound to honor both their mother and their father (Exod. 20:12; Deut. 5:16). In fact, if anything, Mosaic law sought to shore up the rights of women, not tear them down (see, for example, the treatment of divorce in Deut. 24:1–4). The eye-for-an-eye principle of the Mosaic code was clearly more equitable toward women than comparable legal codes of the day (see, for example, favoritism toward nobility in Hammurabi's code).

So, what rights did Jewish women in antiquity possess then? It is difficult to make blanket statements because freedoms varied according to age, marital status, and location. In general, however, Jewish girls below the age of majority (twelve and a half years old) had the fewest rights, married women had more rights, and divorcées and widows had the most rights.

A Jewish girl's father had full authority over her while she was a minor, including the right to sell her into slavery (Exod. 21:7), but he could not sell her into prostitution (Lev. 19:29) or offer her as a child sacrifice (Deut. 18:10). A daughter had no right to her own possessions; even the wages she earned belonged to her father (*m. Ketub.* 4.4; compare *b. Ketub.* 40b). She also had no legal rights beyond those her father exercised on her behalf. If she made a religious vow, her father could render it null and void (Num. 30:3–5). Acceptance or refusal of a marriage contract was her father's prerogative (Deut. 22:16; cf. *m. Ketub.* 4.4; *Qidd.* 2.1)—although she could ask to have that decision deferred until she reached the age of majority. If a Jewish girl was violated, defamed, or injured, the compensation money was paid to her father, not to her (e.g., Exod. 22:16–17; Deut. 22:13–19, 28–29; cf. *m. Ketub.* 4.4).[11]

Once a girl reached the age of majority, her rights increased. She could arrange her own marriage (*m. Qidd.* 2.1; cf. *b. Qidd.* 2b [79a]), keep her earnings (*m. B. Meṣ.* 1.5), testify in court (*m. Ketub.* 2.5–6), and swear an oath (*m. Šebu.* 5.1; *Ketub.* 9.4; *Ned.* 11.10).[12] She had the right to maintenance after her father's death and to receive it before her brothers could inherit, if the property was small (*m. Ketub.* 13.3). She could even inherit her father's property if her father died without a male heir.[13]

The rights of the divorcée and widow were even more extensive. The Babata documents preserved at Qumran show the legal capabilities of Jewish women in the A.D. first and second centuries. Here was a woman in charge of her life—inheriting the properties of two husbands, buying and selling properties, and supervising her holdings. The number of legal transactions she handled is astonishing even by modern standards (thirty-five legal documents were found in her possession). To give an example, on one occasion in court Babata defended her interests against claims from various members of her late husband's family, including the wife of her second husband and the guardians of her son by her first husband.[14]

This level of activity accords with what is found in rabbinic materials. A divorced or widowed woman could bring suit for damages (*m. B. Qam.* 1.3), sell property in her possession (*m. Ketub.* 11.2), testify in court (*m. Ketub.* 2.5–6), swear an oath (*m. Šebu.* 5.1; *Ketub.* 9.4; *Ned.* 11.9), manage her earnings (*m. B. Meṣ.* 1.5), and arrange her own marriage (*m. Qidd.* 2.1).

### EDUCATION

Up until the age of twelve, most Jewish girls received the same education as boys. Primary education for all children in the Roman system amounted to the basics in reading, writing, and arithmetic. A Jewish education went beyond these basics to include religious instruction. Both boys and girls were expected to be able to read, memorize, and recite Scripture.[15] Josephus boasts that if anyone asks "any of our people about our laws, [they] will more readily tell them all than tell [their] own name and this in consequence of our having learned them immediately as soon as ever we became sensible of anything" (*Against Apion* 2.18 §178).

Further education in Roman times included secondary learning (grammar, rhetoric, dialectic, geometry, arithmetic, astronomy, and music) and advanced instruction (physical education, rhetoric, philosophy, law, medicine, etc.). But while a Greek teenager would study Homer and the dramatists, a Jewish teenager would study written law (Torah), oral law (Halakah), and oral interpretation (Haggadah).

Jewish girls did not follow the formal route of a secondary education comparable to that of their male peers, but this did not exclude them from pursuing secondary instruction of an informal kind. The rabbis were known to have debated the value of this. Some like Eliezer ben Hyrcanus (circa A.D. 80–120) thought that giving one's daughter a knowledge of the law was sheer foolishness (*m. Soṭa.* 3.4; *b. Soṭa.* 21a–22a), while others like Simeon ben Azzai (circa 120–140) believed a father should teach his daughter at least some Torah for her own safety and need (*m. Soṭa.* 3.4).

### MARRIAGE

An Israelite woman was inseparably linked to her husband. Even Deborah, who was a prophet, a military general, and a judge, was known as "the wife of Lappidoth" (Judg. 4:4). This was partly because at that time Jewish girls usually married at age twelve and boys between age twelve and fourteen. It had even more to do with the focus in biblical times on the family or household unit rather than on individuals as such.

A person was named by the household to which he or she was attached. Even today people are known by their family connections. "That's Joe's son" or "that's Frank's wife" are familiar comments. The one exception is the head of the household. While today we might say "that is Sue's husband" or "that is Linda's father," such was not the case in biblical times. Women were named in relationship to their father or husband and not vice versa. In part, this was because of the authority attached to heads of households.

This authority impacted the marriage relationship. A woman's vow of submission and the husband's oath of provision was a routine part of the first-century Jewish marriage contract. The routine contract read: "[Mary] shall remain with [Joseph], obeying him as a wife should obey her husband. . . . [Joseph] whether he is at home or away from home shall furnish [Mary] with everything necessary and clothing and whatsoever is proper for a wedded wife, in proportion to their means" (Papyrus Tebtunis 104 [Alexandria 92 B.C.]).

It is important to note, however, that in vowing submission to her husband, a Jewish woman did not give up all personal rights. Some rights were guaranteed to her by law. She had the right to have her physical (food, clothing, shelter) and sexual needs met (Exod. 21:10; *m. Ketub.* 12.3; *b. Ketub.* 77a). Her husband was forbidden by law from striking her. If her husband died leaving only a little property, she had a right to maintenance before her sons could inherit (*m. Ketub.* 9.2; cf. 13.3). She also had a right to medical care (*m. Ketub.* 4.9), a proper burial (*m. Ketub.*

4.4; *t. Ketub.* 4.2), and the payment of a ransom if she were captured (*m. Ketub.* 4.4, 8–9; *t. Ketub.* 4.2). If her husband failed to fulfill her rights, she could demand them in a court of law (*b. Ketub.* 77a).

A woman's dowry was her most important possession. Every Jewish woman brought one into the marriage, retained ownership of it during the marriage, and took it with her after the marriage. The dowry was a deterrent to divorce, abuse, and neglect. It also provided security in the event that she became widowed ( *y. Ketub.* 5.2 [29d]).

What about headship? Where and how does this enter the picture? It is a curious fact that while the husband's headship is implied in certain of the Old Testament stories, nowhere in the Mosaic law is the wife explicitly commanded to obey her husband. Nor do any regulations exist for dealing with a disobedient wife (as exist for dealing with disobedient children; e.g., Exod. 21:15, 17).

Moreover, there are no role distinctions delineated for husband and wife in Mosaic law. Nowhere are domestic and public spheres labeled as specifically male or female. Fathers and mothers are equal parental figures; obedience is commanded equally to father and mother (Exod. 20:12; 21:15, 17; Deut. 5:16). Paul reflects this understanding when he instructs the children in his churches to obey their parents because it is "the first commandment with a promise" (Eph. 6:1–3; cf. Exod. 20:12).

All this would suggest that marital roles and rights were not hard-and-fast rules in biblical times. The ideal wife in Proverbs 31 supports role flexibility as do a number of passages in the Apocrypha. For example, Anna became the family wage earner when her husband, Tobit, was unable to work, and she did not hesitate to rebuke him when he was in the wrong (Tobit 2:9–14; 10:7).

This is not to say that marital inequities did not exist. One such inequity concerned divorce. In Roman times a Jewish husband could divorce his wife for a variety of reasons. The question with which the Pharisees tried to trap Jesus, "Is it lawful for a man to divorce his wife for any and every reason?" (Matt. 19:3), indicates that for the more liberal-minded, legitimate grounds for divorcing one's wife were wide-ranging.

A Jewish man could divorce his wife because of her inability to have children (*b. Yeb.* 63b), going out in public without a head covering ( *y. Soṭa.* 1.1 [16b]; *b. Ber.* 24a), bold speech, bodily defects (like a dog bite that became a scar), an unfulfilled vow, or intercourse during menstruation. In some instances a husband not only had grounds for a divorce but was obliged to do so (e.g., adultery, a childless marriage).

The picture was quite different for the woman; divorce was one right she did not possess. This was the sole prerogative of the husband—a prerogative that Mosaic legislation and Jesus himself recognized but nowhere condoned (Deut. 24:1–4; Matt. 5:31–32). A woman had the right to petition the court for a divorce. The court, in turn, could put pressure on the husband to grant it. It could, for example, scourge, fine, imprison, and even excommunicate him. Grounds for such a petition included cruelty, leprosy, neglect of physical or sexual needs, certain physical defects, occupational handicaps, and overly long separations.[16]

The lot of Jewish women improved somewhat during the Roman imperial period. For example, laws were passed to assure a woman alimony in the event of a divorce. This amount was spelled out in the marriage contract and was to be paid to the woman in addition to the dowry she brought with her into the marriage (*m. Ketub.* 4.7; *Yeb.* 7.1; *b. Ketub.* 82b).[17]

On the other hand, attitudes toward women during this same period reached an all-time low. The grounds for a husband to divorce his wife became so broad that one wonders if the overall devaluation of women offset any gains. A husband, for example, could divorce his wife in the event that anything about her appearance or behavior became displeasing to him. Even "if the wife badly cooks her husband's food by over salting or overroasting it, she is to be put away" (*m. Git.* 9.10).

Legal parity in the marriage relationship also changed. By the end of the A.D. second century, the wife was obliged to obey her husband as master, roles were carefully distinguished, and respect of father came before respect of mother (*b. Qidd.* 31a; *m. Ker.* 6.9). Even the life of the husband took priority over that of the wife—although she must be brought out of captivity sooner than he (*m. Hor.* 3.7).

### FAMILY

"A woman generally stays at home, whereas a man goes out into the streets and learns understanding from people" (*Genesis Rabbah* 18:1). So goes the saying of Rabbi Samuel, the son of third-century Rabbi Isaac. While male and female boundaries were more fluid than this during biblical times, it was still the case that the prime sphere of responsibility for women was in the home.

This was especially true of women during their childbearing and childrearing years. Because of the concern for carrying on the family line, a woman's number one domestic role was to bear children. If a woman remained childless, it was a great sorrow for her, and some even thought it was a punishment from God (Gen. 18:10; 29:31; 1 Sam. 1:5). Hannah, for example, wept and would not eat because she was childless (1 Sam. 1:7).

The birth of a son was held particularly dear. So much was this the case that if a man died before the birth of a son, it was the responsibility of his brother (or nearest relative) and his widow to produce a son so the dead man's name did not die out (Deut. 25:5–10; Ruth 3:12; Mark 12:18–19).

The domestic realm was the sphere where Jewish women were in charge. The family's well-being depended on how well a woman managed her household. Her daily tasks included grinding flour, baking bread, washing clothes, cooking the meals, making the beds, working in wool, attending to her husband's needs, nursing her children, and anything else that kept the family running smoothly (*m. Ketub.* 5.5, late first century).

As a Jewish woman's household expanded with the addition of children, servants, and even relatives, her job became more managerial and less caught up with the daily domestic routines. Sarah, Leah, and Rachel had maidservants (Gen. 16:1; 29:24–29) and Rebekah had her "nurse" (Gen. 24:59). As the domestic sphere enlarged, it took on a public character that is often overlooked when assessing the role of Jewish women in the family. "Mistress of the house" is an appropriate title for these women.

As a wife and mother, the Jewish woman's status was not without honor and dignity. Rabbi Joseph (fourth century) went so far as to equate the sound of his mother's footsteps with the approaching presence of God (*b. Qidd.* 31b).

### Public Roles

> Let no woman busy herself about those things which are beyond the province of economy [the home] but let her cultivate solitude and not be seen to be going about like a woman who walks the streets in the sight of other men, except when it is necessary for her to go to the temple.
>
> *Special Laws* 3.31 §§169–71

Philo's voice is the voice of the idealist. While Philo was of the opinion that women should not move about freely in public, only the rich could afford to remain secluded at home, and in actuality, only a few did. The real lives of women present quite a different picture. For the most part, women commonly helped their husbands with their trade. This was especially the case in rural areas where women worked alongside their husbands in the fields and sold olives at the door. Even in more urban settings, women typically tended the store, kept the shop, and drew water from the local well.

The New Testament depicts urban women (even married ones) as quite mobile and active. Jewish women who lived in Palestine are pictured as pursuing their legal rights (Luke 18:1–3) and managing their financial affairs (Acts 12:12). Jewish women living abroad were just as active. Asian inscriptions depict women involved in the affairs of their community—even to the extent of purchasing burial monuments and owning burial sites. Rufina, for instance, as head of a large household in Smyrna, built a tomb for her freed slaves and all the slaves raised in her house (*CIJ* 741, second century). Jewish women in Greece were no different. Lydia, for example, was a dealer in purple cloth in the leading city of Philippi (Acts 16:14), and Priscilla was a tentmaker (Acts 18:2–3).

Apart from Rome itself, women in Egypt were perhaps the most involved in the public arena. Documents of the day attest to Jewish women owning land and livestock, buying houses, leasing land, contracting and selling debts, and even terminating a marriage. We have, for instance, the legal documentation of a woman named Thases regarding the sale of a two-story house and all its furnishings to a woman named Herieus (*CPJ* 483, 45 B.C.). We also possess the record of a woman named Martha settling her share of a debt (*CPJ* 148, 10 B.C.) and the divorce agreement from Apollonia to her husband Protarchos (*CPJ* 144, 13 B.C.), to note a few.[18]

### In the Final Analysis

Proverbs 31 and the book of Judith need to be taken seriously when assessing the roles of Jewish women. While they present a different role model from that of the traditional one, it is a model that is mirrored in various ways in the lives of the women of antiquity. In Proverbs 31 the woman worth far more than rubies is a wise, hardworking entrepreneur who successfully juggles a family, a business, and a concern for the poor and needy in her community. Her husband earns a seat of respect among the elders because of her. Her children call her blessed. Judith is another example of a Jewish heroine who is a paragon of a woman—wise, righteous, resourceful, independent, intelligent, and wealthy. She brilliantly and courageously saves her people from their attackers and is honored throughout Israel for her intelligence and valor.

Neither woman lacks for traditional virtues either. The seemingly liberated wife in Proverbs 31 still spins thread, manages her household, and cares for and instructs her children. The heroic Judith is the faithful spouse even to the grave. She remains a widow all the days of her life after Manasseh, her husband, dies. Judith also respects the traditional lines of inheritance of her people, dutifully distributing her property before she dies to the next of kin to her husband and only then to her own nearest kindred (Judith 16:21–25).

Both portrayals reflect the tension in Jewish society between the ideal of a stay-at-home mother and the real world of expanding public roles for women. Judith and the proverbial wife are virtual superwomen in their ability to balance both worlds. It was probably just as hard for Jewish women in Roman times to strike this balance as it is for women today, but they did have superb models after which they could pattern themselves.

## Women in Greek Society

When looking at the roles of Greek women, it is important to pay close attention to the questions of *when, where,* and *what:* When does she live, where does she live, and what is her social standing? For example, it has been said that the status of Greek women during the classical period (fifth through fourth centuries B.C.) fared worse than at any other time in Western civilization.[19] While there is some justification for this statement, it needs to be modified to specify Athenian, upper-class women to be accurate.

### THE WOMEN OF CLASSICAL GREECE

Male attitudes toward women in classical times certainly matched and in some cases exceeded the most disparaging comments of Jewish writers. This was especially true of Greek tragedians and comedians. Euripedes's *Medea* 573–75 (484–406 B.C.) contains the famous line: "Would that mortals otherwise could get them babes, that womenkind were not, and so no curse had lighted upon men." A century later, Menander (342–292 B.C.) spoke of woman as "the beastliest of all the wild beasts on land and in the sea." To instruct a woman is "to feed poison to a deadly serpent" (*Fragments* 488, 702). The line from Euripedes is spoken by a character caught up in the heat of passion and desperation. The lines from Menander are not.

There are other writers, however, who laud the virtues of women. This is especially true of the poets of that day. Women such as Niobe, Helen, Penelope, Cassandra, and Iphigenia are portrayed as women of intelligence and determination. Even earlier, Homer portrayed Queen Arete (wife of the king of Scheria) as a woman of great intelligence, who resolved quarrels even among men (*Odyssey* 7.74).[20] Some of the most noteworthy philosophers took up the cause of women during classical times. Socrates (470–399 B.C.) claimed that virtue is the same for women as for men.[21] Plato (427–347 B.C.) argued that a woman had a right to the same educational opportunities as a man (including athletics and the martial arts) and that she had the same civic obligations (including holding public office). This stemmed from Plato's belief that men and women possess the same natural gifts—save that "men are stronger and women are weaker" (*Republic* 451C–461E). Even Aristotle (384–322 B.C.) thought it desirable for women to be in the democratic process—at least within limits (*Politics* 2.6.5–10).

The day-to-day lives of Greek women varied from city to city. The lives of upper-class Athenian women were rather dismal by our standards. They were typically kept in seclusion; some never left their house their entire life. Even at home, they were restricted to a certain section of the house (e.g., a rear room or upper story) far removed from any chance contact with the opposite sex. Husband and wife dined in separate quarters (Herodotus, *Histories* 5.18–20). Those women who did leave the house were always accompanied by a slave. While out of the house, they were not permitted to visit friends or even to chat with them in the park. They also could not engage in public dialogue with the opposite sex. When spoken of in public, they were not referred to by name but were always "the wife of so-and-so."

The education of Athenian women occurred at home and focused on domestic things—although some did learn to read and write. Their sole purpose in life was to manage the female side of the household and bear legitimate children. The key word is *legitimate.* Seclusion had the benefit of assuring the legitimacy of the children born to women of stature in Athens.

The lives of upper-class Spartan women presented quite a different picture. Not only did they have free run of the house, but they moved about openly in public. In fact, they were encouraged to do so. Spartan women could also buy and sell property. The land registers during classical times show that 40 percent of all real estate in the city was owned by women. They also participated in politics, held public office, and were involved in various civic projects.[22]

Spartan girls were encouraged at a young age to develop athletic skills. So it is not unusual to run across female names in the lists of famous Spartan athletes. It is worth noting, however, that the rationale for such training was quite traditional. Physically fit mothers bred strong soldiers. Despite the public activity of Spartan women, their primary roles were still the traditional ones of bearing children and managing their homes.

Athens and Sparta represent the extremes in terms of women's roles in classical Greece. Other Greek city-states of the day fell somewhere between the two. At Argos, for example, the citizens erected a statue to Telesilla in which she is portrayed with her books thrown aside, putting on a helmet for battle.[23]

The lives of lower-class Greek women fit neither Athenian nor Spartan upper-class models. The Athenian life of seclusion was not an option for them, nor did they have the Spartan leisure or the status to be involved in public life to any great degree. Jobs like washing, wool working, horse tending, food vending, dress and accessory making, or acting as nurse-maid or midwife—in addition to domestic tasks at home—were what consumed their time.[24] Work, for them, was not an option—it was an economic necessity, much as it is for many women today.

### The Women of the Hellenistic Period

The rise of Hellenism in the centuries that followed the classical period was a positive development for women throughout the civilized world regardless of their ethnic origin. When Alexander the Great created his Greek Empire in the late fourth century B.C., the feminine model that became the norm was more that of Spartan independence than of Athenian seclusion. The one exception was in Athens, which was slow to make any progress.[25]

The rest of the Hellenistic world experienced something of a women's liberation movement. Women were able to inherit and bequeath property, own and free slaves, buy and sell land, lend and borrow money, and manage their dowries. This expanded public activity brought about an increase in the number of women possessing wealth in their own right.[26]

The inviolable belief in the male guardianship of women also began to lose ground. Initially male oversight was needed because women did not have the legal or financial means to manage their own business affairs. As women gained more and more expertise in handling their own affairs, however, the need for male oversight became moot.

The growing economic power of women during this time period is reflected in the Lydias (Philippi), Chloes (Corinth), Phoebes (Cenchrea), and Nymphas (Laodicea) of the New Testament letters. It can also be seen in the number of Greek women of high standing converted through Paul's preaching (Acts 16:14; 17:4, 12). Most of these women were from the province of Macedonia, where attitudes toward women took an upturn during these centuries. Cassander's naming of the city of Thessalonica after his wife is an indicator of just how favorable this attitude was (Strabo, *Geography*, 7.24).

Another advance for women was in the sphere of public life. The agora (marketplace) and gymnasium, which had been strictly male turf, now saw the entrance of women. The agora was a large rectangular display area for public monuments and statues that was flanked by shops and offices. Much like the public square of the city and the town square in rural America, the agora in antiquity was the center of life—a place to shop, converse, exchange ideas, and carry out financial transactions (cf. Acts 17:17). The gymnasium was an athletic complex that included a track for running, a courtyard for wrestling (and other sports), and a lecture hall devoted to higher education. The involvement of women in these two spheres marked their entrance into the very center of Greek public life.[27]

EDUCATION

The educated women in classical times were the *companions (hetairai)*— those who provided men of means with intellectual stimulus, companionship at the theater, and sexual satisfaction.[28] Little effort was made to educate legitimate wives beyond the basic skills of reading and writing. Emphasis was placed, instead, on learning how to spin wool, weave cloth, and run a domestic household—or at least the female portion of it. Yet within this sphere, the wife was truly mistress of her realm and left to her own devices. Many a tombstone praised a wife's ability to manage her household.

In the centuries prior to Christ, things changed, and women in the Hellenistic period (except Athenians) made great strides in the area of education. For girls who wanted an education, the opportunity was suddenly there for the taking. Eurydice of Hierapolis was one woman who took up the gauntlet. She writes:

> Eurydice of Hierapolis
> Made to the Muses this her offering
> When she had gained her soul's desire to learn
> Mother of young and lusty sons was she
> And by her diligence attained to learn letters
> Wherein lies buried all our lore
> (quoted by Plutarch in *Moralia 14C*)

This is not to say that perceptions about the fundamental differences between the sexes disappeared entirely, but that the opportunities for an education beyond the basics existed for those who were interested. Progress was especially evident in the literary realm. In some places (like Egypt) more women could sign their name than men. Novels with female names began to surface, and poetry penned by a female hand started to appear with regularity.

"Distaff," a poem written in memory of a childhood friend, shows the literary capabilities of educated women. Although the text is frag-

mentary, the age-old games of tag, keeping house, playing with dolls, and
even fear of the bogeyman come through loud and clear:

> I shouted loudly . . . tortoise
> Leaping up . . . the yard of the great court.
> These things, O poor Baukis, . . . in mourning
> These traces . . . lie in my heart warm still
> . . . embers now of dolls . . . in the bedrooms. . . .
> Once at dawn Mother . . . to the woolworkers
> She came to you . . . salted.
> O for little girls . . . Mormo brought fear
> . . . it went around on feet four . . .
> changing its appearance
> > > (Errina of the Dorian island of Telo;
> > > D. L. Page, *Greek Literary Papyri* 1.486–89)

Women philosophers also begin to make an appearance. This was
helped along by supporters like Epicurus, who admitted women into his
school on the same terms as men, and by the acceptance of women into
the ranks of Cynic philosophers.[29]

### MARRIAGE AND FAMILY

Marriage commonly occurred at the age of fourteen for an Athenian
girl and between the ages of sixteen and twenty for girls in other parts
of Greece. Males, by contrast, did not marry until well into their thir-
ties. This was because the training of capable male citizens required
higher education—including a good liberal arts program. Young men
who did not pursue higher education spent those years in a trade appren-
ticeship or learning the family business. As a result, husbands were typically twice the age of their brides when they married. This meant that
men brought a maturity (as well as settled habits) to the marriage relationship that girls did not have. It also meant that men were in a position to rule, while women were not.

The primary responsibilities of the Greek wife were to bear and raise
children and to contribute to the self-sufficiency of the household by
spinning thread and weaving cloth for use in the home. In fact, the distaff
became a symbol of the dedicated housewife in Greek times.[30]

It was typical for a Greek couple to have a marriage contract. Among
other things, it spelled out the obligations of both husband and wife. The
Greek wife was obligated to obey her husband, to remain with him, not
to spend a night or day away from home without her husband's permission, not to have intercourse with another man, and not to ruin the

common household or bring shame on her husband. The husband, in turn, was required to furnish his wife with what was necessary for her well-being as a married woman, to return her dowry should he divorce her, not to bring home another wife, concubine, or boy lover, not to bear children (or maintain a house) by another woman, not to eject, insult, or ill treat her, and not to handle any of their property to her detriment (Papyrus Tebtunis 104.24; Egypt 92 B.C.)

Should the husband not fulfill his obligations, the woman was free to file for a divorce with the local magistrate. At one time, the husband had the option of merely sending his wife away with the words, "I repudiate you," but this changed during the Hellenistic period. By the first century B.C. the marriage could be terminated by either partner.[31]

Although attitudes about the role of women in the marriage and the family remained largely traditional during this time period, there was nonetheless a movement toward a more egalitarian relationship between husband and wife. One evidence of this is the change in the way children related to their parents. While fathers continued to be addressed as "master" *(kyrios),* mothers now began to be called "mistress" *(kyria).* Also, a wife started to eat at the same table as her husband and to be seen in public with him—at dinner parties, the theater, and the like. Some women even became the primary wage earner in the family.[32]

There were also legal developments that benefited women. Women were permitted to bear witness and manage their husband's affairs in his absence. Laws were passed equalizing the inheritance and property rights of men and women. Women could not only buy and sell property and goods but now could will them to others.[33]

Needless to say, not everyone sat quietly by while women were liberated. The traditional family structure was threatened, and some spoke out. Aristotle, who supported the role of women in the democratic process, nonetheless argued against women taking the lead in the family, "for the male is by nature superior to command than the female. . . . the one is ruler and the other ruled. . . . the male stands in this relationship to the female continuously" *(Politics* 1.5.1–1.5.4). Stoic, Peripatetic, and Neopythagorean philosophers who came after Aristotle likewise defended the rule of husbands and the submission of wives. One Neopythagorean, for instance, states, "A woman must live for her husband according to law and in actuality, thinking no private thoughts of her own. . . . If her husband thinks something is sweet, she will think so too; or if he thinks something is bitter, she will agree with him" *(Stobaeus* 4.28.19). Some of the literary giants of the day also followed suit. Menan-

der (342–292 B.C.), for instance, states that a house in which a woman
has the final say will "go to utter ruin" (*Fragments* 484).

### PUBLIC ROLES

Tombstone inscriptions give us a clear picture of the variety of professional roles women filled in Hellenistic times. They were musicians,
poets, doctors, nurses, craftsmen (e.g., goldsmith, armorer), athletes—
even professional charioteers (to name a few).[34]

City records and inscriptions show the civic-mindedness of women.
Their names appear in connection with the underwriting of temples,
theaters, gymnasiums, public baths, and the like. For example, one
woman named Artemis founded the local gymnasium. Another woman
named Plancia Magna built the gate complex at the south entrance to
the city of Perga.

Women also served as civil servants and public officers. Mendora (first
century A.D.) at one time or another served as magistrate, priestess, and
*dekaprotos* (i.e., an official concerned with public revenues and the collection of taxes) of the city of Sillyon (Pisidia, Asia).

Women were active in the economic and business world, matching
men, for example, in money lending to individuals and cities. They also
owned slaves, bought and sold property and goods, managed their own
properties and businesses, and were held responsible for their own debts.
The range of properties in their possession included grainfields, vine-
yards, olive groves, and pasturelands. The women of Asia Minor and
Macedonia, in fact, became renowned for their benefactions of wheat,
wine, oil, and meat.[35]

### Women in the Roman Empire

Why should we pay taxes when we do not share in the offices, honors,
military commands, nor, in short, the government, for which you contend against each other with such harmful results?

Appian, *Civil Wars,* 4.33

It is when we reach the period of the Roman Empire (first century
B.C. to A.D. fifth century) that the activity of women in the public arena,
which was still somewhat novel during Hellenistic times, becomes commonplace. Women in the Roman Empire routinely married and divorced
on their own initiative, chose their own name, bore legal witness, ran
for public office, and even bore arms. Images of leading women appeared
on Roman coins. Educational opportunities were available not merely
for women with initiative but for all. Upper-class women were expected

to be educated (Quintilian, *Institutes of Oratory* 1.1.6), and even girls from lower-class families went to school.[36]

Some of the most sweeping changes occurred in the realm of family life. For one, the position of married women was noticeably higher. The marriage relationship began to be seen as a partnership, and by the end of the A.D. first century, women entered marriage in virtual equality with their husbands. Also, the wife's position in the household was equal to that of her husband. In fact, the woman of the house was addressed as *domina* (mistress) not only by her children but also by her husband. In addition, extramarital intercourse was no longer viewed with the double standard of Hellenistic times, which considered marital infidelity the privilege of the Greek male but illegal for a married woman. Instead it began to be frowned upon for men as well.

There continued to be inequities. Women still needed a male guardian for performing important transactions (such as making a will, selling a piece of land, freeing a slave, entering into a contract, accepting an inheritance)—although this increasingly became a mere formality during the A.D. first century. Women also did not have a voice in the assembly or hold positions of command in the military; and public speaking roles were rare.

Yet, the introductory quote from the speech of Hortensia (the daughter of a famous first-century orator) shows the political and oratorical capabilities of at least one Roman woman. Her speech won the crowd's support, and the following day the ruling triumvirate (Octavian, Mark Antony, and Lepidus) reduced the number of women subject to taxation to four hundred.[37]

Adultery was another area of inequity. For women it was a legal offense. If convicted, they lost half of their dowry and were exiled. Husbands, on the other hand, did not face any legal consequences. Also, while a husband was obliged to divorce an adulterous wife, the wife was merely permitted to do so.

There were a number who spoke out against these inequities. Jurist Ulpian, for instance, argued that it was unjust for a husband to require from a wife a level of morality to which he himself did not live (*Digest* 48.5.1–4; see also Stoic philosophers).

EDUCATION AND LEGAL STANDING

Roman girls were better educated than their Greek counterparts. Both girls and boys ages seven through twelve attended elementary school. Well-to-do children were educated by private tutors, while the others attended public schools located in the forum or marketplace. Some girls went on for further studies and became philosophers, poets, writers, orators, and even doctors. Afrania, for example, was a lawyer of some renown in the first century B.C. Hortensia (mentioned above) became a famous orator.[38]

The legal standing of Roman women exceeded that of their Jewish and Greek counterparts. Most Roman women could manage their own affairs, handle their own property, and make their own decisions. In fact, after the age of twenty-five, they were subject only to the supervision of a guardian with regard to business and legal transactions. Yet even this became increasingly a mere formality. Women bought and sold property, freed slaves, bore witness, and entered into a wide range of contractual relationships. Even daughters fared better; under the Roman law of intestate succession, they and their brothers divided the property equally.

Married Roman women also fared better than their non-Roman counterparts. They retained possession of their property inside and outside the marriage, and they had the power to dissolve their marriage on their own initiative. In fact, it was the married woman with children who had the biggest legal advantage (even over the Jewish and Greek widow). In an attempt to shore up the disintegrating family unit, Emperor Augustus granted mothers of three or more children freedom from all male supervision. A woman who demonstrated responsible behavior by bearing the children Rome needed was deemed capable of acting without a male guardian. This was a far-reaching measure that extended virtual independence to a class of women who had been the most bound by tradition in previous centuries.

The legal strides women made during Roman times can be gauged by the number and range of lawsuits initiated by women. By the turn of the second century, 20 percent of all litigants were women. Some of the litigation pertained to business transactions. For example, a woman named Marcia filed suit against her debtors in the hope of getting satisfaction even though she had lost the IOUs. Other litigation was domestic in nature—having to do with marriage, divorce, dowries, alimony, and child custody.[39]

### MARRIAGE

During classical times the freedoms of Roman women were quite limited. This was especially the case for a married woman. Her husband had absolute authority over her. He even had the right under certain circumstances to take her life.

This did not continue during Roman imperial times. There was a definite shift from an authoritarian to an egalitarian understanding of marriage. Already in the third century B.C. marriage started to be defined as the joining together of a man and a woman in a partnership in all of life (Modestinus [a Roman lawyer], *Digest* 23.2.1).

With Roman marriages (in contrast to Athenian and Jewish marriages) there was genuine equality in daily life. Within the household there were no separate quarters for women. Women and men dined together, spoke their mind to one another, and developed respect for one another. If the marriage was a *free* marriage (requiring the consent of both parties), the wife was not obligated to obey her husband, and the husband had no right to correct or order anything of her. By Jesus' day, the traditional marriage, where the woman passed from the authority of her father to that of her husband, had become quite rare, and *free* marriages were the norm.

Unlike Athenian women, Roman women moved about freely in public. They were at liberty to go to the theater, visit friends, go to the park, or stroll down the promenade. They (not companions) provided their husbands with intellectual stimulus and companionship at the theater, banquets, and the like. Women even began to accompany their husbands when they traveled. Pilate's wife (Matt. 27:19) and Drusilla, Felix's wife (Acts 24:24), are good examples. Women also worked side-by-side with their husbands in a trade (as, for example, the early church tentmakers Priscilla and Aquila).

All the ingredients were there in the Roman marriage for the development of a mutual and abiding love and appreciation. This is rather amazing given that Romans typically married during their teenage years (ages twelve through fourteen for girls and seventeen to eighteen for boys).

One of the consequences of the relative independence of Roman women was that they were less tied to childbearing. On average, marriages rarely produced more than one or two children. As the "sons of Rome" decreased in number, the concern of the government increased. Bachelors were seen as traitors to their civic duties and given inferior positions in the political hierarchy. Women between the ages of twenty-five and fifty were required to be married.[40] Childbearing was rewarded, and adultery committed by a woman was made a capital offense.

Interestingly enough, the marital ideal of marrying only once *(uni-vira)* continued despite the government's best efforts. While Roman law stipulated the remarriage of widows, tombstones praised the once-married woman. This ideal cut across rank and social standing. The tombstones of an upper-class woman named Cornelia, a slave named Tabia, and a freedwoman named Aurelia equally laud the fact that they were once-married.

Even so, reality fell short of the ideal (as it often does). In fact, one husband's epitaph to his wife in the first century B.C. reads: "Rare are marriages so long lasting and ended by death, not interrupted by divorce" (ILS 8393). With freedom of choice also came freedom to divorce. Both Roman men and women exercised this right with astounding abandon (rivaled only perhaps by American society today). Under Roman law, either spouse could dissolve the marriage by mutual consent or unilateral repudiation. A parent (usually the father) could even dissolve the marriage—although this was mostly done by upper-class families seeking a better alliance for their child. In fact, the rate of divorce was so high that every legal effort was made to curb it. Although divorce itself was not outlawed, seven witnesses were required to make it legal.[41]

### FAMILY

At the same time that the marital trend in Roman society was toward mutuality and equality, family values remained largely conservative. Roman men by-and-large measured the success of a woman's life not by her personal accomplishments but by her devotion to her family, her husband, and her children. It was, in fact, the opinion of one second-century B.C. senator that women willingly served men and abhorred the freedom that the loss of husbands and fathers produced (Lucius Valerius; *History of Rome,* Livy 34.7.12–13). It also tended to be the feeling of Roman husbands, regardless of their rank. For example, the husband of Aurelia Domitra, a freedwoman of the imperial household, had inscribed on her tombstone: "a spouse most blessed, most devoted, most proper and respectful to her family" (CIL 6.13303). Another husband claimed that he lived with his wife twenty-four years, six months, and eleven days without any quarrel (CIL 5.7763).

The high value placed on a woman's devotion to her family is explained, in part, by the fact that the family was the basic unit of Roman society. The health of the Roman Empire depended on the health of the nuclear family. The health of the nuclear family depended, in turn, on how well the mistress of the household did her job.

Devotion to family, however, is not to be equated with the American concept of a housewife—that is, diapering babies, cooking meals, clothing the children, running them to this and that activity, washing clothes, cleaning the house, and so on. Nor is it to be equated with the bearing and rearing of many children. *Mistress* (not *housewife*) is the term that sums up the first-century role. The Roman woman's job was to manage the household and to oversee the children's upbringing (see, for example,

Hunt and Edgar, *Select Papyri* #130, Loeb Classical Library, Cambridge, Mass.: Harvard University Press).

*Oversee* is the key word. Not many women assumed the responsibility of personally educating their children, although they did personally discipline their children and train them to be good citizens. They either arranged for a private tutor (in the case of upper-class households) or sent them to the equivalent of public school (in the case of lower-class families). Nor did many wives personally perform the household chores. Even modest households included one or two servants who did most of these tasks. In essence, the mistress's job was a managerial one.[42]

Roman society gave special prominence to the role of mistress of the household. The day after a Roman girl was married, a ceremony was held in which she assumed her new role as mistress. In more affluent houses, the ceremony included a presentation of the domestic staff and being given the keys to the household.[43]

## PUBLIC ROLES

Already in the second century B.C., Cato opined that women ought to stay at home as in the good old days and devote themselves to spinning and other traditional female tasks (Livy, *History of Rome* 34.2–4). His wish was, needless to say, not realized. In fact, Roman women increasingly strove to be free from household chores so they could be out and about.

Women at the top and bottom of Roman society played an active role in the daily affairs of city life. The occupations of women at Pompeii, for instance, ranged from dealers in beans, sellers of nails, and construction workers to dealers in exotic merchandise, manufacturers of bricks and textiles, and owners of stonecutting businesses. For some women, work was an economic necessity. They served in the traditional roles of wool weighers, midwives, seamstresses, hairdressers, shopkeepers, weavers, laundresses, waitresses, and vendors of commodities as wide-ranging as today (e.g., meat, fish, clothing).

For other women, however, work was a matter of professional interest, and they chose non-traditional roles previously restricted to men. From at least as early as the first century B.C., we run across female physicians, instructors, secretaries, and artists. We also find an increasing number of women philosophers, athletes, and writers. Some women became so accomplished in their field of endeavor that they won the praise of the Stoic philosopher Seneca, who remarked, "Who has dealt grudgingly with women's natures and has narrowly restricted their virtues? They have just as much force, just as much capacity . . . for virtuous action; they are just as able to endure suffering and toil" (*To Marcia On Consolation* 16.1).

We also run across women who were heads of their households, ran businesses of all sorts, managed their estates, and traveled with their own slaves and servants. Women of means were in a particularly favorable position to hold public offices and play civic roles and so impact the power structures of their cities and towns. A significant number of women are mentioned on coins and inscriptions as benefactors of civic projects or as holders of a civic office.

There were some limits. Women did not hold a seat in the Roman legislature or serve in a judicial capacity. They were also not to draw attention to themselves in public. Public speeches, demonstrations, or arguing one's own case in court were frowned upon. Women did not have a voice in the governing of Rome, nor could they hold positions in the Roman army (as the opening quote of Hortensia so eloquently points out). Even so, there were exceptions. As early as 195 B.C., women publicly protested the taxation of female luxury items (Livy, *History of Rome* 34). Amasia Sentia, who pled her case before the praetor who presided over the court, was said to have pursued every aspect of her defense diligently and boldly, and Gaia Afrania, the wife of an A.D. first-century senator, always represented herself because "her impudence was abundant" (Valerius Maximus, *Memorable Deeds and Sayings* 8.3).[44]

## The Biblical Perspective on the Role of Women in Society

What is the biblical perspective on the role of women in society? Is marriage figured along egalitarian lines, or is the biblical view hierarchical in nature? Does a woman have a leadership role to play in the family, or is this strictly a male domain? Is a woman encouraged to be a stay-at-home mother following the traditionalist ideal, or does she have the freedom to be an entrepreneurial mother like the woman in Proverbs 31?

The role of women in society is an especially important question given two trends in religious circles today. There is the increasing tendency of biblical feminists to downplay and, in some cases, eliminate sexual distinctions. "Feminism," Virginia Mollenkott states, "involves opposing the age-ist, racist, classist, *heterosexist* systems of patriarchy."[45] It is argued that sexual distinctions had their place in populating the world, but now that the task of propagating the species has been accomplished, sexual distinctions are no longer needed—or even desirable. The goal today is *unisexuality,* with the ideal of a loving relationship between committed partners (same sex or otherwise) and the roles of women and men being equal and interchangeable.

At the same time there is the increasing tendency of traditionalists to overplay sexual distinctions. *Male* and *female* are identified as not merely sexual distinctions but also as role distinctions—roles that are irreversible and noninterchangeable. It is claimed that a man, by virtue of his manhood, is called to lead and direct, and a woman, by virtue of her womanhood, is called to submit and support.[46]

What do the Scriptures say about all this? What is the biblical perspective on male and female? The biblical texts that address this question in a fundamental way are found in Genesis 1–2. It is here that God's creation of the human being as male and female is set forth, the divinely intended relationship between a man and a woman explained, and the social responsibilities of each spelled out. Also, Jesus and the New Testament writers cite these texts in ways that make it clear the early church found them to be normative for their understanding of male-female relations.

### Genesis 1–2

> Then God said, "Let us make human beings in our image, in our likeness, and let them rule over . . . all the creatures that move along the ground." So God created human beings in his own image, in the image of God he created them; male and female he created them.
>
> Genesis 1:26–27

The first thing to note is that the creation of humankind was a calculated act on God's part: "Let us make" (v. 26). The goal of this calculated act was the creation of two sexually distinct human beings—not one bisexual or unisexual person: "God created *hā'ādām* in his own image . . . male and female he created them." God did not create a *him* but a *them*. The plural pronouns in verses 26 and 27 make this clear. Genesis 5:2 (AT) makes it even clearer: "He created them male and female . . . he called *them* 'Adam'" (NIV "man"). The familiar sound of *Adam* should not throw us off. *Ādām* (literally "earth-made") is not the proper name of an individual but a generic term for the human race (NRSV "humankind"; NIV "man"). Jesus affirms this when he states, "The one who made them at the beginning, 'made them male and female'" (Matt. 19:4 NRSV; see also Mark 10:6).

The deliberative "let *us*" (Gen. 1:26 italics added) has intrigued readers for generations. Yet we must not get sidetracked from the key thought: The creation of humankind is distinct from all that precedes it in the creation process. The grandeur of this final creative stage is underlined by the three parallel clauses of Genesis 1:27, which climax in the declaration: "male and female he created them."[47] The creation of humanity as male and female is no incidental fact or afterthought but the very peak of God's creative activity. To suppress (or even to deny) our sexuality—as some are wont to do—is therefore to suppress our humanness.

The creation of two sexually distinct human beings is something Scripture labels as inherently good. After the creation of male and female, "God saw all that he had made, and it was very good" (Gen. 1:31). To be male is good. To be female is good. Nowhere in Scripture are we encouraged to downplay sexual differences and move in a unisex direction—as some feminists would encourage. Moreover, the sexuality that is deemed very good is male plus female. This, at least, is the divine intent—although human intent can make it into something quite different.

Why this sexual differentiation? The command to "be fruitful and increase in number" (Gen. 1:28) points to at least one reason—namely, the propagation of the species. But there is another reason that is just as important. It is summed up in the statement: "A man will . . . be united to his wife, and they will become one flesh" (Gen. 2:24). Simply put, sexual distinction is intended to create unity out of multiplicity. This, along with creation in God's image, is what makes human beings distinct from the rest of creation. After all, God also commanded the creatures of the sea and the birds of the air to be fruitful and increase in number (Gen. 1:22), but only the human being is created with a view to oneness.

It is this very oneness (and not propagation) that is emphasized in the teachings of Jesus and Paul. While culture emphasized the continuation of the family line, it is a curious thing that neither Jesus nor Paul mention fruitfulness when they treat the purpose of marriage. What they do mention is God's intent that the two become one. Jesus states that the union of a man and a woman means "they are no longer two, but one" (Matt. 19:5–6; Mark 10:7–8). Paul goes even further. For him this oneness embodies the union of Christ and his church (Eph. 5:32).

What kind of oneness is intended? Sexual intimacy is undoubtedly one element. Paul makes this clear when he speaks of sexual intercourse with a prostitute as a one-flesh experience (1 Cor. 6:16). Yet sexual activity by no means exhausts what God had in mind. While Westerners tend to think of *one flesh* as purely sexual in nature, the Israelites understood the phrase to mean much more. In part, this is because they did not compartmentalize the human being into body, mind, and soul as we tend to do. Instead, they viewed the human being wholistically from different vantage points. For example, to speak of someone as *flesh* was to look at the person as *mortal,* or *human.* A union of *flesh,* then, is a merging of one human being with another. This merging is so complete that, where there were previously two, now there is only one.[48]

Can two human beings of the same sex experience the kind of oneness talked about here? Friendship can run deep, and love knows no sexual boundaries. But in the created order of things, a one-flesh union can only occur between a man and a woman. In fact, the rest of Scripture knows of no other pairing except that of male plus female—and this despite the numerous changes in the cultural panorama.

This is what the first male recognized when he exclaimed: "This is now bone of my bones and flesh of my flesh" (Gen. 2:23). The language is thoroughly covenantal. In a Near Eastern setting, "bone of my bones and flesh of my flesh" expresses not merely kinship but loyalty—much like our marital vow "in sickness and in health . . . 'til death us do part" (*Book of Common Prayer;* cf. Judg. 9:2; 2 Sam. 5:1; 19:13–14).[49]

Marital loyalty is shown by a man who "will leave his father and mother and be united to his wife" (Gen. 2:24). The NIV's "leave" and "unite" are rather weak (cf. KJV "leave" and "cleave"). "Forsake" and "cleave" is more the sense (compare *ʿāzab* in Josh. 22:3; 1 Sam. 30:13; and *dābaq* in Deut. 10:20; 11:22). The language is covenantal for the severing of one loyalty and the commencing of another; the exclusive loyalty that a son showed his parents is now transferred to his wife. In a society where honoring parents was the highest human obligation, this is quite an outstanding statement.

Is there more to be learned from these texts? Does being male and female distinguish who we are and what we can do in ways that are non-interchangeable and divinely ordered—a biblical manhood and womanhood so to speak? Although some are quick to say *yes,* the creation accounts offer no support. Instead, the note that is clearly sounded throughout Genesis 1 and 2 is that of equality. For one, there is an equality of personhood. Both male and female are created in the image of God. A straightforward reading of Genesis 1:27 excludes any other understanding: "God created humankind in his image . . . male and female he created them" (NRSV). And he did it by divine fiat: "*Let us* make" (v. 26 NRSV). Although there is a great deal of debate about what creation in "God's image" means, the Genesis account is unequivocal in affirming that women and men equally share it.

There is also equality in the social realm. Both male and female are commanded to exercise dominion over creation. Although some claim that male headship is intrinsic to the creation accounts, quite frankly the only time this kind of language appears is when it is used of the joint dominion of male and female: "Let us make human beings in our image, in our likeness, and let them rule over the fish of the sea" (Gen. 1:26). There is no division or distinction of roles here. The woman is given the same task and level of responsibility as the man.

Two verbs define this task. Both are imperatives: "Rule over" (vv. 26, 28) and "subdue" (v. 28). The first translates a Hebrew term that is used twenty-two times in the Old Testament of human dominion (*rādâ*, e.g., Ps. 110:2; Isa. 14:2, 6). "Let them *rule over* the fish of the sea and the birds of the air, over the livestock, over all the earth, and over all the creatures that move along the ground" (Gen. 1:26 italics added; cf. v. 28). The second verb, which occurs fifteen times in the Old Testament, means to bring into submission by brute force (*kābaš*, e.g., 2 Chron. 28:10; Neh. 5:5; Jer. 34:11, 16). The implication is that creation will not do the bidding of human beings gladly or easily.[50]

The ability of male and female to rule over creation stems from their creation in God's image. Although God's image and dominion are sometimes equated, the passage makes it plain that it is God's image that enables dominion to be exercised. "Let us make human beings in our image" comes first, and "Let them rule . . . over all the earth" comes second (Gen. 1:26). The assumption is that women and men have what it takes to rule and subdue the entirety of what God has created.

There is likewise an equality in the family realm. Both male and female share joint responsibility in the bearing and rearing of children. The idea that it is the woman's job to bear and to raise the children and the man's job to work the land is simply not found in the text.[51] Both are called to be fruitful, and both are called to enjoy the produce of the land. The pronouns are plural throughout: "God . . . said to *them,* 'Be fruitful and increase in number. . . . I give *you* [plural] every seed-bearing plant on the face of the whole earth and every tree that has fruit with seed in it. They will be *yours* for food'" (Gen. 1:28–29 italics added). Nor is fruitfulness an idle responsibility. The link between descendants and dominion is an important one. Fruitfulness in childbearing is the means by which the earth is brought into submission.

Finally, there is an equality in the spiritual realm. Both male and female are blessed by God (Gen. 1:28). Both relate directly to God: "The LORD God called to the man. . . . The LORD God said to the woman" (Gen. 3:9, 13). Both are addressed personally by God when they disobey: "To the woman he said, . . . to the man he said" (Gen. 3:16–17 NRSV).

The equality of male and female arises, in part, from their sameness. Sameness is emphasized at two key points in the narrative. There is, first, a sameness of origin. Both male and female can be called '*ādām* ("earthling," Gen. 1:26, 27; 5:2) because they are formed from the '*ādāmâ* ("earth," "dust"). There is also a sameness of nature. The *'îš* ("man") recognizes this when he calls what God has created *'iššâ* ("wo-man"); for she was "taken out of man" (Gen. 2:23). She is "bone of [his] bones and flesh of [his] flesh" (v. 23). She is "that which corresponds to the him" *(kĕnegdô)*—a personal counterpart in every way.[52]

What about distinctions? Are there differences between male and female that go beyond the obvious biological ones? The creation of woman as a "help" seems to point in this direction: "It is not good for the man to be alone. I will make a help corresponding to him" (Gen. 2:18, 20 AT). But what does it mean to be a "help"? Is the woman's function similar to that of the hired help in our society? Is her position one of subservience? Some would say *yes* and claim that subservience is implicit in the idea of a helping role. The one who receives help, so it goes, has a certain authority over the one who gives help. But while help can come from a subordinate, it need not. Nor is subordination implicit in the idea of helping. If the help is in the form of aid or deliverance, then it is more likely to come from a peer or a superior.

The translation "a helper" (NIV, NASB, NKJV, NRSV, RSV) is partly to blame for the notion of subservience. The REB's and CEV's "a partner" and the NEB's and NLT's "a companion" are closer to the mark. In actuality, the KJV's "a help" or the ASV's "a succor" is exactly what the Hebrew term *'ēzer* means. In all of its other seventeen occurrences, it is used of the assistance one of strength offers to one in need (i.e., help from God, the king, or an army). The words of the psalmist are perhaps the most familiar:

> I lift up my eyes to the hills—
>> where does my *help* come from?
> My *help* comes from the LORD,
>> the Maker of heaven and earth.
>> Psalm 121:1–2 italics added

Since most of Old Testament references have to do with the help God alone can provide (e.g., Exod. 18:4; Deut. 33:7, 26, 29; Pss. 33:20; 89:19 [20];115:9–11; 121:1–2; 124:8; 146:5; Hos. 13:9), we do well to not read subordination into the language of Genesis 2:18–20. We also do well not to read female superiority into the text. The woman was created as a help *in correspondence to* the man. This is the language of sameness, not superiority.

What kind of help does the woman provide? Elsewhere in the Old Testament the help offered is deliverance from a predicament. For example, David is on the run from enemies (Ps. 70:5), Jerusalem is attacked

(Isa. 30:5), the armies of Israel face certain defeat (Ezek. 12:14). So what is the man's predicament? The key word is *alone:* "The LORD God said, 'It is not good for the man to be alone'" (Gen. 2:18). This is the only time in the creation process when something is said to be less than satisfactory. Only after the creation of both male and female is the verdict of "good" rendered (Gen. 1:31).

In our society the dog is often named "man's best friend." This, however, is not how God intended it to be. God created woman to play this role. Nor is it how the man understood it. For from among all the beasts of the field and all the birds of the air, the man could find no help for his aloneness (Gen. 2:19–20). Only bone of his bones and flesh of his flesh could deliver him from this predicament.

Is there anything in the created order of things that would suggest male headship and female subordination? Some have said that the use of *'ādām* in Genesis 1:26–27 "whispers male headship."[53] The English translation "man" is perhaps to blame for this mistaken understanding of the Hebrew term. *'Adām* is not a term that denotes gender. It literally means "earth-made" or "earthling" and is properly translated with a generic term like *human* or *humankind.* When gender comes into play, the Hebrew terms *zākār* ("male") and *něqēbâ* ("female") are used—as in the last part of Genesis 1:27: "male and female he created them." That *'ādām* is a gender-inclusive term is clear from the repeated reference to *'ādām* as "them" (Gen. 1:26–27; 5:2). The Septuagint's consistent choice of the generic term *anthrōpos* ("person," "human") to translate *'ādām* points to the same thing.

What about the fact that the male names the female? "She shall be called 'woman,'" the man said, "for she was taken out of man" (Gen. 2:23). In so doing, is the man not exercising a headship of sorts? Is he not bringing the woman under his control? Yet right before this, the man states, "This is now bone of my bones and flesh of my flesh"—hardly something one would say about a subordinate.

Perhaps with the recognition of equality also came the attempt to put the woman in her place. This assumes, however, that there is power in the naming of the female as "woman." Although some have so argued, there really is no evidence that this was the case in biblical times. As recent scholarship has shown, naming back then was a way to memorialize an event or to sum up a distinctive personal trait. It was not an act of control or power.[54] For instance, Isaac named the well he had dug in the Valley of Gerar "Esek" ("dispute") because he and the herdsmen of Gerar had argued about who owned it (Gen. 26:20; cf. vv. 21–22). Hagar named a well "Beer Lahai Roi" ("well of the Living One who sees me") to commemorate the place where God spoke to her in the desert (Gen. 16:13–14), and her son was named "Ishmael" ("God hears") as a reminder of God's intervention on Hagar's behalf (Gen. 16:11).

In none of these instances is naming an act of control or an exercise of headship. Nor is the naming of woman such an act. "Woman" was the man's response to the creation of a companion who was his personal counterpart in every way. It also summed up that which distinguished her from the rest of creation. She was called "wo-man" because she was created from the rib of the "man." In like manner, the animals were named, not as an exercise of headship but as the means by which the man sought to discern an associate from among them. It is worth noting that in Genesis 2:20 the Hebrew states that the man found no "counterpart" *(kĕnegdô)* to relieve his aloneness, and not that he found no "subordinate" to do his bidding.

What about the fact that the man was created before the woman? Is the man's temporal priority God's way of saying he should take the lead? That first is best is certainly the way we are educated to think. Graduating first in one's class, placing first in a sporting event, or being first in line is part of the American competitive mind-set. But is this what God intended? Does the male by virtue of being created first go to the head of the class—so to speak? Jesus' teaching that the first shall be last and the last first should warn us to tread carefully. The account in Genesis 2 certainly attaches no significance to the order of male then female.[55] Indeed, the fact that the animals were created before the male should caution against drawing a conclusion of this kind.

What Genesis 1–2 does emphasize is the human completeness that occurs after the creation of woman. Man alone is "not good" (Gen. 2:18). Man plus woman is "very good" (Gen. 1:31). If there is any subservience to be found in the creation accounts, it is not that of the woman to the man but that of both the woman and the man to God. It is God who commands, and it is the man and the woman who are expected to obey.

*Genesis 3*

> To the woman he said,
> "I will greatly increase your pains in childbearing;
>     with pain you will give birth to children.
> Your desire will be for your husband,
>     and he will rule over you."
>
>                               Genesis 3:16

A word must be said about Genesis 3:16. While Genesis 1:27 and 2:23–24 figure prominently in the New Testament understanding of male and female relations, Genesis 3:16 does not. Adam's sin is noted (Rom. 5:12–19; 1 Cor. 15:20–22), and Eve's deception is mentioned (2 Cor. 11:3; 1 Tim. 2:14), but a wife's desire for her husband and the husband's rule over the wife (Gen. 3:16) are not cited even once. This is important to see, since both ideas tend to play a prominent role in evangelical thinking and are often treated as factual statements about the way God intends things to be between a husband and a wife.

Michael Stitziner, for example, maintains that the wife's desire and the husband's rule are best regarded as statements of fact, reminding the first woman that the subordinate principle still remains in effect after the fall.[56] Robert Culver claims that the husband's rule over his wife is a statement of fact, which neither the Industrial Revolution nor the feminist movement is likely to overturn.[57] Susan Foh asserts that "rule over" describes the fight the husband must engage in to claim a headship rightfully his own.[58]

What the New Testament lifts up as normative, however, is not Genesis 3:16 but Genesis 1:27 and 2:23–24. Male and female relations are lived out not in light of the fall but in light of God's intent to create two sexually distinct beings in a mutual relationship with one another. This is clear from Jesus' declaration that God from the beginning had made them male and female (Matt. 19:4; Mark 10:6). It is also clear from his teaching that the marriage relationship is a functional *oneness,* not a hierarchical *twoness.* "They are no longer two, but one," says Jesus (Matt. 19:6; see Mark 10:7–8). In response to the liberal rabbinic notion that a man had the right to divorce his wife on any grounds he thought suitable (Matt. 19:3), Jesus declared that this was not God's creative intent. What God deemed suitable—and therefore normative—is that a man "forsake" father and mother and "cleave" to his wife (the reverse of the societal norm even today) and that he do it in such a way that the two become one (Matt. 19:5–6; Mark 10:7–8). What God also deemed suitable is marriage for life. Marriage is a divine union that is not to be separated by any human agency: "What God has joined together," Jesus states, "let no one separate" (Matt. 19:6; Mark 10:9 NRSV).

Genesis 3:16, on the other hand, does not figure into the marital scheme of things at any point in the New Testament. The statements "your desire will be for your husband" and "he will rule over you" just do not appear. No New Testament writer cites them; no New Testament writer treats them as theologically significant. Yet, they do raise questions that need to be addressed regarding social implications for male-female relationships.

The first thing to notice about Genesis 3 is that (contrary to popular opinion) the woman is not cursed. The serpent is cursed (v. 14, "cursed are you above all the livestock"), and the ground is cursed (v. 17, "cursed is the ground because of you [the man]"), but neither the man nor the woman are cursed. There were, however, serious consequences for both. A divine command had been given: "You must not eat from the tree of the knowledge of good and evil" (Gen. 2:17). Disobedience on the part of the man and the woman followed (Gen. 3:6–7), and there was a price to pay as a result (Gen. 3:14–19).

The consequences for the woman strike at the heart of her role as wife and mother. Painful toil in childbearing and dominance by her husband would be her lot (Gen. 3:16). Both the man and the woman were called to be fruitful (Gen. 1:28), but childbearing was the woman's distinctive task. The consequences for the man strike at the heart of his role as caretaker of the Garden of Eden. Although both the male and female were given the larger task of subduing the earth, the specific job of working the ground was distinctively the male's (Gen. 2:15–16). Painful toil as ground keeper would be his lot after the fall (Gen. 3:17–19).

At first glance, the results are not dissimilar. Both are consigned to weary toil—the same Hebrew word (*'iṣṣābôn*) appears in both instances. In the case of the woman, there is the prospect of "greatly increased toil" (AT; not NIV "pain") in bearing children (Gen. 3:16).[59] In the case of the man, the ground will yield its food but not without "toil . . . all the days of [his] life" (v. 17 NRSV).

Even so, there are unique aspects. The impact on the man (*'ādām*) is related to the ground from which he was taken (*'ădāmâ*, Gen. 2:7): "Cursed is the ground [*'ădāmâ*] because of you [*'ādām*]; through painful toil you will eat of it all the days of your life" (Gen. 3:17). The impact on the woman (*'iššâ*) is related to the man (*'iš*) from whose rib she was formed: "I will greatly increase your toil in childbearing; with toil you will give birth to children. Your desire will be for your husband, and he will rule over you" (Gen. 3:16 AT).

Because of the postfall implications of Genesis 3:16 for the marriage relationship, we need to look at this text more closely. Two statements are made. The first is a statement about the woman's marital desires: "Your desire will be for your husband" (Gen. 3:16). Some take this to be some sort of punishment. Yet, God's intent that the two become one flesh surely indicates that sexual desire was a key element of the prefall relationship (Gen. 2:24). Part of the difficulty is that the Hebrew term

*tĕšûqâ* ("desire," "yearning") is found only two other times in the Old
Testament, and neither is an exact parallel. In Genesis 4:7 God says to
Cain that sin is like a crouching beast *hungering* for him. The other use
in Song of Solomon 7:10 is interesting because it speaks of the bride-
groom's (not the bride's) *desire* for his beloved.

What kind of desiring is in view in Genesis 3:16? Some think the
woman's desire is to dominate her husband.[60] This produces a good link
with what follows. The translation would run: "Your desire will be to
rule your husband, but he will rule you." The difficulty is that nothing
prepares us for the idea of wifely domination. Nor does the Hebrew
term itself suggest it. Others suppose the wife's desire is "for what your
husband desires," but this introduces an idea that is extraneous to the
passage. The text is literally: "for your man [is] your yearning." Still others believe the text should be translated: "You will be desirable to your
husband."[61] This, though, imports a passive idea that hardly fits the active
notion of the noun *yearning*.

What is left? Since the immediately preceding clause has to do with
childbearing, it is quite natural to think in terms of the wife's desire for
sexual intimacy. This is plainly how the term is used in the Song of
Solomon ("I am my beloved's, and his *desire* is for me," 7:10 NRSV italics added). A yearning for sexual intimacy makes good sense in the context.[62] A yearning for personal intimacy—that is, for a companionship
that includes sexual intimacy but goes beyond it—makes even more
sense. The wife's desire is as God intended—a desire to become "one
flesh" with her husband (Gen. 2:24).

So the relational problem is not the woman's desire for her husband.
After all, this is why God created her. It is found, rather, in what follows:
"and he will rule over you" (Gen. 3:16). This text has been the source
of no little controversy. Is the man's *rule* a good or a bad thing? Is it—
as some say—a positive statement about the man's intended role as head
of the wife? Or is it—as others say—a negative statement about the
man's perversion of the created equality of male and female? Then too,
is this text descriptive or prescriptive? Does it describe the way things
will tend to be after the fall, or does it prescribe the way things must be?

One thing to note is that the Hebrew term *māšal* ("rule") is not inherently negative. We are not talking about a word that refers to spousal
abuse or oppression. It does not even mean to bring into submission by
brute force—like the word *kābaš* ("to subdue") in Genesis 1:28. Instead
it is the standard term for *rule* or *reign,* which occurs seventy-six times
in the Old Testament. This speaks against Genesis 3:16 having to do with
the corruption of a benevolent rule given to the male at creation. If this

were the case, then the term *rule* would be modified by an adjective like *harsh* or *domineering*, but all we have is the word *rule*.

It is the context, not the term *māšal*, that determines whether the rule in question is good or not. For example, *māšal* is used of Joseph's good administration of Egypt (Gen. 45:8), but it is also used of the Philistines' oppressive rule over Israel (Judg. 14:4; 15:11). The context of Genesis 3 is human disobedience and its impact. It is, therefore, difficult not to see the husband's rule as something different than the divine intent of Genesis 1–2. There would be no point to merely repeating the marital norms of Genesis 1–2. There is also no way to get around the fact that Genesis 3:16 involves the subordination of the woman to the man—something foreign to Genesis 1–2. The creation order is that of cleaving, oneness, and companionship.

Some would protest this, but the simple fact is that subordination finds no place in Genesis 1–2. One can claim allusions to male headship—as some are inclined to do. Yet to find a verse that explicitly puts forward male headship and female subordination as the norm is another matter entirely.

What does the husband's *rule* actually entail? Some suppose the husband's rule takes the form of sexual demands.[63] This provides a good link with what precedes. The translation would then be: "Your desire will be for your husband, and he will rule over that desire." It is also consistent with the context. Childbirth, sexual desire, and sexual demands are related ideas. Others think the husband will rule over his wife by requiring her obedience to his decision making. They claim headship is God's way of keeping the postfall woman faithful and submissive.[64] But this interjects an idea that has little connection with the immediate context.

A plausible suggestion is to read the pronoun *hû'* as *it* (neuter), rather than *he* (masculine). The wife's desire will be for her husband, and *it* (the desire) will rule her. This nicely fits the context. It is also quite close to the wording of Genesis 4:7, "Sin's desiring [*tĕšûqâ,* same noun] is for you but you will master it [*māšal,* same verb]" (AT).[65]

The first and last interpretations seem the likely options. Increased pain in childbearing is offset by God giving the woman an increased desire for sexual and personal intimacy with her spouse. The husband, in turn, takes advantage of this increased sexual appetite to make demands of his own. Or, alternatively, the woman's desire for her husband in the end gives him the upper hand over her.

What we want to avoid is lifting "he will rule over you" out of the context and making this statement a freestanding prescription for marital relationships. All too often, however, this is exactly what is done. We must remember that Genesis 3:16 is not God's intent for the marriage relationship. Genesis 1–2 define the marital norm. We do a tremendous disservice to the church's witness when we put humanity's fallen condition forward as God's intent for male-female relations.

The fact that the husband's rule over the wife does not reappear in the Old Testament should also caution us about reading Genesis 3:16 as prescriptive. The wife is nowhere commanded to obey her husband; the husband is nowhere commanded to rule his wife. On the other hand, the fact that the husband's rule is part of the fallen condition does indicate something of the direction human nature will incline given any encouragement. If we glean anything at all from Genesis 3:16, it should be a realistic understanding of dysfunctional capabilities of male-female relations. Perhaps one way to look at this text is similar to the way Jesus viewed divorce: "Moses permitted you [Pharisees] to divorce your wives *because your hearts were hard*" (Matt. 19:8 italics added). The divine standard is marital mutuality and oneness. The human reality all too often is marital subordination and twoness.

To summarize, the creation order of male and female is an egalitarian one. This comes through loud and clear in the accounts of Genesis 1–2. Equality is the key note—an equal task in society, an equal role with regard to family, equally created in God's image, and spiritual equals in God's sight. Sameness is also a common thread. "Bone of my bones," "flesh of my flesh," "wo-man," "in correspondence to," are phrases that drive this point home. Yet there is distinction; there is a *she* and there is a *he*. The *she* is created to relieve the aloneness of the *he*. Such an affinity exists between this *she* and *he* that the two can become one—soul mates as it were. So strong is this affinity that it leads the *he* to forsake the greatest of social obligations to forge a lifelong commitment to the *she*.

## The New Testament Perspective

Something other than a mutual and equal relationship between male and female first appears in the New Testament letters, and then only where marital correction occurs. This correction is specifically directed at wives. In four passages wives are called to be submissive to their husbands—a call that at face value assumes a hierarchical, not reciprocal, structuring of the marriage relationship: "Wives, submit to your husbands" (Eph. 5:22; Col. 3:18; see also Titus 2:5; 1 Peter 3:1).

The command itself is somewhat puzzling in that it stands side-by-side with clear statements of marital parity. *Oneness* is what both Jesus and Paul affirm as God's intent for the marriage relationship—and this despite the fall. Four times "and the two will become one flesh" is found in their recorded teachings (Matt. 19:5; Mark 10:7–8; 1 Cor. 6:16; Eph. 5:31). Also, equality and mutual responsibility are familiar parts of the New Testament marital landscape. Both the husband and wife are commanded to fulfill their marital duty to one another (1 Cor. 7:3–5). Neither husband nor wife is to divorce an unbelieving spouse (1 Cor. 7:12–13). "In the Lord, . . . woman is not independent of man, nor is man independent of woman" (1 Cor. 11:11), and both the husband and wife are to submit to one another "out of reverence for Christ" (Eph. 5:21). How, then, do we reconcile these seemingly conflicting expectations?

### JESUS' TEACHING

For Jesus there was no conflict. In the five recorded instances in which he treated the topic of marriage (most often under provocation), subordination did not make an appearance (Matt. 5:27–32; 19:1–12; Mark 10:1–12; 12:18–27; Luke 16:18; cf. Matt. 22:23–33; Luke 20:27–40). Instead, his language was that of mutuality and equality. This is quite remarkable given the strongly hierarchical character of the first-century Jewish male-female relationship.

When the Pharisees brought up the male prerogative to divorce a wife "for any and every reason" (Matt. 19:3; cf. Mark 10:2), Jesus rejected this assumption and recalled them to the fact that "the Creator 'made them male *and female*'" (Matt. 19:4). The creation order knows nothing of male priority or prerogatives. God created two sexually distinct beings on equal footing. It is this that motivates the male to forsake father and mother and to cleave to his wife (Matt. 19:5). It is also this that allows for oneness (Matt. 19:6).

Jesus went even further. He not only rejected the male prerogative to divorce but attributed the impulse to human hardness of heart.

> "Why then," they asked, "did Moses command that a man give his wife a certificate of divorce and send her away?" Jesus replied, "Moses permitted you to divorce your wives because your hearts were hard. But it was not this way from the beginning."
>
> Matthew 19:7–8; cf. Mark 10:4–6

God created man and woman to live in a monogamous union severed only by death. This is why Jesus was so tough on adultery (Matt. 5:27–32; 19:9; Mark 10:10–12). There is no male prerogative. There is no female prerogative for that matter. The prerogative is God's alone. God alone is the one who joins together. God alone is the one who severs this joining (Matt. 19:6).

Jesus was not the only one to think this way. While the men of mainline Judaism may have treated marriage lightly, the men of sectarian Judaism called the taking of a second wife while the first was alive *fornication*. What the creation order dictates is male and female for life (*Damascus Document* 4.21).

Jesus went on to affirm the legal parity of husband and wife. At the conclusion of his dialogue with the Pharisees, his disciples questioned him about his teaching. Although his answer was unequivocal—divorce and remarriage amounts to adultery in God's sight—what is sometimes overlooked is the legal parity of male and female that Jesus acknowledged. It was not just the man who wanted to divorce his wife but also the woman who wanted to divorce her husband who received Jesus' attention. The statements are finely balanced: "Anyone who divorces his wife and marries another woman commits adultery against her. And if she divorces her husband and marries another man, she commits adultery" (Mark 10:11–12).

Jesus could have cited Jewish scribal law, where the initiative to divorce lay wholly with the husband. Instead, his words recalled Roman law, where the initiative to divorce lay with either husband or wife. The divorce of Herod from his wife and of Herodias from her husband is most assuredly in the background, but Jesus' evoking of Roman law is a tacit acknowledgment of the parity—and hence equal responsibility—of husband and wife in God's eyes. The same measure of fidelity and commitment was expected of both.

Jesus' disciples responded with dismay. "If this is the situation between a husband and wife," they said, "it is better not to marry" (Matt. 19:10). The indissolubility of marriage was apparently not an agreeable idea to the average first-century Jewish male. The fact that Jewish marriages were typically contracted between families and often when the children were quite young undoubtedly has something to do with this attitude. But it also shows how far afield from Genesis 1–2 God's people had gone.

To a certain extent, Jesus agreed with his disciples. It is indeed better for some not to marry. The *some*, however, are not men who would find a lifetime commitment to a spouse well nigh intolerable but "those to whom it has been given" and who "have renounced marriage because of the kingdom of heaven" (literally, "those who have made themselves eunuchs," Matt. 19:11–12). In short, Jesus recognized an alternative path to marriage when there was a commitment to advance the work of God's kingdom. He also was realistic about this path. Those who choose it cannot go it alone; they need God's enabling ("to whom it has been given").

Celibacy for the sake of the kingdom of God is not something Jesus presented as a distinctively male commitment. Jesus saw women as equal to the call. Mark 10:29–31 is particularly instructive, for here Jesus states that no one who has left house, brothers or sister, mother or father, or even their children for the sake of the gospel will fail to reap a reward. The household (*oikia*) was the domain of the woman, and the bearing and raising of children was her primary responsibility. So Jesus' teaching is particularly relevant for women.

Jesus' teaching is phenomenal in two respects. First, celibacy was not something upon which the Roman government at this time looked favorably (see p. 93), so advocating a path other than marriage was in essence defying Rome. Second, Jesus was a Jew, and Judaism viewed the continuation of the family line of the utmost importance and the highest of obligations (see, for example, Gen. 38:8; Deut. 25:5–6; Ruth 4:5). To advocate something other than marriage would have been perceived as antifamily. The family, after all, was looked on as the most sacred of social institutions. Of course, Jesus did not do this lightly or even hypothetically. The priority he personally placed on ministry over family ties made his own mother and siblings think he was insane (Mark 3:21).

The parity Jesus accords women extends beyond the realm of marriage and singleness. Women are nothing less than social equals. This is clear from the utmost respect Jesus showed women. He talked with them (e.g., John 4:6–26), traveled with them (e.g., Luke 8:1–3), and developed close friendships with them (e.g., John 11:5). While we might not think this strange today, it was very unusual in the first century. Back then, Jewish men and women simply did not mix in public. It was looked on as a social affront for a Jewish man to even talk with a woman.

Jesus did not confine his social mixing to the feminine elite of his society. Women from all ranks and walks of life received his attention. Jesus associated with married women (e.g., Matt. 20:20–21; Mark 1:30–31; 15:40; Luke 8:3), unmarried women (Mark 15:40; Luke 8:2–3), ritually defiled women (e.g., Mark 5:25–34), non-Israelite women (e.g., Mark 7:24–30), and even women prostitutes (e.g., Luke 7:36–50).

Jesus also treated women with dignity. The domestic routines of women were highly valued (Matt. 13:33; 24:41; Luke 15:8–10). Jesus even likened himself to a mother hen gathering her chicks under her wings (Matt. 23:37–38). He called a crippled woman (Luke 13:16) and a ritually unclean woman (Mark 5:34) "daughters," and he said that a lustful look at a woman—which would tend to be written off as no big deal today—was sin (Matt. 5:28).

APOSTOLIC TEACHING

What about Paul? How do women fare socially in his teaching? Let's start with marriage. Although Paul is commonly accused of having a low view of marriage and an even lower view of a woman's place in it, his teaching on both accounts suggests just the opposite. For Paul, the marriage union is something created by God and good (1 Tim. 4:3–5). The married couple is no longer "two" but "one flesh" (Eph. 5:31), and the relationship of husband and wife mirrors the relationship between Christ and the church (Eph. 5:32). This sounds like a high, not a low, view of marriage.

This high view extends to the woman's role in the marriage. It is interesting to note what Paul does not say. For one, he does not say that the primary responsibility of the wife is to bear and raise children. He does advise young widows at Ephesus to marry, have children, and manage their homes (1 Tim. 5:14), but this is because they were bringing disrepute on the gospel through their disdain of marriage (1 Tim. 4:3) and their going from house to house "saying things they ought not to" (1 Tim. 5:13). Otherwise, Paul does not identify childbearing as a duty of the woman. This is rather amazing given the importance of family in that day.

Additionally, Paul does not include anything about wifely submission to a husband's sexual demands. This is striking even by today's standards, where sex is still commonly viewed as the husband's privilege and the wife's obligation. One also looks in vain for the marital prerogatives and rights that men took for granted in the first century. In fact, Paul is so bold as to say that the husband has no rights in the sexual arena. In 1 Corinthians 7:4, for example, he states, "The husband has *no* authority over his body" (a literal translation of the Greek text). Instead, it is the *wife* who holds this authority (and vice versa). The use of *exousiazei*—the standard Greek term for *power* or *authority*—is particularly eye-catching. The end result is a far cry from the pronouncement in Genesis 3:16: "He shall rule over you." It is also at odds with first-century male expectations and attitudes.

### The Husband's Duties

What Paul sets forth as the husband's role in the marriage is equally illuminating. Three duties are listed. The first duty of the husband is not to rule over his wife but to satisfy her sexual needs: "The husband should fulfill his marital duty to his wife" (1 Cor. 7:3). The Greek word is actually a verb of command ("let him fulfill"); and it is in the present tense, indicating that sexual fulfillment is the husband's ongoing duty. In fact, Paul calls the withholding of sex from one's wife an act of fraud (*apostereite,* 1 Cor. 7:5).

Paul also states (as a second duty) that the husband must release an unbelieving wife if she wishes to leave (1 Cor. 7:15). And he cannot divorce a believing wife, even if she leaves him (1 Cor. 7:10–11). This is quite astonishing considering that the religious convictions of the man of the house ruled the day. As the first-century historian Plutarch said, "It is becoming for a wife to worship and to know only the gods that her husband believes in and to shut the front door tight upon all queer ritual and outlandish superstitions" (*Moralia* 140D).

The third duty of the husband is to love his wife (Eph. 5:25–33). This was quite a tall order for the average male of that day, and probably why Paul takes nine verses to drive it home. Roman marriages were increasingly contracted by mutual consent, but this was not typically the case with Greek marriages. The wife was not viewed as a life partner or close companion but rather as the head of the domestic household and the mother of a man's legitimate children. It was not uncommon for upper-class Greek men to seek companionship and sexual gratification from someone other than their own wife (see p. 87). This means that Paul's love command targets a real need at that time.

Paul's instruction to the husband takes the form of a command. The husband *must* love his wife. An act of the will is required to carry out this duty. Although this may sound strange to our ears, it makes perfect sense in the first-century context. Not many couples at that time married out of love. Marriage contracts outlined marital duties and obligations, but love was not one of them. Marriage vows contained nothing like our "to love and to cherish 'till death us do part" (*Book of Common Prayer*). Love sometimes developed once two people were married, but not always.

The term Paul picks is also surprising to our Western way of thinking. We might expect him to speak of romantic (*eros*) or affectionate (*philos*) love in connection with marriage. Instead, he chooses a word that denotes the intentional giving of self for the sake of another (*agapē*)—a love that was supremely seen in the person of Jesus Christ. Paul goes even further, to insist that the husband must not only love his wife sacrificially, but he must do so "just as" (*kathōs*) Christ loved the church (Eph. 5:25). To love like Christ is to take the form of a servant (Phil. 2:7), to put the interests of one's wife first (Phil. 2:3–4), and, if need be, to die for her, "just as Christ loved the church and *gave* himself up for her to make her holy" (Eph. 5:25–26 italics added).

The husband is also to love his wife as he loves his own body—feeding and caring for it (Eph. 5:28–29). Initially, love of self sounds a bit at odds with the idea of sacrificial giving. Paul may be thinking of what he had said in the previous chapter about Christ as the head from whom the whole body (the church) is nourished and sustained (Eph. 4:16).

Yet the fact that he goes on to cite Genesis 2:24 ("the two will become one flesh," Eph. 5:31) points in a different direction. The variant reading in some early manuscripts and versions (א<sup>c</sup>, D, G, itala, Vulgate, Syriac) is revealing: "We are members of his flesh and of his bones" (Eph. 5:30). This is what the first man recognized in the first woman—someone so akin to himself that nothing would do short of forsaking mother and father, cleaving to her, and becoming one with her (Eph. 5:31; citing Gen. 2:23–24). To love one's wife as oneself, therefore, recalls the creation order of male and female. For a husband to love his wife in this fashion is to vow loyalty to her as "bone of his bones and flesh of his flesh."

The complete absence in Paul's writings of *rule* or *authority over* a wife as a duty of the husband must be duly noted. Self-sacrifice, unswerving loyalty, personal intimacy, and sexual satisfaction are the extent of the responsibilities Paul lists for the husband.

Peter adds the duty of living with one's wife, literally "according to knowledge" (1 Peter 3:7). While this could be knowledge of her needs and desires, it could also refer to a knowledge of God's intent for the marriage relationship. Husbands are likewise to "honor" their wives as "the weaker vessel" (1 Peter 3:7 KJV, NKJV). Some translations have "the weaker partner" (JB, NJB, NIV). The Greek term actually refers to something that is delicate and easily broken—like a fragile vase.[66] It has nothing whatsoever to do with weaker intellect, greater emotional vulnerability, nonassertive behavior, or less objectivity. The term is used elsewhere in the New Testament for what is mortal and perishable (e.g., Acts 9:15–16; 2 Cor. 4:7; Rev. 2:27; 18:12). Physically weaker is surely what Peter had in mind.

### The Wife's Duties

What about the woman's duties? With one exception, they are identical to those of the man's. As Paul puts it, she is to function in the very same way (*homoiōs,* 1 Cor. 7:4). To start with, the woman has the same responsibility to enter into a monogamous marriage: "Each man should have his *own* wife, and each woman her *own* husband" (1 Cor. 7:2 italics added). God's people are not to have multiple husbands or wives. In ancient times this was almost always a male phenomenon. Polygyny ("many wives") was (and is) a way to exercise control over women (compare Mormonism). It was against the law in Roman times, but the Jews tolerated the polygamous practices of rulers like Herod the Great (37–4 B.C.).

Paul tolerates no such state of affairs. He puts it in the form of a command: *Let each* have his or her *own* spouse (see 1 Cor. 7:2). Sectarian

Judaism did not tolerate polygamy either—not even for the king of Israel. One of the statutes in the *Temple Scroll* states: "He [the King of the New Jerusalem] is not to take another wife in addition to her; no, she alone shall be with him as long as she lives" (57.17–18).

The wife's first marital duty is to satisfy her husband's sexual needs, just as her husband's duty is to satisfy her sexual needs (1 Cor. 7:3). She must not "defraud" him of it except by mutual consent (v. 5). She cannot insist on her rights in this area any more than he can, for she—as he—has no authority over her body (v. 4).

The wife's second duty is to preserve, where possible, the marriage union and to maintain the family unit. She is to devote herself to pleasing her husband—just as he is to devote himself to pleasing her (1 Cor. 7:34). She is not permitted to divorce him, regardless of whether he is a believer (1 Cor. 7:10) or an unbeliever (1 Cor. 7:13). On the other hand, she must permit an unbelieving husband to leave, if he so desires (1 Cor. 7:15). Her presence has a sanctifying effect on the family. Just as the unbelieving wife is sanctified through her believing husband, so the unbelieving husband is sanctified through his believing wife. Even the children are "holy" because she is there (1 Cor. 7:14).

The wife's third duty is to love her husband and her children. This, in fact, was a part of the social training that a younger woman received from an older woman. In Titus 2:3–5, Paul instructs the pastor of a recent church plant to "teach the older women" so that "they can train the younger women to love their husbands and children." The term for *love (philos)* more properly refers to affection and friendship, rather than the *agapē* that husbands are commanded to show their wives (Eph. 5:25–33; Col. 3:19). Paul does not detail what this training in affection would involve; he simply states that this is a duty they must learn.

Some see a fourth duty in 1 Timothy 5:14, where Paul advises the younger widows to marry, to have children, and to manage their homes. It is erroneous, however, to call this a duty. Paul's instruction was specifically aimed at young widows who were engaging in socially disruptive activities that brought the gospel into disrepute (1 Tim. 5:13–15). He nowhere commands women on general principle to marry and have children. In fact, in 1 Corinthians 7 he counsels just the opposite. The higher calling is celibacy for the sake of God's kingdom. A married woman is concerned about the affairs of the world—how she can please her husband. An unmarried woman is concerned about the Lord's affairs; her aim is to be devoted to the Lord in both body and spirit (1 Cor. 7:34).

Although marriage and children are not incumbent on women, the married woman nonetheless is duty bound to family and household. The term Paul uses in 1 Timothy 5:14 is *oikodespotein*. The NIV's translation, "to manage their homes," is rather weak. A more rigorous translation would be "to rule their house" (compare our English word *despot*). Yet, whatever the translation, a leadership capacity is clearly in view. We are not just talking about cleaning the house, watching the children, and cooking the food. The first-century wife was in charge of running the entire household. Epictetus stated that the *oikodespotēs* of the house "assigns each and every thing its place" (*Fragment* 3.22.4). This fits New Testament usage. All twelve occurrences refer to the master or owner of the household in the widest sense.[67]

The ancient household was much larger than the typical Western home. Even modest households included one or two servants in addition to a husband and children. More typically, a household included relatives, servants, children, and guests. When her husband was away, the wife's responsibilities also included managing the estates and running the family business. This meant the wife needed extensive administrative skills and explains the need for training young women to be "good managers of the household" (*oikourgous agathas,* Titus 2:5 NRSV).

The phrase is literally "works the household well." "Busy at home" (NIV, NEB) falls short. "Home-lovers" *(Phillips)* is also wide of the mark. Accuracy is important because some have understood this text to be instructing women to stay at home. Paul is concerned, rather, with women who would bring social disgrace on themselves and the newly planted church by neglecting their managerial duties at home ("so that no-one will malign the word of God," Titus 2:5).

Managing the household included managing the children. To this end Paul commands the children of his churches to obey their parents—not just their father (Eph. 6:2; Col. 3:20). Paul grounds this obedience first and foremost in God's law (not merely in societal norms): "'Honor your father and mother'—which is the first commandment with a promise" (Eph. 6:2; citing Deut. 5:16). To do so is "righteous" *(dikaios),* not merely "right" (v. 1 NIV) or "proper." What this means is that maternal authority and responsibility are part of the divine order of things. It also means that the children grow spiritually in relationship to both the mother and the father.

Paul does single out the father in one area. In Ephesians 6:4 fathers are commanded not to provoke their children to anger *(para* plus *orgizō)* but to discipline *(paideia)* and admonish *(nouthesia)* them in a godly fashion (cf. Col. 3:21, *erethizō,* "rouse to anger"). By this Paul does not exclude the mother as a disciplinary figure. What he targets is the father's apparent tendency to be too heavy-handed in the area of discipline.

The key note throughout these texts is that of marital and familial mutuality. Paul insists on absolute reciprocity in the marriage and equal respect in the family. There is no ground that the husband or wife can claim as his or her own; each marital norm is carefully and precisely balanced. It is always "each man should" and "each woman should" (1 Cor. 7:2), "the husband must" and "the wife must" (v. 3), "the wife's body does not" and "the husband's body does not" (v. 4). Mutuality extends even to the matter of initiating (or not initiating) a divorce. A wife must not divorce her husband, and a husband must not divorce his wife (vv. 10–11). A husband must not divorce his unbelieving wife, and a wife must not divorce her unbelieving husband (vv. 12–13).

A word must be said about the matter of decision making in the marriage. While "wives, submit to your husbands" might come immediately to mind, three words in 1 Corinthians 7:5 need to be given careful attention. These three words are: "by common consent." Paul's statement is quite straightforward—decisions in the marriage are to be arrived at by mutual agreement. Marriages that operate by common consent require work. It is no wonder many gravitate toward "wives, submit to your husbands." It is so much easier for all concerned. But is this what God intended for the marriage?

## Submission and Headship in the New Testament

There are five passages in the New Testament that seem to be in conflict with the principle of mutual consent: 1 Corinthians 11:3, Ephesians 5:22–24, Colossians 3:18, Titus 2:3–5, and 1 Peter 3:1–6. Three command the wife to submit to her husband (Eph. 5:22; Col. 3:18; 1 Peter 3:1), one counsels training in wifely submission (Titus 2:3), one speaks of the husband as the wife's "head" (Eph. 5:23), and one talks about the man as the woman's "head" (1 Cor. 11:3).

Wifely submission is quite in line with the culture of that day. Although first-century Roman marriages were increasingly egalitarian in character, the ideal nonetheless remained that of a devoted mother and dutiful wife. What is surprising, however, is the presence of such language in Scripture, for apart from these five New Testament passages, the biblical materials are wholly devoid of such instruction.

### Submission

"Is the head of the house at home?" "May I speak to the head of the house?" Such questions by telephone solicitors never fail to puz-

zle—especially given the high percentage of two-income families, highly
positioned women, and single-parent families in our society. Are solicitors out of touch with American life? For whom exactly is the person
asking—the primary breadwinner, the decision maker, or the family
manager?

Part of the difficulty is that the term *head* is a common one in our
society. We have heads of corporations, department heads, office heads,
head coaches, headmasters, and so on. But is there any biblical mandate
for speaking of the head of a household? The following four passages are
often taken to be that mandate:

> Wives, submit to your husbands as to the Lord (Ephesians 5:22).

> Wives, submit to your husbands, as is fitting in the Lord (Colossians
> 3:18).

> Train the younger women . . . to be subject to their husbands (Titus
> 2:4–5).

> Wives, in the same way be submissive to your husbands (1 Peter 3:1).

That wives are called to submit to their husbands can hardly be questioned. There are a couple of qualifications to note though. For one, the
term is *submit*, not *obey*. The distinction is an important one. Obedience
is something demanded of someone in a lesser position. Slaves (Eph.
6:5; Col. 3:22) and children (Eph. 6:1; Col. 3:20), for example, are commanded to *obey* their superiors. Submission, on the other hand, is a voluntary act of deferring to the wishes of an equal (BAGD 1bβ p. 848).
As such, wives are addressed in all four passages as free and responsible
agents; at least this is what the Greek term denotes (middle voice of
*hypotassō,* "to place oneself under").

There is a second qualifier. Wives are called to submit themselves
to their husbands, but what the wife is being asked to do to her husband is no different from what believers are called to do to one another.
Both Paul and Peter preface their instructions to wives with a call for
mutual submission: "Submit to one another out of reverence for Christ"
(Eph. 5:21), and, "Submit yourselves to every human creature *[ktisis]*
for the Lord's [Christ's] sake" (1 Peter 2:13). This ties the submission
of wives closely to the idea of service. The English translation "be subject to" (Eph. 5:21 NEB, REB, RSV, NRSV) for this reason is inaccurate.
Putting the interests of another ahead of one's own interests is the
basic notion.

THE CULTURE

One must still ask why the wife is singled out and the husband is not. Does it have to do with the culture of that day? Or is wifely submission the biblical norm for marital relationships in any age?

In the case of 1 Peter 3:1–6, the social context is quite clear. Peter urges wives to submit themselves to their husbands so that their socially appropriate behavior might provide a continuing witness where the gospel message has fallen on deaf ears. A proper understanding of the Greek is crucial here. Some render verse 1, "Wives submit to your husbands, so that *if perhaps* any of them [the husbands] do not believe the word they may be won over" (italics added). What we have, however, is a condition of fact (*ei* plus the present indicative). Peter is not presenting a hypothetical situation (*ean* plus the subjunctive) but the real dilemma of married women in his congregations. A more accurate translation would read: "So that even though some of them have rejected the word [of God], they may be won over without talk by the behavior of their wives."

This places a completely different spin on things. We must keep in mind that the husband's rule and the wife's obedience were the social norms for the Greek and Jew of that day. For a wife to reject this norm in the name of Christian freedom would in most cases be a real obstacle to the husband's receptivity. For that matter, should any of the married women in Peter's congregations do this, the impact would be quite predictable. There was no lack back then of religious cults whose rites encouraged women to cast aside their personal inhibitions and domestic duties. If its women shirked their familial responsibilities, Christianity (and its message) would be labeled as just another feminist cult.

This is surely why Peter begins with a general command to all the married women in the congregations of Asia Minor: "Wives submit yourselves to your husbands" (1 Peter 3:1 AT). It is also why he appeals to the obedience of Sarah (as "Sarah obeyed Abraham and called him lord," 3:6 NRSV). Wifely submission was also the social norm in Sarah's time. (There is certainly no biblical command calling for her submission.) Although Abraham believed in God, the country in which he and his wife sojourned did not (see, for example, Genesis 13). Sincere and respectful behavior on the wife's part would have been an important evangelistic tool in a traditional social context such as theirs.

There are several indications that the other submission passages equally reflect the social norms of their day. First, in no instance is the call for wifely submission grounded in the creation order of male and female. When Paul does appeal to the creation order, it is to stress marital mutuality (e.g., Eph. 5:31; citing Gen. 2:24). The submission passages, on the other hand, lack any appeal to the creation order. There is a simple explanation for this: The creation order of male and female is a mutual, not a hierarchical, one.

Second, each of the submission commands is part of what has come to be known as the "household code"—the rules by which wives and husbands, children and parents, and slaves and masters were to conduct themselves. The interesting thing to observe is that the rules for husbands and children are grounded in biblical teaching, while those for wives and slaves are based in social propriety. Children are to obey their parents because Mosaic law requires it: "'Honor your father and mother'—which is the first commandment with a promise" (Eph. 6:2; citing Deut. 5:16). Husbands are to love their wives because God intended that "the two . . . become one flesh" (Eph. 5:25–31; citing Gen. 2:24). Wives and slaves, on the other hand, are to submit because it is "fitting" (Col. 3:18) and "commendable" (1 Peter 2:18–19) to do so.

Third, the rationale for submission is socially based. Wives in Crete were to submit to their husbands "so that no-one will malign the word of God" (Titus 2:5). Wives in Asia Minor were to submit so their husbands "may be won over without words" (1 Peter 3:1). Young widows in Ephesus were to marry, have children, and rule their households so as "to give the enemy no opportunity for slander" (1 Tim. 5:14). Evangelistic strategy was the bottom line for the early church. If the gospel was to gain a hearing, Christians could not behave in socially offensive ways.

Fourth, the submission of wives and of slaves is talked about in virtually identical language. Both wives and slaves were to submit "in every way" (*en panti,* Eph. 5:24; Col. 3:22; Titus 2:9). Both were to do so for evangelistic reasons: to "make the teaching about God our Savior attractive" (Titus 2:10); to win them over (1 Peter 3:1). Both wives and slaves submitted "as to the Lord" (that is, as part of their service to Christ; Eph. 5:22; see also 6:5; Col. 3:23, 24) and "with respect" (that is, in a courteous fashion; Eph. 5:33; 6:5; 1 Peter 2:18).

So then, whatever we do with slaves, we must do with wives. For centuries various governments and churches justified slavery and the subordination of women on the basis of these biblical texts. Today we are quick to jettison slavery as antithetical to the gospel, yet we treat women's submission as God ordained. On what basis, though?

### THE CHRISTIAN COUNTERCULTURE

The ancient world (and modern world up until recently) thought that a well-ordered society and a fitly structured household had the pattern of superiors, inferiors, and equals.[68] At first glance the submission texts seem to support this mind-set. A closer look, however, shows that, in fact, they are strikingly countercultural. About the only traditional element is the command itself—"Wives submit to your husbands"—and even this has a nontraditional verb. Virtually everything else is new.

The linking of wifely submission to the command that believers submit themselves to one another out of reverence for Christ (not because of societal place or position) is new. This makes the wife's submission merely one example of mutual submission (and the husband's love another example). The lack of a verb in Ephesians 5:22 reinforces this. The text merely reads: "wives to your husbands." Most translators supply the word *submit* from verse 21 ("Submit to one another"). But the main verb (and therefore, the main command) is actually found back in verse 18: "Do not get drunk on wine. . . . Instead, *be filled with the Spirit*" (italics added). What follows in verses 19–22 (all participles) are examples of the Spirit-filled life, namely, "speaking to one another with psalms . . . singing and making music . . . giving thanks . . . submitting to one another" (AT).

Also new is the redefining of wifely submission in terms of service to Christ. Yes, the wife is to submit to her husband, but she is to do it "as to the Lord" (Eph. 5:22), "as is fitting in the Lord" (Col. 3:18), and "as the church submits to Christ" (Eph. 5:24). By submitting, then, she serves Christ (and only secondarily her husband).

New as well is the call to *submit,* as opposed to *obey.* This places the wife on the same level as her husband and addresses her as capable of making her own decisions (see p. 118).

The end result is a strikingly different view of the marital relationship than the prevailing one of the day. What Paul in essence does is level the playing field. Husbands are called to self-sacrifice ("love your wives, just as Christ loved the church," Eph. 5:25). The wife is called to self-sacrifice ("submit to your husband out of service to Christ"). Both are called to mutual submission, and both are called to lay aside self-interest. While this may seem to fall short of the modern, liberated woman, it also falls short of first-century dominant male. Christ is the only *lord* in this picture. Our role (be it husband or wife) is that of servant. As Paul states in 1 Corinthians 6:19–20, we are not our own; we were bought at a price.

### HEADSHIP

A word must be said about headship. Two New Testament passages speak of the man as the head of the woman. In Ephesians 5:23 Paul states that "the husband is the head of the wife as Christ is the head of the church." In 1 Corinthians 11:3 he asserts that "the head of every man is Christ, and the head of the woman is man, and the head of Christ is God."

Today a *head* of something or someone is commonly understood to be the CEO or controlling person or thing. But is this the biblical use of the term? There are those who say that the Greek term *kephalē* can mean nothing else,[69] and there are those who say that it means virtually everything but this.[70] The debate has been a heated one. This undoubtedly is because of the profound impact the answer has on that most sacred of human institutions—the family. Responses, however, tend to be an unqualified *yes* or *no* with very little—if any—middle ground. Can the biblical texts sustain an absolute *yes* or *no?*

Part of the difficulty is that the Greek term *kephalē* rarely means anything other than the physical head of the body—be it human or otherwise. Yet metaphorical uses are wide-ranging in meaning. Most have to do with the idea of "chief" or "prominent"—like the top of a mountain (e.g., Gen. 8:5), pride of place (e.g., Deut. 28:13; Isa. 7:8–9; Jer. 31:7 [38:7 LXX]), the foremost position in a column or formation (e.g., Job 1:17), the capstone of a building (Ps. 118:22 [117:2 LXX]), or the end of a pole (e.g., 2 Chron. 5:9). Others have to do with the idea of "beginning" or "origin"—like the progenitor of a clan (e.g., Philo, *The Preliminary Studies* 12 §61; Hermas, *Parable* 7.3), the starting point of a river (Herodotus, *History* 4.91), or the source of evil (*Life of Adam and Eve* 19.3).

In some instances *kephalē* can stand as a part for the whole ("to count each head" is to count each person; e.g., Judg. 5:30) or for the "self" or one's "life" (Isa. 43:4). There are also a few passages where *kephalē* appears to mean "leader." Jephthah, for example, was chosen to be the "leader" of the people of Gilead (Judg. 11:11), and David was the "leader" of nations (2 Sam. 22:44; Ps. 18:43; cf. Jer. 52:31). The one surprising aspect is that the only times *kephalē* is used to mean "master" or "ruler," it is in a negative sense. For instance, those who would be Israel's master are her foes (Lam. 1:5).

Another problem in understanding headship is the interconnectedness of *origin, prominent,* and *leader.* Privileges often accompany being the first or origin of something. The Greek god Zeus is a good example; there is no doubting the prestige and power that go along with being the "beginning *[kephalē]* of all things" (*Orphic Fragment* 21A). Stature also can easily follow from being the progenitor of a clan. Christ, for instance, is the beginning, the firstborn from the dead in order that he might be preeminent or foremost in everything (Col. 1:18). This interconnection is a primary reason why scholars have reached different conclusions about the metaphorical meaning of *kephalē* in various texts.

An additional hurdle is the tendency to read one's cultural understanding back into the text. Virtually all English translations render *kephalē* as "head." Yet it is difficult to translate it this way without suggesting a position of authority (or even dominance) to the average English reader. The simple fact is that *kephalē* is rarely used to describe the relationship of one individual to another, let alone the relationship of a superior to a subordinate. Can we distance ourselves from Western culture long enough to be accurate to the Greek text?

In terms of the Pauline texts, opinions, with rare exception, divide into one of three camps: *Kephalē* means either (1) "source/beginning," (2) "leader/ruler," or (3) "prominent/preeminent." *Prominent* is by far the most common usage (see above). *Source* and *leader,* on the other hand, are quite rare—although examples can be found which show the currency of both meanings in the first century A.D. For example, in a Jewish work contemporary with Paul's writings, while recalling her experience with the serpent, Eve says, "For desire is the source *[kephalē]* of every kind of sin" (*Life of Adam and Eve* 19.3), and the first-century historian and moralist Plutarch recounts Catiline's proposal to become the "leader" *(kephalē)* of the republic of Rome (*Cicero* 14.5).

What all this means is that Paul's uses of *kephalē* must be decided on a case-by-case basis. Six of Paul's eighteen uses clearly refer to a physical head (Rom. 12:20; 1 Cor. 11:4a, 5a, 7, 10; 12:21), while two others might (1 Cor. 11:4b, 5b). This leaves eight to ten passages where *kephalē* is used in a metaphorical way. In some cases the exact meaning is difficult (if not impossible) to determine definitively.

Three of these texts speak of Christ as the *kephalē* of the church:

> And he [Christ] is the *kephalē* of the body, the church; he is the beginning and the firstborn from among the dead.
>
> Colossians 1:18

> They have lost connection with the *kephalē, from* whom the whole body, supported and held together by its ligaments and sinews, grows as God causes it to grow.
>
> Colossians 2:19

> Instead, speaking the truth in love, we will in all things grow up into him who is the *kephalē,* that is, Christ.
>
> Ephesians 4:15

A close look at parallel language in the surrounding context shows that the primary idea is "first" or "origin." Christ is the "firstborn" of all creation

(Col. 1:15). Everything was created and then reconciled "through" him (Col. 1:16, 20). He is the "beginning" (Col. 1:18). He is also the source of the church's cohesion and ongoing life, for "from him" *(ex hou)* the church is supported, held together, and grows (Eph. 4:16; Col. 2:19).

Two other texts speak of Christ as the *kephalē* of all power and authority:

> You have been given fullness in Christ, who is the *kephalē* over every power and authority.
>
> Colossians 2:10

> God placed all things under his feet and appointed him to be *kephalē* over everything for the church, which is his body, the fullness of him who fills everything in every way.
>
> Ephesians 1:22–23

While *kephalē* could mean the "source" of all rule and authority, the broader context points in another direction. God seated Christ *"far above* all rule and authority, power and dominion" (Eph. 1:21 italics added). God also placed all things *"under* his feet" (Eph. 1:22 italics added). *Kephalē* most certainly is used here in its predominant metaphorical sense, namely, to be "preeminent" or "foremost."

### EPHESIANS 5:22–23

This brief overview of Christ as *kephalē* is important background for Ephesians 5:22–23, where Paul states, "Wives, submit to your husbands as to the Lord. For the husband is *head* of the wife as also [*hōs kai*] Christ is the head of the church, his body, of which he is the Savior" (italics added). While our English understanding of *head* might lead us to think in terms of a CEO, Paul's use of *kephalē* elsewhere in Ephesians challenges us to broaden our horizons. By *head* does Paul mean *source*—as in Ephesians 4:15–16, where the church's life and growth come *from him?* Or does the term mean *preeminent*—as in Ephesians 1:20–23, where Christ is seated *far above* all cosmic power and authority?

It is instructive to note that in Paul's letters where *kephalē* defines the relationship of Christ and the church, the primary idea is source, not preeminence. As Savior, Christ is the source of the church's existence. He brings forth the church from himself as his "fullness" (Col. 2:10) and his "body" (Eph. 5:23). As sustainer (Eph. 5:29), he is the source of the church's life and health. It is from him that the whole body is "supported and held together by its ligaments and sinews" and "grows as God causes it to grow" (Col. 2:19).

This is not to say that Christ is not Lord of the church. He is. The fact that Paul greets all his churches with the "grace of our Lord Jesus Christ" drives this home as a point of first importance. Yet it is doubtful that lordship is what Paul means by the term *kephalē*. While our twentieth-century thinking might lead us in this direction, the context of Ephesians 5:23–33 does not (nor does first-century usage).[71]

*Savior* and *sustainer* are the key concepts in these verses. Christ is *kephalē* of the church in that he is its savior.[72] The lack of the article is significant. If the text read "the *kephalē* of the church," we might think in terms of a CEO. The absence of the article, however, means that the noun *kephalē* describes rather than defines. *Savior* also lacks an article, so we want to be careful not to capitalize this word. While the term can mean "deliverer," in this context it has to do with preserving that which is near and dear—even to the point of death. The husband is commanded to love his wife even "as Christ loved the church and *gave himself up for her*" (v. 25 italics added).

Preserving a living being requires nourishment and tender loving care. It is for this reason that Paul goes on in Ephesians 5:28–31 to talk about Christ as the source of the church's well-being. Just as Christ feeds and cares for the church, so the husband is to feed and care for his wife (vv. 29–30). The text is literally "to nourish and cherish" and has in the background the kind of tender loving care that a mother gives to her children.[73]

The parallel idea is caring for one's own physical body. As the church becomes Christ's own body, so the wife becomes the husband's own body (Eph. 5:30–31). The use of *body* is more than analogical. In a very real sense the marital union creates one where there had been two ("the two will become one flesh," v. 31, citing Gen. 2:24).

What of a husband's rule over his wife? No such command appears. Instead, the husband is called to love his wife as Christ loved the church. Not one but three times Paul urges husbands to do this (vv. 25, 28, 33). Indeed, the example of Christ virtually excludes all notions of rule and authority, for to love like Christ loves is to take the form of a servant, to put the interests of another ahead of one's own (Eph. 5:21), and to sacrifice oneself for the sake of another (Eph. 5:25).

Nor is it possible to read into *head of the body* the idea of rule and decision making. While the idea of the head as the decision-maker of the human body was current in the first century, it is absent in Paul. For Paul it is the heart, not the head, that is the seat of the human will. It is the heart that makes decisions (1 Cor. 7:37 NASB), the heart that believes (Rom. 10:9–10), the heart that becomes foolish and darkened (Rom.

1:21) or wise and enlightened (Eph. 1:18), and the heart on which the law is written (Rom. 2:15).

There is perhaps no clearer indication that *kephalē* means *source* in these verses than Paul's statement that "we [the church] are members of his [Christ's] body, that is, his flesh and his bones."[74] The allusion to Genesis 2:21–23 and the creation of the woman from the rib of the man is unmistakable, and so is the notion of *source.* The church is the Eve of the second Adam, bone of his bones and flesh of his flesh. How this comes to be is on the order of a "profound mystery" (Eph. 5:32). The church as Christ's submissive servant is no mystery at all; the church as Christ's flesh and bone is a mystery indeed.

One final thought: If to be *head* is to be source and sustainer, why then is the wife called to *submit?* Is this not more consonant with the husband as CEO? It might be, were it not for the fact that Ephesians 5:22–33 is to be read in light of Paul's command in verse 21 to submit to one another out of reverence for Christ.

### 1 Corinthians 11

First Corinthians 11:3–16 is distinctive in that the husband-wife relationship does not seem to be primarily in view. For this reason it is perhaps the most critical New Testament text to look at with respect to male-female relations.

> Now I want you to realize that the head of every man is Christ, and the head of the woman is man, and the head of Christ is God. Every man who prays or prophesies with his head covered dishonors his head. And every woman who prays or prophesies with her head uncovered dishonors her head—it is just as though her head were shaved.
>
> 1 Corinthians 11:3–5

The RSV, NRSV, TEV, LB, and NLT translate the initial verse as the head of a woman is "her husband."[75] Yet such a reading becomes untenable farther along in the passage. The difficulty is that the Greek terms *male (anēr)* and *female (gynē)* can also mean *husband* and *wife.* Paul normally adds a possessive word like *own, her,* or *their* to distinguish the two (e.g., "If they want to learn, let them ask their *own* males [i.e., husbands] at home," 1 Cor. 14:35; cf. 7:2 AT), but there is no such addition here— and rightly so. Otherwise Paul would be speaking of some nonexistent religious taboo regarding husbands (as opposed to other males) covering their heads in public worship (1 Cor. 11:4). He would also be saying that husbands (as opposed to other males) are the image and glory of God (1 Cor. 11:7), are birthed by their wives (1 Cor. 11:12), and cannot by the laws of nature have long hair (1 Cor. 11:14). This makes an already difficult text incomprehensible.

It is sometimes said that virtually all women were married in the first century, so it is not a stretch to understand "the man" as "her husband." But this overlooks the many women in the early church who were widowed or divorced (see, for example, 1 Cor. 7:39–40; 1 Tim. 5:3–16). It also discounts Paul's statement four chapters earlier that virgins, widows, and divorcees do well to remain unmarried (7:8, 11, 25–26, 39–40).

One suspects that "her husband" is an attempt to bring verse 3 in line with other husband-wife passages in the New Testament. Otherwise, 1 Corinthians 11 stands alone in defining the male-female relationship in terms of headship. But stand alone it must. Rather, the question is why Paul tackles this topic here and not elsewhere. What is going on in the Corinthian situation that leads him to insist that the head of a woman is the man?

The basic situation is easy to grasp. The social world of Paul's day had fixed ideas about appropriate dress for men and women. It was not so long ago that it was considered unbefitting for a woman to appear in an American worship service without a hat, and in some circles it is still judged to be rude behavior for a man not to remove his hat at an indoor public event (sports games excepted). That Paul is likewise upholding a firmly established social custom seems clear from terms like *shameful* (1 Cor. 11:6), *proper* (1 Cor. 11:13), and *disgraceful* (1 Cor. 11:14).[76] "Judge for yourselves: is it proper?" (1 Cor. 11:13) especially points in this direction.

Even so, Paul's appeal to the creation order of Genesis 2 shows that something more than unbefitting behavior is at issue. "A man ought not to cover his head . . . for man did not come from woman, but woman from man; neither was man created for woman, but woman for man" (1 Cor. 11:7–9). Nature itself teaches that women and men are to coiffure themselves differently (1 Cor. 11:14–15). This suggests that a blurring of the created distinctions between the sexes is at stake.

What created distinctions does Paul have in mind, though? There is nothing in the passage to indicate that they are functional in nature. Paul distinctly approves of women praying and prophesying alongside men (1 Cor. 11:4–5). What they have (or do not have) over their heads when they engage in these public activities is the issue. This means that the mention of Eve coming *from* Adam and being created *for* Adam is not an attempt to put women in their place. Paul is also concerned to show from the creation order that men in public worship should not cover their heads. Creation in the image and glory of God demands it (1 Cor. 11:7) and "nature" confirms it (1 Cor. 11:14).

To treat such matters at length—as Paul does here—leads one to think that some sort of sexual identity confusion lurks in the background. It may be that the Corinthians took "there is not (ουκ) male and (και) female, for you are all one in Christ Jesus" (Gal. 3:28 AT) literally to mean they should seek to do away with gender distinctions. In a culture where dress signaled maleness and femaleness, cross-dressing would certainly be a step in that direction.[77]

The part of the dress code that Paul targets is headgear: Female worship leaders are to have their heads covered, and those who are male are not. But what kind of headgear are we talking about? Were women being asked to wear some sort of hat or veil, or does the problem have to do with hairstyles (as some argue)? Were men letting their hair grow long and women cutting their hair boyishly short, or were the men aping the upswept feminine fashion and the women loosing their plaited buns and letting their hair hang down?

The Greek term (katakalyptomai) is hard to nail down. It is not really used either of a veil or of hair. A literal rendering would be something like "down from the head." Men are not to have "down from the head," while women are. The typical hairstyle shown in portraits of upper-class Greek and Roman women involved twisting the hair into a roll at the top of the head and then looping it to form a raised ridge. Upper-class men had short locks combed forward to frame the forehead.[78] Such styles, however, have more to do with formal wear and leave us wondering how hair was worn on a day-to-day basis. To complicate matters, social standing tended to dictate both clothing and hairstyle in the Roman world.

There are a number of places in 1 Corinthians 11:3–16 that seem to demand a covering other than hair. One is verses 14–15. That women should cover their heads is shown by the long hair (komē) with which nature endowed them. Hair is nature's equivalent to a head covering (anti plus the genitive), not the head covering itself.[79] A second place is verse 6, where Paul states that if a woman will not cover her head, she should cut her hair. This assumes a covering distinct from her long (able to be cut) tresses. A third place that demands something other than hair is verse 10, where Paul states that a woman "ought to have authority [or power, KJV; exousia] on her head [epi tēs kephalēs]."[80] There is nothing in the literature of the day to connect hair with authority or power. On the other hand, it is a well-known fact that both Roman clergy and laity veiled their head before performing liturgical functions.[81]

While the language of *veiling* might conjure up images of the Roman Catholic habit or the Islamic head and face covering, such was not the case for Roman women in the first century. Portraits show that Roman women usually wore no head covering at all in public. Functionaries (both religious and civic) did, on the other hand, cover their heads. This was done by pulling up their toga far enough over their heads to cover to the middle of the ear. The fact that the outer garment draped the head at about the same point as long hair explains how it is that Paul could speak of long hair as an equivalent form of head covering (1 Cor. 11:15).[82]

Given this custom, it is surprising that Paul labels the action of men who cover their heads in a Christian worship service as dishonoring (1 Cor. 11:4). The fact that Jewish priests officiating in the temple wore turbans makes Paul's statement doubly surprising (Ezek. 44:18; cf. *m. Yoma* 7.5). It may be that Paul felt Roman religious practice blurred the sexual distinctions implicit in the creation order of Genesis 1–2. Paul does not say that a man praying or prophesying with his head covered stigmatized him in the eyes of society. What he does say is that such an action disgraced *Christ* (1 Cor. 11:3–4). We cannot know for certain why this was.

All this talk of headgear should not sidetrack us from what this passage says about societal roles for women. For one, it is clear there is a leadership role for women in society. In Paul's day, such leadership was not merely tolerated but applauded. Paul begins this section of the letter with words of praise. The Corinthians are holding to "the traditions" (*paradoseis*) exactly as Paul had "passed on" (*paredōka*) to them (1 Cor. 11:2). "Passed on" is an important statement. It means that women in leadership was quite agreeable not only with what Paul instructed but with what the apostles as a whole taught and practiced.

It is also clear the relationship of male and female is one of mutuality and equality. Paul begins and ends this passage with an emphasis on the functional equality of the sexes within the community of God's people. Both women and men are expected to pray and prophesy (1 Cor. 11:4–5). Both men and women are mutually dependent on one another. The woman may have come "from" the man initially, but every man has come "through" women ever since (1 Cor. 11:11–12 NRSV).

It is likewise clear that God intends for us to maintain a distinction between the sexes. Paul's appeal to Genesis 1–2 ("from man" and "for man") makes this quite plain. Mention of the "practice" of all "the churches of God" (1 Cor. 11:16) suggests the same.

Finally, it is clear that both men and women are called on to act in a responsible fashion: "A man *ought* not to cover . . . a woman *ought* to . . ."

(1 Cor. 11:7, 10 italics added). The language of obligation assumes that women could and would act responsibly on their own behalf.

How does all this help us understand what Paul means when he says the head of a woman is man? Whatever meaning we attach to Paul's statement, the context rules out any and all notions of male superiority—be they personal or functional. The woman may be the glory of the man (by virtue of her creation out of him), but she is also the image of God (1 Cor. 11:7–8). She may have been created *from* the man, but all men have come *through* her from that point on (1 Cor. 11:12).

It is also important to see that *headship* is a new teaching. The opening phrase, "Now I want you to know that" is the way Paul routinely introduces new information in his letters. It is wrong, therefore, to connect (as some do) male headship with the apostolic tradition passed on to all the churches (1 Cor. 11:2).

So what does the man is "the head of the woman" mean (1 Cor. 11:3)? Although some are quick to insist that *head* must mean "authority over," it is a conclusion drawn more from English usage and Western experience than from the passage itself. Paul introduces this as a new idea and then goes on in the subsequent verses to explain this new idea. It is imperative, therefore, that we look for explanatory phrases in verses 4–16. There are two such phrases: (1) "The woman is the glory of man" (v. 7), and (2) the woman is "out of" the man and created "for his sake" (vv. 8, 12). In fact, the connections can be drawn even more closely. The reason ( *gar,* "for") the woman is the glory of the man is because she was created from him and for his sake (vv. 8–9).

What does it mean to be the *glory* of someone? The term can mean to reflect someone's splendor—like our phrase, "He is a chip off the old block." The more common meaning of *praise* or *honor,* however, better fits the contrasting idea of *dishonor* in verses 4, 5, and 14. The woman brings praise or honor to her *head* (the man) by virtue of her creation *from* and *for* him. There can be little doubt that Paul has Genesis 2:21–24 in mind and in particular the phrase "bone of my bones and flesh of my flesh." The difficulty, though, is that all honor and praise in public worship should go to God.

Commentators too often lose sight of Paul's theological focus. Paul tells the Corinthians just a few verses earlier, "Whatever you do, do it all for the glory of God" (1 Cor. 10:31). A little farther on he asserts that "everything comes from God" (1 Cor. 11:12), and he concludes with concern about how one prays "to God" (v. 13) and with reference to "the churches of God" (v. 16). So here is the problem: A woman who uncovers her physical head draws attention to her masculine origin or *head* (i.e., "from the man," v. 8), and this is wholly inappropriate in God's realm (in the Lord). She must cover herself so that all attention is focused on God.

The theological focus of 1 Corinthians 10:31–11:16 encourages us to assign *head (kephalē)* its most common metaphorical meaning, namely, that of "preeminent" or "foremost" (see p. 122). *Head* and *glory* are really two sides of the same coin. When a woman uncovers her head in the worship service, she draws *inappropriate* attention to her foremost part— the man, but when a man uncovers his head, he draws *appropriate* attention to his foremost part—God. Is this not, after all, what Paul means when he says the man is the "glory of God" (v. 7)? Perhaps comparison with the top or head of a mountain is not far afield. All attention is draw to the highest of its snowcapped peaks—as any tourist viewing Mt. Rainier or Mt. Everest knows.

To understand *head* as "preeminent part" helps us with verse 3. As many have pointed out, there are difficulties with construing *kephalē* as either "source" or "authority over." The order in verse 3 does not really support the latter. Instead of God—Christ—man—woman, we have Christ—man—woman—God. (There is also the difficulty of explaining how exactly God rules over Christ.) Nor is there any notion of male rule or authority in the verses that follow.

What about *kephalē* meaning "source"? *Source* and *head* are indeed connected in verses 8–9 ("from man"), but the connection is not one of identity. While the man's headship results from being the physical source of the woman, one is hard pressed to say the same of Christ's headship of the man, and Paul does not. He does not say in this or in any other letter that Christ's headship is the result of being the literal and physical source of the man. The church may be bone of his bones and flesh of his flesh (see Eph. 5:30), but the male is not. On the other hand, Christ as the preeminent member of the relationship fits quite nicely.

All this leaves little room for the traditional notion of male headship as "rule over." This should not be troublesome—unless we have become overly attached to a strongly hierarchical view of male-female relations. In the final analysis, whatever meaning we attach to the man is "the head of the woman" (1 Cor. 11:3), this state of affairs does not hold true "in the Lord." Mutual dependence is what should characterize life in community, for "in the Lord" a "woman is not independent of man, nor is man independent of woman" (1 Cor. 11:11).

# Can Women Hold Positions of Authority?

A third crucial question to raise is what, if any, positions of authority can women hold? This is an especially important question when it involves the church. Can a woman preach God's Word? Can she teach an adult Sunday school class? Can she serve as an elder? Can she chair the church council? Can she serve communion, baptize, usher, or lead in worship? These are the questions that end up dividing churches, friends, and families today. The issue for many is not whether the Spirit gifts women in the same way he gifts men but whether a particular activity is authoritative in nature. If it is, then women are excluded.

Should this be so? A lot depends on how we define the term *authority* and who we believe rightfully holds it. There are some who argue that authority is a God-given right to rule and that it is only men who possess this right. To be a male, then, is to possess authority; to be female is not to possess authority. There are others who think along these same lines but see both women and men as invested with this God-given right. God, after all, did command both male and female to subdue the earth and rule over it (Gen. 1:28–30). There are still others who believe authority is intrinsic to the office, not the person. The president of the United States or the prime minister of England are good examples. It is not a matter of being male or female but being charged with a sacred trust.

Which (if any) of these definitions is the biblical one? That is our first task. And what about offices? Are there leadership positions in the New Testament that we can legitimately call an office, and are there leadership activities that are distinctly authoritative in character? That is our second task. Finally, there is the question of limits. Does the Bible limit the roles women can play? First Corinthians 14:33–35 and 1 Timothy 2:12–15 are often cited as providing clear limitations, but is this the case? That will be our third task.[1]

## Authority: A Matter of Definition

The term *authority* is found over one hundred times in the New Testament.[2] While current church practice might lead us to think that most of these references have to do with the authority of pastors, elders, deacons, bishops, and the like, one searches in vain for the biblical passages that would validate such thinking. The fact of the matter is that the language of authority is simply not connected with church leadership in the New Testament.[3] This, if nothing else, should caution us to tread carefully. The closest we come is Titus 2:15, where Paul instructs his second-in-command to "rebuke with all authority." Yet Titus possessed this right as Paul's deputy, not as a local church leader. Then, too, the term for authority is not *exousia* ("the right to govern") but *epitagē* ("the right to command"), so a better translation would be, "show that you have every right to command when you rebuke."

It is the church, not individuals, that has authority. Perhaps the most familiar texts are Matthew 16:18–20 and 18:18–20, in which Jesus gives the church the "keys of the kingdom" and the right to "bind" and to "loose." Other passages bear this out as well. It is the corporate responsibility of God's people to test (1 Thess. 5:19–22) and weigh prophecies (1 Cor. 14:29), to warn the idle, encourage the timid, and support the weak (1 Thess. 5:14), to delegate responsibility (Acts 6:1–6), to empower for missionary work (Acts 13:1–3), to choose representatives (Acts 15:22–23; 20:4–5), to discipline (2 Cor. 2:6), to excommunicate in the case of persistent sin (Matt. 18:17; 1 Cor. 5:2, 9–13; 2 Thess. 3:6, 14–15; cf. 2 John 10–11), and to reinstate the penitent (2 Cor. 2:7–8; cf. Matt. 18:10–14). The church's authority derives from the power of the Lord Jesus that is present with believers gathered in his name (Matt. 18:20; 1 Cor. 5:4) and from corporate possession of the "mind of Christ" (1 Cor. 2:16).

Congregations and churches can, of course, choose individuals and groups to represent their interests and to work on their behalf, as in the case of the seven deacons in the Jerusalem church (Acts 6:1–7), the missionaries from Antioch (Acts 13:1–3), and the Jerusalem collection representatives (Acts 20:1–6). Yet in no way do these individuals possess authority over the congregation. Nor is this authority an authority to rule or govern. It is, rather, an empowerment to do the work of ministry and to be a servant of the church. As Paul states, Christ "gave some to be apostles, some to be prophets, some to be evangelists, and some to be pastors and teachers, to prepare God's people for the work of the ministry" (Eph. 4:11–12 AT).

Ultimate authority resides in God and Christ alone. The New Testament references (with few exceptions) are references to Christ's authority. Jesus possessed and exercised authority during his earthly ministry. He taught with authority (in contrast to the legal and theological experts of the day; Matt. 7:29; Mark 1:22; Luke 4:32). He had the authority to judge (John 5:27) and to forgive sins (Matt. 9:6; Mark 2:10; Luke 5:24). Even demons obeyed him (Mark 1:27; Luke 4:36). After Jesus' death and resurrection, *all* authority was given to him (Matt. 28:18). Perhaps the most sweeping statement along these lines is found in Philippians 2:9–11:

> Therefore God exalted him to the highest place
>> and gave him the name that is above every name,
> that at the name of Jesus every knee should bow,
>> in heaven and on earth and under the earth,
> and every tongue confess that Jesus Christ is Lord.

If one can speak of a God-given authority or a rule by divine right, this applies more properly to secular authority. Both Peter and Paul call their respective congregations to submit to the political powers in authority over them (Rom. 13:1–5; Titus 3:1; 1 Peter 2:13–17). "Let everyone be subject to the governing authorities," Paul tells the Roman Christians, "for rulers hold no terror for those who do right, but for those who do wrong" (Rom. 13:1, 3). Even so, this is a delegated authority. There really is "no authority except that which God has established" (v. 1). Secular rulers could claim to possess authority—as Pilate did ("I have power either to free you or to crucify you"). But Jesus was quick to remind Pilate (and others) that all authority is given "from above" (John 19:10–11; cf. Luke 20:20).

Who else possesses authority? The apostles certainly did. References to apostolic authority, however, are surprisingly few in number. All three Gospel writers record that the Twelve were sent out by Jesus with "authority to drive out evil spirits and to heal every disease and sickness" (Matt. 10:1; see also Mark 3:14–15; 6:7; Luke 9:1; 10:19). It is interesting, though, that the Twelve were also sent out to preach and teach, yet authority is not mentioned in conjunction with these two activities.

Only exorcisms and healings were done with authority. Yet some today are quick to identify preaching and teaching as authoritative activities.

What about the apostle Paul? Didn't he speak often of his authority as an apostle? Paul certainly laid claim to apostleship. The vast majority of his letters begin with "Paul, an apostle of Christ Jesus by the will of God" (see Rom. 1:1; 1 Cor. 1:1; 2 Cor. 1:1; Gal. 1:1; Eph. 1:1; Col. 1:1; 1 Tim. 1:1; 2 Tim. 1:1; Titus 1:1). But is this a claim to authority? Some of his letters open with "Paul, a *slave* of Christ Jesus" (Rom. 1:1; Phil. 1:1; Titus 1:1; Philem. 1). Two letters start with both "Paul, a slave" *and* Paul "an apostle" (Rom. 1:1; Titus 1:1)—which would suggest that *apostle* and *slave* (not *apostle* and *rule*) are two sides of the same coin.

The very few times that Paul mentions his or another's apostolic authority also gives one pause. Twice he speaks of the authority the Lord gave him for building up, not tearing down, the church (2 Cor. 10:8; 13:10), but that is all. He does use equivalent language on occasion. For example, he tells Philemon that he could order him to do the right thing (Philem. 8–9), and he points out to the Thessalonians that he could make demands on them as an apostle of Christ (1 Thess. 2:6). But *could* and *did* are two different matters. Paul, in fact, was characterized by his opponents as timid and unimpressive because he did not throw his weight around as an apostle: "I, Paul, who am 'timid' when face to face with you, but 'bold' when away!'" (2 Cor. 10:1–2; see also v. 10).

There is a good reason why Paul and the other New Testament writers shied away from talk of authority. It concerns the *how* of leadership. The early church simply refused to buy into the prevailing style of leadership, which was to lead by force of will. When James and John came to Jesus asking to sit at his right hand and his left hand in his kingdom, he reminded his disciples that the rulers of the Gentiles lord it over them and their high officials exercise authority over them, but this was not to be so with them (Matt. 20:20–26). The key terms are "lord it over" (*katakurieuō*) and "exercise authority over" (*katexousiazō*). The first verb means to gain or exercise dominion over or against someone, while the second verb denotes the exercise of rule or authority. Inherent in neither term is the misuse or abuse of power. Both terms merely denote its rightful possession and exercise (LSJ s.v.).

A top-down management style is as much a part of our culture as it was part of first-century culture. What should we put in its place? What Jesus put in its place is probably the last thing some of us would associate with leadership today, namely, servanthood. Perhaps one of the best examples of this kind of leadership is found in Matthew 20:26–27, where Jesus teaches, "Whoever wants to become great among you must be your servant, and whoever wants to be first must be your slave." The point is quite clear. Those who lead by force of will do so to advance themselves and their ego. Their desire is "to become great" and "to be first."

Sometimes we try to fool ourselves into thinking our motives for wanting control and power are laudatory ones, and they might well be at the start. But "power has the tendency to corrupt, and absolute power corrupts absolutely" (Lord Acton, 1830–1905). This is why Jesus opted for something else. "The Son of Man," he said, "did not come to be served, but to serve, and to give his life as a ransom for many" (Matt. 20:28). The giving of oneself for others was not something to which Jesus merely gave lip service. It was a reality he lived out in his daily life.

Paul also rejects a top-down style of leadership. In 2 Corinthians 1:24, he told the Corinthians that his aim, as an apostle to the Gentiles, was not to rule over their faith but to work with them for their joy. Paul saw his relationship to his churches as that of a partnership (working alongside them) and not that of a commander in chief (ruling over them). Peter opts for this same style of leadership. In his letter to the churches of Asia Minor, he exhorts the elders to "be shepherds of God's flock . . . *not* ruling over [*katakyrieuō*] them but being examples to the flock" (1 Peter 5:2–3 AT).

How then can we explain those passages in the New Testament that call for submission and obedience to local church leadership? They are not many in number—actually only two—but they still require an explanation. In the letter to the Hebrews, the readers are instructed to "remember" (*mnēmoneuete*), "pay attention to" (*peithesthe*), and "submit to" (*hypeikete*) their "leaders" (*hēgoumenoi;* Heb. 13:7, 17). In one of Paul's letters to the Corinthians, the congregation is called on to "submit" (*hypotassēsthe*) to "such as these" (i.e., the household of Stephanas; 1 Cor. 16:16).

What is sometimes overlooked is the reason for the submission. In neither instance is the submission based on the possession of authority or the holding of an office. Instead, the context makes it clear that submission is the appropriate recognition of pastoral service. The "such as these" to whom the Corinthians were to submit were "everyone who joins in the work, and labors at it" (1 Cor. 16:16). The leaders to whom the Hebrews were to submit were those who "keep watch over" them (Heb. 13:17). The NIV's "devoted themselves to the service of the saints" catches the meaning quite well (1 Cor. 16:15).

Another thing to note is the absence of the verb *obey* (*hypakouō*). The response that is called for is submission—a voluntary act of deferring to the wishes of an equal (see p. 118). The distinction is an important one. Obedience can be willingly or unwillingly given. It can also be something demanded of someone in a lesser position (for example, a boss to a worker today). Submission, on the other hand, is the action of a free and responsible agent.

## *Leadership and Offices*

What about leadership language in the New Testament? *Bishop, elder, pastor, deacon,* and the like surely define offices that are authoritative in character, don't they? They tend to do so in many church contexts today. In my local church, for example, all those who serve on boards gather once a year for what is called a *governance* retreat. Article 3 of our constitution concerns the *officers* of the church. The chairperson is "the Chief Executive Officer" who "presides at all the business meetings of the church and of the Council" and has "the authority to convene an executive session" of either body (*Constitution and Bylaws,* 1990). Although leadership language may vary from one congregation and denomination to another, governance structures, church officers, and chief executives are a familiar part of the workings of most churches today.

To govern, to officiate, to wield authority—are these secular ideas, or is there a biblical basis for such thinking? There are five terms in the New Testament that have been commonly understood to provide such a basis: *leader/guide (proistēmi), shepherd (poimainō), overseer (episkopos), elder (presbyteros),* and *deacon (diakonos).* We will look at each in turn to see what is involved, whether the involvement is official, and if the role is an authoritative one. We will also see if these are roles that women can or cannot assume.

### *Leader/Guide (proistēmi)*

In 1 Thessalonians 5:12–13 Paul uses three words to describe the leadership task. Leaders are those who "work hard," "admonish," and "go before." The first of these stresses the exhausting and tiring character of leadership (*kopiaō;* cf. 1 Cor. 16:16; 1 Tim. 5:17). The second has to do with correction and redirection of wrong behavior (*nouthesia;* cf. 1 Cor. 4:14; Titus 3:10). The third means "to stand or go before someone" so as to "lead the way," "protect," and "care for" ( *proistēmi;* the NIV "over you" does not catch the sense).[4] The fact that all three terms are also used of the work of the congregation at large means Paul is not talking about a leadership role that is distinctive in any way (see Col. 3:16; 1 Thess. 1:3; Titus 3:8).

The key term here is *proistēmi*. In 1 Thessalonians 5:12 it is commonly translated to be "over" (KJV, RSV, NIV), "above" (JB), or in "charge of" (NRSV). In 1 Timothy 3:4–5 and 12 it is frequently rendered "to manage" (e.g., TEV, NIV, RSV, NASB, NRSV) and sometimes even "to rule" (e.g., KJV, NKJV). But does the term carry these commanding overtones?

*Proistēmi* is found seven times in Paul's letters (Rom. 12:8; 16:2; 1 Thess. 5:12; 1 Tim. 3:4, 5, 12; 5:17) and nowhere else in the New Testament, so the sample is quite small. In Romans 12 it is a spiritual gift. In Romans 16 the noun is used of the help that Phoebe gave to both Paul and the broader Christian community. In 1 Timothy 3 it is a qualification of an overseer and a deacon. In 1 Timothy 5 it is something that elders do.

All this clearly points to a leadership capacity of some sort. But what kind? Is it a leadership that rules (i.e., makes the decisions), or is it a leadership that guides (i.e., leads the way)?

Several things suggest the latter. For one, *proistēmi* is grouped with the spiritual gifts of offering practical assistance to those in need ("give generously," "showing mercy," Rom. 12:8). Also, the *prostatis* (the noun form) in the culture of the day was someone who provided patronage and protection (see chapter 1, pp. 50–53). Further, the parallel words define pastoral activities. In 1 Timothy 3:4–5, for example, to *proistamenon* the church is to "care for" *(epimelēsetai)* it.[5]

All in all, the kind of leadership this term points to is pastoral, rather than authoritarian, in nature. This makes translations like "to rule," "to be in charge of," and "to manage" less than desirable. The TEV's "to guide" in 1 Thessalonians 5:12 is closer to the mark. Since *proistēmi* appears as a qualification for both an overseer (1 Tim. 3:4–5) and a deacon (1 Tim. 3:12) and identifies a function of an elder (1 Tim. 5:17), it is important to accurately define what it means. This is especially so given the tendency today to construe these roles in strictly authoritarian and hierarchical ways. There is a world of difference between, "If someone does not know how to care for and protect his own family," and, "If someone does not know how to rule his own house" (see 1 Tim. 3:4–5).

### Shepherd (poimēn)

In Acts 20:28 and 1 Peter 5:2, the task of the local leaders in the churches of Asia Minor is summed up by the command: "Be shepherds of God's flock." The Greek word for *shepherd* is found about forty times in the New Testament and about two hundred times in the Septuagint (the Greek translation of the Old Testament). For this reason, it is one of the most easily grasped concepts of leadership in Scripture.

Psalm 23 has immortalized the role of shepherd:

> The LORD is my shepherd, I shall not want.
> He makes me lie down in green pastures,
> he leads me beside the still waters.
>
> verses 1–2 NRSV

Green pastures and still waters vividly call to mind the familiar image of one who guides, protects, and cares for the flock. It was the job of the first-century shepherd to find pasture for the sheep, to protect them from marauding animals, and to restore any sheep that strayed from the fold. Although sheep still dot the American landscape, the modern farmer is a far cry from the ancient shepherd. It is perhaps for this reason that pastors today often look more like the entrepreneur of Luke 12:18 (out to build bigger and bigger barns) than the shepherd of Psalm 23.

What is involved in shepherding God's flock? Are *leader* and *shepherd* congenial ideas? If one thinks of pastoring in terms of running the church, then they most certainly are not. Shepherding in the New Testament is in marked contrast to calling the shots and running the show. "Do not try to rule over those who have been given into your care," Peter instructs the elders in Asia. Instead, "be examples to the flock" (1 Peter 5:3 TEV; cf. 2 Cor. 1:24).[6]

To be a shepherd is to be an example. Today we might use the phrase "role model." Rock musicians, movie stars, and athletes are commonly lifted up as role models. What is involved in being a Christian role model? Fortunately, Paul spells it out quite clearly for two of his associates. His instruction to Timothy is to set an example in speech, conduct, love, faith, and purity (see 1 Tim. 4:12). For Titus the challenge is to set an example in everything by doing what is good (Titus 2:7). So to be a shepherd is to lead in thought, word, and deed. In this we take our cue from Jesus, the chief Shepherd, whose life of verbal integrity, moral conduct, and personal sacrifice becomes a model for the would-be leader of any local congregation (John 13:5, 14–15; 1 Peter 2:21).

To be a shepherd is also to be a teacher. In writing to the Ephesians, Paul states that Christ "gave some to be apostles, some to be prophets, some to be evangelists, and some to be [pastors-teachers]" (*tous de poimenas kai didaskalous,* Eph. 4:11). The single Greek article before "pastors and teachers" should give us pause; it serves to conceptually unite the two nouns. What this means in practical terms is that the task of pastoring is inseparable from the task of teaching.

This should come as no surprise, especially if we remember that it was the shepherd's task to protect the flock from predators. Beware of "savage wolves [who] will come in among you and will not spare the flock," Paul warns the leaders at Ephesus. They will "distort the truth in order to draw away disciples after them" (Acts 20:29–30). The teaching that Paul has in mind is not an authoritative word of knowledge (1 Cor. 12:8) but sound doctrine. This is why qualifications for an overseer and an elder include the ability to teach (1 Tim. 3:2) and the capacity to refute unsound instruction (Titus 1:9).

### Overseer (episkopos)

"Paul . . . to all God's people in Philippi together with the overseers and deacons" (Phil. 1:1 AT). In distinction from the previous two leadership terms, *overseer* not only describes the task involved but also designates a specific group within the local church.

Although it is commonly translated "bishop" (KJV, *Phillips,* RSV, NRSV, NEB, REB) and traditionally regarded as defining a position of rule and authority, in reality this word describes a pastoral function and so is more properly translated "overseer." In essence, the *episkopos* is a person who "watches over" or "looks after" *(epi* plus *skopeō)* those in his or her care.[7] The rest of the New Testament bears this out. The Greek term is used of God's renewed concern for his people (Luke 7:16; Acts 15:14), of caring for the needy of society (the sick, the prisoner, the widow, the orphan; Matt. 25:36, 43; James 1:27) and of the care that Paul and Barnabas gave the newly founded churches in Galatia (Acts 15:36).

That the task of overseer is essentially a pastoral one is clear from the descriptive terms in Acts 20:28 and 1 Peter 5:2.[8] Overseers are *shepherds* of God's people. They are not appointed or elected by the congregation but put there by the Holy Spirit. Their job is to keep watch over and to pay close attention to the flock. In carrying out this role they are to follow the example of Christ, who is the preeminent "Shepherd and Overseer" (1 Peter 2:25).

Quite frankly it is hard to see how exactly *overseer* and *shepherd* differ. The only obvious difference is that Paul lists qualifications for the former but does not for the latter. Perhaps *overseer* defines a position of leadership, while *shepherd* merely describes the task. The difficulty, though, is that the qualifications listed by Paul for an overseer are hardly ones we would associate with an office. For one, there is no job description. The closest we come is Paul's statement that overseers must be hospitable and able to teach (1 Tim. 3:2). For the rest, the emphasis is on their reputation inside and outside the church. They must be above reproach, con-

siderate, and well thought of by outsiders (1 Tim. 3:2–3, 7). They are to
be family oriented—faithful in marriage, have obedient and respectful
children, and be good caregivers of the family (1 Tim. 3:2, 4–5). They
are to act respectably and with self-control (not given to excesses; 1 Tim.
3:2–3). They should not be recent converts (1 Tim. 3:6).

How then is the singling out of a specific group of leaders within the
local congregation to be explained? After all, Paul does address a letter
to the "overseers and deacons" of the Philippian church. Do we not have
something of a pastoral office after all? If by *office* we mean a duty or service, then the answer is *yes*. But if (as is more commonly the case today)
we mean a specific position that carries authority, then the answer must
be *no*. For even though *overseers* does single out a group within the local
congregation (Phil. 1:1; 1 Tim. 3:1–7; Titus 1:7–9), it is a group defined
by a common task rather than by an appointed office. "If anyone is eager
to be an overseer," Paul states, "that person desires a *noble task*" (1 Tim.
3:1 AT).

The task-oriented nature of the overseer is clear in other respects.
For one, the work of an overseer is not the exclusive right of any particular group within the church. Passages like Hebrews 12:14–15 make it
a responsibility of the whole congregation: "Look after each other *[episko-
pountes]* so that none of you will miss out on the special favor of God"
(NLT). Nor is it an incidental responsibility. In Matthew 25:43, caring for
those in need *(epeskepsasthe)* becomes the basis for Christ's acceptance
or rejection of us on his return.

Can women be overseers? One of the qualifications of both an overseer and a deacon is "the husband of one wife" (1 Tim. 3:2 KJV, RSV,
NASB, NIV). Are women thereby excluded? While this is a common understanding, the broader context points in another direction.

The key lies in seeing two things. First, the ministry of widows required
that a woman be "the wife of one husband" (1 Tim. 5:9 RSV). So the
standard is not exclusively a male one. The NIV obscures this fact, when
it translates the Greek phrase, "has been faithful to her husband." The
wording of 1 Timothy 3:2, 12 and 5:9 is exactly the same in the Greek:
*mias gynaikos andra* (3:2, 12) and *henos andros gynē* (5:9). Second, women
were not excluded from serving as deacons in their churches. Paul not
only recognizes their place in the church (1 Tim. 3:11, "likewise women
[deacons]"), but he gives concrete qualifications for selecting them ("worthy of respect, not malicious talkers but temperate and trustworthy in
everything").

The curious thing is not the presence of "the husband of one wife"
(for male overseers and deacons) but the absence of "the wife of one

husband" (for female deacons). Paul quite obviously did not think that this qualification applied to married women. Why not, though? One explanation is that women overseers (and deacons) were largely drawn from the ranks of the unmarried. A more likely possibility is that marital faithfulness was a greater challenge for the males in that society. In a Greek city like Ephesus, where men were still by and large the initiators in matters of divorce (as well in philandering), marital faithfulness would be an important part of a man's Christian witness.

### Elder (presbyteros)

"To the elders among you, I appeal as a fellow elder" (1 Peter 5:1 NIV). Here perhaps we approach something like an office. For unlike the other terms for leadership, *elder* alone is not set forth as a responsibility of the congregation. Also, of all the named leadership positions, elder alone is by appointment. Paul appointed elders in the churches he founded (Acts 14:23), and his coworkers were instructed to do the same (e.g., Titus 1:5).

Another thing to note is that *elder* (unlike the other leadership terms) is consistently plural in form. It defines a corporate entity *(the elders)* rather than a specific function (like *eldering*). The leadership of the Jerusalem church consisted of "the apostles and the elders" (Acts 15:2–6, 22–23; 16:4). The elders were part of the leadership team of the well-established church at Ephesus (Acts 20:17–38; 1 Tim. 5:17–20) and of the newly established church on the island of Crete (Titus 1:5). James instructs his churches to "call the elders of the church" to the bedside of the critically ill (James 5:14). Peter appeals to the elders of the churches of Asia Minor as a fellow elder (1 Peter 5:1).

So who were the elders, and what did they do? Were they in charge of the spiritual life of the church (like they are in many churches today)? Were they authority figures as so often is the case now?

The Greek term for *elder (presbyteros)* is commonly used in the New Testament of those who are older in age and, by extension, valued and respected within the community of God's people.[9] In Jesus' day, elders were found in the Sanhedrin ("chief priests, scribes, and *elders,*" e.g., Mark 8:31; 11:27; 14:43, 53; 15:1 NRSV) and in the local governing councils (e.g., Luke 7:3).

Elders in Greco-Roman society similarly were civil servants. In Sparta, for instance, *elder* was a title given to the presiding magistrate. In Egypt *elder* was used of the annually elected officials of village councils, who had judicial and administrative duties.

Oddly enough, the elders of the church did not follow the cultural norm. They were not civil servants. It is true they were part of the decision-making process in the Jerusalem church, but they did not rule or govern like their Jewish and Greek counterparts. Also, church elders played an official role in their local congregation, while Jewish elders did not. In fact, elders were second only to the apostles in the leadership structure of the early church ("the apostles and the elders," Acts 15:2–6, 22–23; 16:4).

When and where do elders appear? The early chapters of Acts do not mention elders. The apostles seem to be the movers and shakers (along with the seven chosen to "wait on tables" in Acts 6:1–6). Elders first appear as a distinct group when James takes the helm of the Jerusalem church (Acts 11:30; 15:2–6, 22–23; 16:4; 21:18). Yet elders were not unique to the mother church. They were present in churches scattered throughout the Roman Empire—be they Jewish (James 5:14) or Gentile (Acts 14:23; 20:17–38; 1 Tim. 5:17–20; Titus 1:5; 1 Peter 5:1). They also popped up in a wide range of locales and were found in churches young (Titus 1:5) and old (1 Tim. 5:17).

What exactly did elders do? The fact that they were appointed by the apostles (and their successors) suggests they were to a certain extent guardians of the apostolic tradition (Acts 20:17–18, 29–31).[10] Beyond this, their role was far-reaching and diverse. They were called upon to pray and care for the critically ill (James 5:14), to help the weak (Acts 20:35), to refute error (Titus 1:9), to commission for service (1 Tim. 4:14), to preach and teach (1 Tim. 5:17), and to be shepherds (1 Peter 5:1–2) and guides ( *proestōtes,* 1 Tim. 5:17) of the flock. Peter's concern about greed suggests that they also handled the money (1 Peter 5:2).

It is to be noted that all these leadership roles were pastoral in nature. Elders may have been appointed, but their functions were essentially practical (rather than official) in nature. The qualifications Paul sets forth reinforce this impression. In the first place, there is no job description. The closest we come is Paul's statement that elders must be hospitable, able to refute false teaching, and be committed to sound doctrine (Titus 1:8–9). Otherwise, the emphasis is on character and lifestyle. Elders must be blameless, upright, and holy; they must not be overbearing or quick-tempered, but must love what is good; they must be faithful to their spouse, and have obedient and believing children; they are to be self-controlled and not given to excesses (Titus 1:6–8).

Who then were the elders? At heart, this was a group whose responsibility was to care for the spiritual life of the local congregation. The key word is *care for.* Their job was to shepherd God's flock (Acts 20:28; 1 Tim.

5:17; 1 Peter 5:2). The language throughout is that of pastoring and serving, not that of ruling or governing. Nowhere are elders and authority connected. In fact, when elders are singled out, it is because of the job they do, not the position they hold or the authority they wield. "The elders who do their job well deserve to be paid twice as much," Paul says, "especially if they work hard at preaching and teaching" (1 Tim. 5:17 AT).

How, though, do elders differ from the overseers of the church? Overseers are also called to watch over the flock. They too must be able to teach. Some would say there is no difference; others would say each is a distinct position. There is truth in both. *Elder* actually appears to be an umbrella term for a wide range of functions that a number of leaders performed in the early church. The character of these functions is captured by words like *guiding, shepherding,* and *overseeing* (1 Tim. 5:17; 1 Peter 5:1–2; Titus 1:5–7; Acts 20:17, 28). *Elder,* however, does not describe a function. Protectors protect. Shepherds shepherd. Overseers oversee. Elders alone do not *elder.* The fact that Paul calls only for "the elders" of the Ephesian church (Acts 20:17) and that Peter appeals solely to "the elders" of the Asian churches (1 Peter 5:1) indicates that *elder* is the overarching leadership capacity.

## Deacon (diakonos)

*Deacon* is the fifth and final term for leadership in the New Testament. It derives from a Greek word that means "to serve" or "to wait on tables" *(diakoneō).* This was the role Stephen, Philip, Procorus, Nicanor, Timon, Parmenas, and Nicolas were asked to assume during the Jerusalem church's early years (Acts 6:1–7).

The role of deacon has a complex history that is not always easy (or even possible) to track. In part this is because the Greek noun *diakonos* can be translated "minister," "deacon," or "servant." While the New Testament writers did not really attempt to distinguish the three (in essence they simply mean "to serve"), we tend to draw hard-and-fast distinctions among them today.[11] In addition, there were no deacon prototypes in Greco-Roman religion or Judaism, which makes our job even tougher.

What the New Testament writers do distinguish, however, are kinds of service. For example, in Acts 6:1–6 two kinds of serving are identified. Seven were chosen to serve tables *(diakonein trapezais),* while the apostles devoted themselves to serving the Word *(tē diakonia tou logou).*

What did deacons specifically do? Surely they did more than wait tables? This is a tough question to answer because the New Testament (once again) simply does not provide any sort of job description. In the case of the seven in Acts 6, their job was initially to care for the material needs of Grecian widows who were being neglected in the daily distribution of food and other basic necessities. Yet it is far from certain that this was what all deacons did. In fact, Luke does not even use the term *deacon.* The emphasis in Acts 6 is on what they did (serve), not on who they were (deacons). It was also too early in the church's history to have anything like an office of deacon.

*Deacon* is not the only leadership position that is hard to nail down; *elder* and *overseer* are equally elusive. The early church was simply not concerned, as we are today, with offices and the like. It is only in the postapostolic period that there is an attempt to define this and other positions more precisely.

Even so, there were those in the early church who were recognized for the servant leadership they provided. In the church at Philippi, for instance, one of two identified leadership positions in the church was that of deacon. Paul addresses his letter to "all the saints in Christ Jesus at Philippi, together with the overseers and deacons" (Phil. 1:1). In 1 Timothy 3:8–13 the qualifications of a deacon are spelled out in some detail, although the exact duties are not.

The requirements for a deacon are very close to those listed for overseers and elders. The focus on character and lifestyle is identical. Deacons are to be above reproach ("nothing against them," 1 Tim. 3:10). They are to have strong family values—faithful in marriage and good caregivers of their family (1 Tim. 3:12). They are to act respectably and with self-control (1 Tim. 3:8, 11) and be committed to sound doctrine (1 Tim. 3:9, 11).

The two qualifications unique to deacons are that they must be "sincere" (literally, "not double-tongued"), and they must be tested over a period of time (1 Tim. 3:8, 10–11). Both are understandable if the job included some house-to-house visitation. Not prone to gossiping ("sincere"), not given to much drinking, and a Christian life that is above reproach are all qualities that would be essential for this sort of ministry (1 Tim. 3:8, 10).

What exactly did deacons do, though? As best as can be determined, the primary responsibility of a deacon was to care for the material needs of the local body of believers. This is suggested by Acts 6:1–4, in which caring for physical needs is distinguished from preaching the Word. It is also suggested by 1 Peter 4:11, in which the ministries of *speaking* and *serving* are differentiated. Beyond this, care needs to be taken. It is very hard, for example, to say what exactly distinguished a deacon from an elder during the apostolic period. That both were serving roles is clear from James 5:13–18, in which part of the elder's task is identified as caring for the critically ill ("pray . . . and anoint him with oil").

One wonders whether deacons and overseers were subcategories of elders. It would explain why elders and overseers needed to be able to teach sound doctrine, while deacons merely needed to be committed to it (1 Tim. 3:9, 11; Titus 1:8–9). In all fairness, though, it must be said that the boundaries (not to mention the relationship) among *overseer, elder,* and *deacon* are beyond precise definition—at least at this early stage in the church's history.

## Women and Leadership Language

What about women? Were there any women overseers, elders, or deacons? Are leadership terms used to describe their ministries? Of the five leadership terms surveyed, two are explicitly used of women. Phoebe (as we noted in the first chapter) was a deacon of the church at Cenchrea (Rom. 16:1). Paul spells out qualifications for women deacons in his first letter to Timothy: "Male deacons must be . . . women [deacons] likewise must be" (1 Tim. 3:8, 11 AT). So Phoebe was hardly an exception in this regard.

Phoebe was also a *prostatis* or "benefactor" to Paul and to many (Rom. 16:2 NRSV). It is hard to nail down how much was involved (see chapter 2), but there is no disputing the high profile role she played (LSJ s.v.; see also chapter 1).

*Shepherd, overseer,* and *elder* are not used of any women, but then neither are they used to single out specific men. In fact, men are not even singled out as deacons or benefactors as is Phoebe. Peter calls himself an elder (1 Peter 5:1), but he names no others.

This undoubtedly was because *deacon, elder, overseer,* and the like did not define offices in the way we define them today. Webster's Collegiate Dictionary, tenth edition, defines "office" as "a position of authority to exercise a public function." An office, then, is a position of some prestige. This is why, for instance, we address judges as "your honor" and pastors as "reverend." This was not the case back then. There was no great honor attached to being a pastor, elder, or deacon. Today, however, it is not uncommon to hear statements such as, "Bill is an elder of his church," "Frank is the pastor of his church," or "Harriet is a deacon of her church." For these people, the honor lies in the holding of a particular position. The honor in the first century lay not in the leadership position itself but in serving the church to the best of one's ability.

Again we are back to the notion of service (as opposed to rule or authority). It was "those who have served well" who gained an excellent standing in the community of believers in Paul's day (1 Tim. 3:13). If serving well is the key, then names are unimportant—be they male or female.

Even so, there may be more to be seen in the case of women. It all depends on what one understands by the role of overseer. If, as some believe, the first-century overseer supervised the church that met in their homes, then women are indeed singled out as serving in this capacity.[12] In fact, more women are named than men. The New Testament writers mention six churches meeting in the home of a certain person (Acts 12:12; 16:15; Rom. 16:3–5; 1 Cor. 16:19; Col. 4:15; Philem. 2), and five of these six homes were the homes of women (or couples).

What about qualifications for leadership positions? Are there any that would exclude women? The fact that women deacons must exhibit the same character and lifestyle qualities as their male counterparts suggests otherwise (worthy of respect, not double-tongued, temperate, faithful in everything; 1 Tim. 3:8–9, 11). In fact there are some more suitable to women than to men. For instance, hospitality would be a natural for women. The ability to care for one's household (as indicative of ability to care for the church) would also be a good fit. In fact, the term used for the leadership role of the mother in the home (*oikodespotein* "to be master of a house," or "head of a family," 1 Tim. 5:14) is much stronger than that used of the father ( *prostēnai,* "to guide," "care for," 1 Tim. 3:5).

The qualification "able to teach" has provoked doubts in the eyes of some, but one only need look at Priscilla, who did this very thing with Apollos (Acts 18:24–26; cf. Acts 28:23). "The husband of but one wife," as a qualification for overseers, deacons, and elders has also raised some eyebrows (1 Tim. 3:2, 12; Titus 1:6). Why would Paul give this qualification, if he envisioned women serving in these capacities? The point is a good one and requires an explanation. A reasonable one is that Greek married women were not prone to multiple marriages (or illicit unions) to the same degree that Greek men were. Its omission from the qualifications of a woman deacon in 1 Timothy 3:11 would support such an interpretation (see chapter 2).

Yet what about Jesus and the twelve apostles? Did not Jesus by his own maleness and in choosing twelve males as apostles ordain a patriarchal pattern of leadership for the church?[13] This is a common way of thinking today, but it is one that possesses a fatal flaw. For Jesus did not merely choose twelve men but twelve *Jewish* men, and he himself was not merely a male but a *Jewish* one. Yet no one argues that Jewish leadership is thereby ordained. Why then male leadership?

This line of thinking also ignores the biblical symbolism of twelve Jewish males to represent the twelve tribes and their patriarchal heads. It is the twelve apostles who will sit on thrones, judging the twelve tribes of Israel (Matt. 19:28; Luke 22:30). The new Jerusalem will have twelve gates, twelve angels, twelve foundations, and on them the names of the twelve apostles (Rev. 21:12, 14).

It is important not to make a leap from the twelve apostles to male leadership in the church. The leap, instead, should be from twelve apostles to the church of Jesus Christ. It is not male leaders who will serve as judges in the future, nor, for that matter, is it female leaders. "Do you not know," Paul says, "that *the saints* will judge the world? . . . Do you not know that we will judge angels?" (1 Cor. 6:2–3 italics added). This is what we saw in looking at the word *authority* in the New Testament: The apostles possess it. The church possesses it. Church leaders do not possess it—be they male or female.

If there were no first-century leadership activities that were distinctively male in character, why all the fuss about women in leadership? If there are no qualifications that would prohibit women from serving as leaders, why do some persist in excluding them today? At least one explanation comes to mind: Power and control are difficult to share. A solo pastorate is easier than a team ministry. A CEO-run company is easier than an employee-run company. Male headship in the marriage is easier than decisions reached by mutual consent. In short, it is easier to call the shots than to share the job—whether it be in marriage, in the workplace, or in the church. In some instances it is not even a gender issue; it is a control issue.

Sometimes, however, it is both a gender issue and a control issue. This is especially the case when *to lead* is *to rule*. As soon as church offices appeared on the scene, fewer and fewer women seemed to find their way into leadership positions. And, as soon as leadership was viewed as exercising authority (rather than serving to the best of one's ability), the number of women among the ranks of church leaders decreased sharply. For that matter, any time the leadership playing field is narrowed to a powerful few, *church* becomes a spectator sport rather than a shared ministry, and *ministry* becomes a survival of the fittest rather than the empowerment of the whole.

All this is a far cry from New Testament teaching and early church practice. Ministry is the job of the whole congregation. Pastoring is the job of the whole congregation. Service is the job of the whole congregation. Some may feel called to devote themselves full-time to such a job, and in such cases the congregation is called upon to submit to, highly esteem, and love those who do (see, for example, 1 Thess. 5:12–13). Yet it is not the person or the position that is esteemed; it is the hard work and devoted service that earns such respect.

## Women and Authority: Passages That Suggest Limits

Does the New Testament place any limits at all on women? Are women excluded from any church roles? Examination of the evidence so far indicates they are not. Both women and men are acknowledged in and commended for exactly the same roles (patrons, evangelists, apostles, prophets, teachers, deacons). What then is the source of the debate today?

The November 1995 issue of the Council on Biblical Manhood and Womanhood Newsletter (*CBMW News*) identified in list form what women can or cannot do in the church. (The CBMW is a group of evangelicals committed to the functional separation of women and men in the church.) Where the CBMW draws the line has to do solely with the *degree* of governing or teaching authority attached to each activity.

Three lists are given with rankings from greater to lesser. The first ranks governing activities in terms of the perceived degree of authority; the second ranks teaching roles in terms of perceived responsibility and influence; the third ranks public acts in terms of perceived recognition and visibility. Of the list of twenty-eight governing activities, six (perhaps as many as eight) are prohibited for women. These include being president of a denomination, a member of a denominational governing board, a regional governing authority (such as bishop or district superintendent), a member of a regional governing board, senior pastor of a local church, and a member of a local governing board (such as elders, deacons, or council members). Of the list of twenty-four teaching activities, five are prohibited for women. These include teaching Bible or theology in a seminary or Christian college, preaching or teaching at a denominational or regional meeting, and preaching to or teaching the whole church on a regular basis on Sunday mornings. Of the list of twenty public activities, only one is prohibited: ordination as pastor or clergy member in a denomination.

Listings of this sort remind me in two respects of the Jesus Seminar (a group of scholars who attempt to determine which of Jesus' sayings are authentic and which are not). For one, both the CBMW and the Jesus Seminar assume objectivity when in fact the whole enterprise is subjective from start to finish. *Greater* and *lesser* are subjective judgments and personal perceptions. Drawing lines is an arbitrary exercise.

A few examples will suffice. According to the CBMW, it is okay for a woman to direct Christian education in her local church, but it is not okay for a woman to direct Christian education for her region or denomination. On what basis? The *perceived* degree of governance involved. Yet, in a congregational context, it is actually the local church that makes the decisions, not regional or denominational boards or councils. Also, CBMW says it is okay for a woman to be a Bible professor on a secular campus but not on a Christian campus. On what basis? The *perceived* degree of teaching authority. (A secular school has "no church-authorized authority or doctrinal endorsement.") Then too, it is okay for a woman to do pastoral ministry with a denominational license but not with denominational ordination. On what basis? The *perceived* degree of public recognition.

Two, both the Jesus Seminar and the CBMW impose a modern mindset on the biblical texts. The Jesus Seminar assumes the Bible (like any other ancient document) cannot be taken at face value and that we are in a position to determine scientifically which parts are authentic and which are not. The CBMW also assumes a modern mind-set. It assumes the structures of today's society are appropriate ones for the church— whether they be governing boards, chief executive officers, ruling elders, etc. It also assumes the Bible speaks in an authoritative way about these modern structures.

This is all rather mystifying for a couple of reasons. First, as we noted earlier, Jesus taught his disciples that they were *not* to structure themselves after the governance and CEO cultural models of their day. Secular authorities may rule over their constituencies, and high officials may exercise authority, but this was not to be so with the disciples (Matt. 20:25–26). Yet, we as evangelicals are quick to adopt such governing structures and equally quick to decide gender appropriateness. On what basis?

Second, the leadership language of the New Testament is the language of serving, not governing or ruling, of being last, not first (Matt. 20:26–28). Authoritative local church leadership is simply not a New Testament concept. Offices with governing authority are foreign to the New Testament. Even "the governing authority of a senior pastor" (*CBMW News,* November 1995, p. 3) is a modern convention. "All authority in heaven and on earth has been given to me," Jesus said. Our job (including but not limited to senior pastors) is to "go and make disciples" (Matt. 28:18–19).

What then is the biblical basis for excluding women? The CBMW lists five New Testament passages: Matthew 10:1–4; 1 Corinthians 14:33–35; 1 Timothy 2:12; 3:1–7; and Titus 1:5–9. Matthew 10:1–4 is the passage in which Jesus calls his twelve disciples and gives them authority to drive out evil spirits and to heal every disease and sickness.

How exactly one gets from driving out evil spirits and healing to governing authority and teaching is far from clear (see the earlier section on authority). First Timothy 3:1–7 and Titus 1:5–9 have to do with the qualifications for overseers and elders, but again, it is difficult to see how the qualifications Paul lists exclude women from these roles. "Husband of one wife" has already been dealt with (see above), and "able to teach" and "refute those who oppose sound doctrine" (1 Tim. 3:2; Titus 1:9) are hardly gender-exclusive activities. They may be perceived to exclude today, but this wasn't the case in Paul's time.

To be honest, there are really only two New Testament passages that are consistently claimed to address women and authority roles: 1 Corinthians 14:33–34, in which women are commanded to be silent in the church, and 1 Timothy 2:12, in which women are not permitted "to teach or to have authority over a man." Of these two, 1 Timothy 2:12 alone has a Greek term that can be translated "authority"—and even this is far from certain. In fact, there is very little that is certain about either 1 Timothy 2:12 or 1 Corinthians 14:33–34. The meaning of virtually every word is debated—as attested by over one hundred articles on these texts. This alone should give us pause. Yet over and over again these two passages are cited as absolute biblical proof that women cannot hold positions of authority in the church.

These texts do raise legitimate questions and need to be considered, but it is vital that such consideration be done in light of the biblical "cloud of witnesses" (Heb. 12:1) that we have already considered. One or two debated passages cannot hold hostage a host of clear passages. Yet this is precisely what all too often happens. Firm decisions about meaning are reached, translations are made, and the church is left to believe that all is crystal clear.

### 1 Corinthians 14:33–35

"Women should remain silent in the churches. They are not allowed to speak" (1 Cor. 14:34). Paul's statement seems pretty straightforward. Women are not permitted to speak out in church. They can visit shut-ins, organize potlucks, run a food pantry, serve in the nursery, and even teach a Sunday school class, but when the congregation meets for worship (or any other formal activity), women are not to open their mouths.

If we stopped our reading of 1 Corinthians 14 at verse 34, this would be exactly what Paul is saying. Fortunately, Paul himself does not stop here, and neither can we. I say *fortunately* because verse 34 by itself flatly contradicts what Paul says earlier in the letter: "every woman who prays or prophesies . . ." (1 Cor. 11:5).

As we noted in the previous chapter, Paul supports the involvement of women in the worship service. He begins 1 Corinthians 11 with the words: "I praise you for remembering me in everything and for holding to the teachings, just as I passed them on to you" (1 Cor. 11:2). He also quite matter-of-factly speaks of women praying and prophesying in the church—albeit with heads covered. Then too he says this is the "practice" of "all the churches of God" (1 Cor. 11:16 AT). So Paul takes issue not with *what* women are doing but with *how* they are doing it. Women (and men for that matter) can pray and prophesy in the church, but they must not flaunt the social conventions of the day in so doing.

It would be rather incomprehensible for Paul to affirm women praying and prophesying in 1 Corinthians 11:5 and then command their total silence three chapters later. What, then, is a reasonable explanation? Some think Paul is affirming women in one situation and silencing them in another. Women can pray and prophesy in informal settings, but in formal settings women are to be silent.[14] There is no doubt, however, that both chapters 11 and 14 deal with the *same* setting. Prophecy, by definition, is a spiritual gift intended to build up the church. Paul says that speaking in tongues is self-edifying, but prophecy edifies "the church" (1 Cor. 14:4). The gift of prophecy is exercised when believers "come together as a church" (1 Cor. 11:17–18; 14:26–33). There is not much way around this.

Others believe Paul is encouraging one set of activities for women and discouraging another. Prophecy and prayer (it is claimed) are vertical in their orientation (i.e., talking to God and for him) and therefore allowed, but teaching and preaching are horizontal in their nature (i.e., exercising authority over another person) and so are disallowed. Nowhere, however, does Paul make such a distinction. Prophecy and teaching are equally horizontal in nature. Paul makes it quite clear that both build up the church, and both are instructional in their focus (cf. 1 Cor. 14:2–6, 26). To prophesy is to speak words of instruction (*katēchēsō,* 1 Cor. 14:19, 31) to the church "for its upbuilding, exhortation, and encouragement" (1 Cor. 14:3 AT). What, in fact, Paul distinguishes in chapter 14 is the horizontal character of prophecy and the vertical nature of tongues (without interpretation). "Those who speak in a tongue" Paul states, "do not speak to other people but *to God.* . . . On the other hand, those who prophesy speak *to other people*" (1 Cor. 14:2–3 NRSV italics added).

Still others gravitate toward the command for silence in chapter 14 and explain away chapter 11. They argue that Paul is speaking only hypothetically in chapter 11. If women *should* pray and prophesy (which they do not), then their heads must be covered. They then claim that truth is found, instead, in Paul's command that women remain silent in the church.[15] This, of course, is unacceptable. There is nothing at all hypothetical about fifteen verses devoted to the issue of what women should wear on their heads when they pray and prophesy (1 Cor. 11:2–16), nor is it possible to understand the grammar in this way. Paul puts everything in the indicative (the mood of fact) and not in the subjunctive (the mood of possibility).

There is an even more fundamental problem. To focus solely on the prohibition is to ignore the broader context of chapter 14 and misunderstand what Paul is saying in this section of the letter. In the immediately preceding verses, Paul sets out some guidelines for participation in the worship service. "When you gather," he says, "*each* has a psalm, a teaching, a revelation, a tongue, or an interpretation" (1 Cor. 14:26 AT italics added). Had Paul intended to limit involvement to men, this would have been the place to do so. Instead he emphasizes that men and women alike must speak out, if the church is to be built up.

Paul does set some limits—although once again they deal not with the *who* or *what* but with the *how*. In this case the *how* is "in a fitting and orderly way" (1 Cor. 14:40; cf. v. 33). Each is to make a contribution, but all contributions must be made in an orderly fashion. Two or three at the most can speak and then only one at a time. If the speaking is in tongues, there must be someone who can interpret. If there is no interpreter, the speaker must keep quiet in the church and speak to themselves and God (1 Cor. 14:26–28). If the speaker is a prophet, the others should weigh carefully what is said (14:29).[16] If a prophetic revelation comes to someone who is sitting down, the first speaker must stop (14:30–31), "for God is not a God of disorder but of peace" (14:33). Whatever Paul is saying about women, these verses show the issue is how one contributes, not whether one can contribute at all.

What comes after the prohibition in 1 Corinthians 14:34 must also be carefully considered. Paul concludes chapter 14 with a word of rebuke for the whole congregation: "Did the word of God originate with you? Or are you the only people it has reached?" (1 Cor. 11:36; the masculine plural *you* is to be noted). Paul anticipates there will be some at Corinth who reject what he has to say (cf. 1 Cor. 4:18, "some of you have become arrogant"). They do this because they think they are spiritually superior to Paul ("if someone thinks he or she is a prophet or spiritual," 1 Cor. 14:37 AT). His challenge to them is to use their spiritual abilities to affirm that what he has been saying is "the Lord's command" (v. 37). The essence of that command is that "everything be done in a fitting and orderly way" (v. 40 AT).

Thus Paul begins this section with practical instructions about the orderly contribution of speech gifts (psalms, teachings, revelations, tongues, interpretations), and he concludes with a challenge to those with the gifts of prophecy and spiritual insight to heed what he says. Sandwiched in between are two short verses about women speaking in the church:

> Women should remain silent in the churches. They are not allowed to speak, but must be in submission, as the Law says. If they want to inquire about something, they should ask their own husbands at home; for it is disgraceful for a woman to speak in the church.
>
> 1 Corinthians 14:34–35

The very brevity of Paul's instruction causes problems. Even a quick glance shows that his words are far from clear. They undoubtedly made sense to the Corinthians, but to an outsider (not to mention a twentieth-century reader) the best that can be done is to hazard an educated guess.

For instance, Paul says that the women at Corinth should "be in submission" (v. 34), but he fails to say in submission to what or to whom. He also states that women are to submit "as the Law says" (v. 34), but he does not specify whether this is Mosaic law, church law, or the laws of the land. He notes that the Corinthian women "want to learn something" (v. 35 AT), but he does not say what that something is. Paul maintains that it is disgraceful for a woman to speak in church, yet he does not indicate why this would be so. On the face of it, silent women doesn't fit with known religious propriety in the Roman world (see chapter 1). Nor does it match up with the charismatic, inclusive character of early Christian worship ("when you gather, each has a psalm, a teaching," 1 Cor. 14:26 AT).

The incongruity of verses 34–35 also causes difficulty. It is not immediately clear how these two verses fit into the broader context of chapter 14. They seem to rudely interrupt the topic at hand. What, after all, do the questions of inquisitive women ("let them ask at home," v. 35 AT) have to do with the need for orderly prophecy and tongue speaking? There is also an awkward change of subject:

> When *you* [plural] gather (vv. 26–33)
> Let *them* [the women] be silent (vv. 34–35)
> Did the word of God originate with *you* [plural] (vv. 36–40)

This is hardly what one would call a smooth train of thought. Did Paul snatch the pen from the hand of his secretary at verse 34 and give it back at verse 36? The abruptness almost gives this impression. In fact, if these verses were removed, it is doubtful their omission would be noticed:

> Two or three prophets should speak, and the others should weigh carefully what is said. And if a revelation comes to someone who is sitting down, the first speaker should stop. For you can all prophesy in turn so that everyone may be instructed and encouraged. The spirits of prophets are subject to the control of prophets. For God is not a God of disorder but of peace, [as] in all the congregations of the saints. Did the word of God originate with you? Or are you the only people it has reached? If anybody thinks he is a prophet or spiritually gifted, let him acknowledge that what I am writing to you is the Lord's command.
>
> 1 Corinthians 14:29–33, 36–37 NIV

So what are we to make of verses 34–35? We can take comfort in the fact that copyists in the early centuries asked the same question. This is obvious from the different places these verses appear. In some of our earliest manuscripts and versions, verses 34–35 follow the final verse of chapter 14 (D F G itala, a vulgate manuscript). In other early manuscripts and versions, verses 34–35 come after verse 33 (P[46] ℵ A B Ψ K L itala, Vulgate, Syriac, Coptic, and others).[17] The Latin text of codex Fuldensis (a sixth-century manuscript of the Vulgate) directs the reader to skip from the end of verse 33 to verses 36–40 and so omit verses 34–35 altogether.[18]

All this has led some scholars to conclude that verses 34–35 are not original to 1 Corinthians.[19] There is certainly merit in this. Could it be that Paul's concern for orderly worship prompted a copyist to think of the disorder that outspoken women can cause and then pen words to this effect in the margin? Later copyists, then, placed them after verse 33 (or, in some cases, after verse 40), thinking their presence in the margin signaled an inadvertent omission. Alternatively, some think the redactor of the Pauline letters[20] or even Paul himself (as a last-minute inclusion)[21] is responsible for their presence.

The theory of a marginal gloss is not without its difficulties though. Why, for example, would a later copyist move these verses from the margin to a position after verse 33 or verse 40? If it is hard to imagine Paul placing them in either spot, it is even harder to picture a later copyist making this change. One also wishes for early manuscript support. We simply do not have any Greek manuscripts that lack these verses.

Then, too, the language is Paul's, even if the connections are not entirely smooth. There are strong links between verses 27–33 and verses 34–35 that would support their inclusion. The word *submission* appears twice—first of the spirits of the prophets (v. 32) and then of the women in the congregation (v. 34). *To learn* comes up twice (vv. 31, 35). *To speak* turns up five times (vv. 27, 28, 29, 34, 35). The command for *silence* occurs three times: Those who speak in tongues are silenced (v. 28), prophets are silenced (v. 30), and women are silenced (v. 34).

Until further evidence comes to light, it is best to suppose that these verses are from Paul's hand. If this is the case, then some decisions have to be made about what the passage is actually saying. The first issue is where to begin a new paragraph. The text of 1 Corinthians 14:33–34 (AT) reads as follows:

> For God is not a God of disorder but of peace.
> [as in all the congregations of the saints]
> Women should remain silent in the churches. They are not allowed to speak, but must be submissive, as the law says.

What does "as in all the congregations of the saints" go with? Does it end a paragraph or begin a new one? Is it Paul's way of driving home his point about the need for orderly worship, or does it introduce a prohibition regarding the silence of women?

The decision is an important one. If the phrase goes with what follows, then Paul is saying that the silence of women in the church is a matter of universal practice: "As in all the congregations of the saints, the women should remain silent in the churches" (ASV, RSV, NRSV, TEV, CEV, JB, NEB, REB with minor variations). If it goes with what precedes, then Paul is saying that orderly worship is a matter of universal practice: "God is not the author of confusion but of peace as in all the congregations of the saints" (KJV, NKJV, NLT, *Phillips* with minor variations).

A logical question to ask is whether Paul tends to use *as* phrases to conclude or to begin a thought. But here we get no help for both are equally his practice. In Ephesians 5:1 he states: "Be imitators of God, therefore, *as dearly loved children*" (italics added). Yet seven verses later he says: "*As children of light,* so walk" (5:8 AT italics added).

What about appeals elsewhere to church practice? Here we get quite a bit more help. The other appeals also appear in 1 Corinthians and come as a concluding point:

> Timothy will remind you of my way of life in Christ Jesus, *as I teach everywhere in every church.*
>
> 1 Corinthians 4:17 italics added

Each should retain the place in life that the Lord assigned . . . and *so I command in all the churches*.

1 Corinthians 7:17 AT italics added

If anyone wants to be contentious about this, we have no other practice—*nor do the churches of God*.

1 Corinthians 11:16 italics added

"For God is not a God of disorder but of peace *as in all the congregations of the saints*" fits this pattern exactly (1 Cor. 14:33 italics added).

On top of this, it would be very poor style to begin a new paragraph at verse 33b because it would result in a redundancy that is quite unlike Paul: "As *in all the churches* of the saints, let the women *in the churches* be silent." Why repeat *in the churches* twice in one sentence? Could Paul's diction really have been that sloppy? On the other hand, "Let the women . . ." is a typical Pauline start to a new paragraph (see, for example, Eph. 5:22 and Col. 3:18) and should be taken as such here.

A second decision to make is what Paul means by "let them submit" and "as the law says" (AT). Here the best decision is no decision. It is very easy to read back into the text what we would like to hear Paul say. All too often it is just assumed Paul is commanding women to submit to their husbands as the "law" of Genesis 3:16 states ("he will rule over her"), yet this is highly unlikely. As we noted in chapter 2, there simply is no Old Testament law commanding women to submit to their husbands, and Genesis 3:16 is nowhere understood this way—be it in the Old or New Testaments. The context deals with childbearing and sexual intimacy. So it is far more likely that Genesis 3:16 has to do with the husband's tendency to take advantage of the wife's desire for intimacy. Then too the translation could just as easily be "it" (rather than *he* or *husband*), in which case the husband would not even be in view. It could be the woman's "desire for her husband" that ends up "ruling her" (see chapter 2, pp. 104–9). Even so, it must be remembered that the context is one describing a fallen relationship. It certainly is not the way God intends husbands and wives to relate. This is clear from the fact that when the topic of marriage surfaces elsewhere in Scripture, it is Genesis 2:24, not Genesis 3:16, that is lifted up as the divine norm.

In any event, whatever law of submission Paul is noting (if indeed he is referring to wifely submission), it is not Old Testament law.[22] Nor is it a commandment of Christ. Jesus nowhere commands women to be submissive to their husbands. Paul certainly urges wives to submit to their husbands (Eph. 5:22; Col. 3:18; Titus 2:5), but nowhere does he equate his instruction with "the law" *(ho nomos)*. So we are left with either church law or the laws of the land. Greek and Jewish marital contracts included wifely obedience, yet Roman contracts typically did not.[23]

Since the word *husband* is lacking in 1 Corinthians 14:34, it is best to think more broadly. To what or whom could women in the church be asked to submit? To make it more complicated, the command could be either "let them submit themselves" (a voluntary action, middle voice) or "they are to be kept submissive" (a forced action, passive voice).

A look at how Paul uses the verb *submit* elsewhere in his letters is a first step. Virtually all have to do with voluntary submission (i.e., middle voice). Congregations are urged to submit to their leaders (1 Cor. 16:16), believers are commanded to submit to secular authority (Rom. 13:1), slaves are called to submit to their masters (Col. 3:22), and wives are asked to submit to their husbands (Eph. 5:22; Col. 3:18; Titus 2:5).

The immediate context is a further help. In 1 Corinthians 14:32 Paul states that the spirits of the prophets are submissive to the prophets. When another prophet receives a revelation, the first prophet is to sit down and be silent. Those who speak in tongues are also commanded to be silent if there is no one to interpret.

If one follows Paul's thinking carefully, submission and silence are two sides of the same coin. To be silent is to be submissive. This is evident from the parallel in verse 34 between "they [women] are not to speak" and "let them be submissive" (AT). The basic principle is one of control over the tongue so as to preserve order in the worship service. This is what all three groups have in common—tongue speakers, prophets, and women. They are able to be silent for the sake of orderly worship.

"As the law says" still leaves us with a puzzle. There simply was no law—social, religious, or otherwise—commanding the silence of women.[24] So we need to look more carefully at what Paul means by *silence*. That the silence is not absolute is clear from 1 Corinthians 11:5 ("every woman who prays or prophesies"). What, then, is being forbidden?

Scholars tend to gravitate toward one of three possibilities (excepting those who do not think these verses are original to 1 Corinthians). One group thinks in terms of some form of inspired speech. Paul may be barring women from mimicking the ecstatic frenzy of certain pagan cults.[25] Or he may be silencing the women who speak in tongues without interpretation. In verse 28 he states, "If there is no interpreter, the speaker should keep quiet in the church and speak to himself and God" (1 Cor. 14:28 NIV).[26] Or yet again he may even be disallowing women from being part of the prophetic examination process spoken of in verse 29: "Two or three prophets should speak, and the others should weigh carefully what is said" (a rather popular position today). To sit in judgment over the prophecies of men (so it is argued) would be to disregard a woman's subordinate role.[27]

The second group of scholars argue for some form of disruptive speech. The Corinthian women were publicly contradicting or embarrassing their husbands by asking questions about a particular prophecy or tongue.[28] Or Paul may be thinking of the tendency of women to chatter during worship and so disturb those around them.[29] Or yet again, he may be barring a more formal activity like that of teaching or preaching. Women may have been flaunting the social conventions by taking on themselves the role of instructors and thereby discrediting Christianity.

One novel (and increasingly popular) interpretation is that verses 34–35 are actually the position of certain members of the Corinthian congregation, which Paul cites ("Let the women in the churches be silent . . ." AT) and then responds to in verse 36: "Did the word of God originate with you [Corinthians]? Or are you the only people it has reached?" The idea is that certain members of the Corinthian congregation were preventing women from active participation in the speaking ministries of the church by appealing to a biblical (or cultural) tradition of female submission.[30]

So what can we conclude from the context? Several things are clear. First, the context is that of public worship. "When you gather as a church" makes this quite clear (1 Cor. 14:23, 26 AT; cf. 11:17–18; 12:7, "for the common good").

Second, the speaking is almost certainly of a disruptive sort. Paul is concerned throughout this chapter with orderly speaking. "Be eager to prophesy, and do not forbid speaking in tongues. But everything should be done in a fitting and orderly way" (1 Cor. 14:39–40).

Third, the source of this disruptive speaking is married women. Single women—be they widows, divorcées, or the never-married (of which there were many; see 1 Cor. 7:8–11, 25–40) are not the problem. The women creating the disturbance are those who can "ask their *own husbands* at home" (1 Cor. 14:35 italics added).

Fourth, the motive for disrupting worship was "to learn" (*manthanō;* the NIV "to inquire" captures the action but not the meaning of the Greek verb). This rules out inspired speech (ecstatic or otherwise). Paul is not addressing women who are exercising their spiritual gifts—those with "a hymn, a word of instruction, a revelation, a tongue or an interpretation" to share with the congregation (1 Cor. 14:26). Nor is he speaking to women exercising a gift of discernment by judging the truthfulness of the prophetic word (vv. 29–30). These are, rather, married women in the congregation who are speaking out in church because they want

to learn. Their fault was not in the asking per se but in the inappropriate setting for their questions. It would also seem that these questions
were directed at men other than their husbands, for Paul instructs them
to ask their *own* men. This would have been considered shameful behavior even to a Roman.

Such disruptive behavior is not such an unlikely scenario even today.
While the worship service tends to be a fairly staid affair in more traditional churches (and so an unlikely context for talking), as an instructor
I inevitably encounter one or two people in Sunday school classes who
constantly whisper to their spouse or friend the entire time. I also have
students (both male and female) who do this during class. Most are simply asking questions of the person sitting next to them and are totally
unaware of how disruptive their activity is to the instructor and to those
around them. When the volume gets above a whisper, it is hard not to
attach the label *disrespectful* to the talking—even though the whisperers
involved may be oblivious to the impact on those around them. So it is
easy for me to see why Paul would use the term *disgraceful* of this kind of
activity. It is not appropriate today, and it was not acceptable back then.

This kind of disruptive activity also compromises the church's witness. Paul is keenly aware of this and says so earlier in the chapter. "If
the whole church comes together and everyone speaks in tongues, and
some who do not understand or some unbelievers come in, will they not
say that you are out of your mind?" (1 Cor. 14:23). A similar state of
confusion would result from women asking questions during worship.

Moreover, such activity would have been perceived as disgraceful. Public speaking by women was discouraged to begin with. Even the more
progressive first-century Roman did not go out of his way to encourage
women to choose public speaking as a career path. Nor did women blurt
out questions during pagan worship. The native cults were strictly regulated, and such interruptions would most certainly have been frowned
upon. Even in the oriental cults, matters of worship were in the hands of
the professional clergy (i.e., the priests and priestesses) and not the laity.

To whom were the Corinthian women's questions directed? They
could well have been directed to those instructing the congregation.
While today we might picture someone interrupting the preacher at a
confusing spot in the sermon, back then it would likely have been a question directed to those instructing the congregation through a hymn,
teaching, revelation, tongue, or interpretation (1 Cor. 14:26).

Women were the ones inclined to ask questions back then. Formal
instruction stopped for most of them at the marriageable age of twelve
(Jewish) or fourteen to sixteen (Greek and Roman). Lower-class women,

in particular, would not have been in a position to pursue a career path that involved formal instruction (1 Cor. 1:26, "not many of you are wise by human standards" AT). Add to this the all-consuming task of raising children and running a household. This group of women, after tasting freedom in Christ to grow their minds, grabbed the opportunity—albeit in a less than suitable fashion.

If we put all these contextual pieces together, a plausible picture emerges. Married women, in exercising their newly acquired freedom to learn alongside the men, were disturbing the orderly flow of things by asking questions during the worship service. Eugene Peterson's *The Message* captures the sense with his paraphrase: "Wives must not disrupt worship, talking when they should be listening, asking questions that could more appropriately be asked of their husbands at home."

Sometimes in the heat of debate, several aspects of these verses are overlooked. It is important to notice that Paul affirms the right of women to learn and be instructed. This, in and of itself, is a progressive rather than a restrictive attitude. Nor is it merely the exceptional or gifted woman whom Paul affirms. "If they [the women at Corinth] want to learn, let them ask" is wholly inclusive (1 Cor. 14:35 AT). Paul also affirms the right of women to ask questions. He does not question the *what* (women asking questions) but the *where* (during the worship service). We also should remember that it was not merely inquiring women who were silenced but also long-winded prophets (1 Cor. 14:29–30) and unintelligible speakers (vv. 27–28). Paul's target was anyone and anything that would compromise the instruction and edification of the body of believers (1 Cor. 14:12, 32, 40).

The fact that Paul concludes this section with a rebuke for the congregation would seem to indicate the Corinthian church was actually encouraging an undisciplined flow of charismatic expression and the questions that came in its wake. This is still the case in some charismatic contexts today. The solution, however, is not to fixate on one aspect of Paul's corrective ("let the women be silent in the churches") and ignore the rest ("if they [the married women] want to learn, let them ask their own husbands at home" AT). While the Corinthian women in their eagerness to learn may have been at fault back then, it could easily be a different group today.

### 1 Timothy 2:11–15

One of the most hotly debated passages on women's roles in the church is 1 Timothy 2:11–15. In language quite similar to 1 Corinthians 14:34–35, Paul seems once again to forbid women from speaking in a congregational setting. In this case, however, the prohibited speaking is of an instructional nature:

| 1 Timothy 2 | 1 Corinthians 14 |
|---|---|
| v. 11—let a woman learn quietly | v. 35—if women want to learn something |
| v. 11—in full submission | v. 34—let them submit themselves |
| v. 12—I am not permitting a woman to teach | v. 34—it is not permissible for a woman to speak |

The similarities (striking as they may be) end here, but the problems do not. For one, the most common translation of this text stands in stark contradiction to the wide-ranging leadership roles Paul acknowledges for women elsewhere in his letters ("I do not permit a woman to teach or to have authority over a man"; 1 Tim. 2:12 TEV, *Phillips*, RSV, NRSV, NIV, NASB, NJB, NKJV, with slight variations). How we reconcile Paul's words here with a Junia (who was outstanding among the apostles, Rom. 16:7), a Deborah (who was a prophet and judge of Israel, Judg. 4:4), or a Priscilla (who expounded the Scriptures to Apollos, Acts 18:26) is problematic indeed.[31]

Also, the meanings of the key words in this passage are in question. Perhaps the best way to show this is by comparing four English translations of 1 Timothy 2:12:

I am not [at this time] giving permission for a woman to teach or to tell a man what to do. A woman ought not to speak, because . . . (JB).

I do not permit a woman to teach or to have authority over a man; she must be silent (NIV).

I do not permit a woman to . . . domineer over man (NEB).

They should be silent and not be allowed to . . . tell men what to do (CEV).

It is important to realize that our understanding of a text like this one is largely determined by the translation we use. If it is the NKJV, RSV, NIV, or TEV, then we are left with a categorical prohibition. "I do not permit a woman to teach or to have authority over a man; she must be silent" leaves little to the imagination. Women are not permitted to teach or to lead men; it is as simple as that. If, however, it is the Jerusalem Bible, then verses 11–12 read as a temporary restriction. Paul at the time of writing does not feel comfortable with having a woman in the church at

Ephesus tell a man what to do (undoubtedly tied to the problem of false teachers).

Even identifying the issue will be decided by the translation in hand. If we use the NEB, we will think the issue is women who lead in an over-bearing fashion. On the other hand, if we use the CEV, the issue will seem to be women leading men per se.

The scholarly community has done little to help the average layperson. In some cases it has done more harm than good. It is one thing to have honest disagreements (as we do over issues like baptism and the Lord's Supper); it is another thing to charge evangelicals who take a differing position with a denial of biblical authority or with abandoning a high view of Scripture. Lamentably, this happens all too often. It would be one thing if the Greek text were clear, but it is not. Even more, the key term in verse 12 *(authentein)* is found nowhere else in the New Testament, and elsewhere (i.e., in the LXX and in secular Greek literature) it is used in a way that does not even come close to what we find in most Scripture translations. Yet it is the rare translation that alerts the reader to the discrepancy.

Additionally, the number of interpretive decisions that have to be made is quite overwhelming. Few laypeople today are aware of this unless their translation alerts them via footnotes. Unfortunately, very few translations do this. The major interpretive decisions include:

1. Is Paul addressing his comments to *wives* specifically or to *women* generally *(gynē* can mean either)?
2. In verse 11 does Paul command a woman to learn *in silence* (i.e., she is not to speak out in public) or to learn *quietly* (i.e., she is not to disrupt worship)?
3. To whom or what is she to be in "full submission"?
4. Is the verb in verse 12 to be translated "I am not permitting" (i.e., a temporary restriction) or "I do not permit" (i.e., a habitual practice)?
5. Does *to teach* carry official or unofficial connotations?
6. Does verse 12 prohibit one action ("to teach a man in an authoritarian fashion") or two actions ("to teach" and "to have authority over a man")?
7. Does *authentein* in verse 12 have a positive ("to have authority over") or a negative ("to dominate") meaning?
8. Is the connection with Genesis 2–3 in verse 13 a causal one ("because Adam was created first") or an illustrative one ("for example, Adam was created first")?

9. Is "Adam was created first" (AT) a historical observation or a statement about rank?

10. In verse 14 is "the woman was deceived and became a transgressor" (AT) a warning from history or a statement about the nature of all women?

11. Is it that women will be "kept safe" through childbearing or "saved" through childbearing (v. 15)?

## THE CONTEXT

The first step in getting a handle on 1 Timothy 2:11–15 is to be clear about where it fits in the letter as a whole. Although some are quick to dismiss the importance of this step, the problem-solving nature of Paul's letters compels us to do so.

Why does Paul write this letter? In 1 Timothy 3:15 he tells Timothy that he is writing so he "will know how people ought to conduct themselves in God's household." Some conclude from this that Paul's aim is to provide his stand-in with a manual on church order. There is some truth to this. One does not have to go very far in the letter before running across qualifications for local church leaders (like overseer and deacon) and the duties of a pastor.

Yet this is not the whole picture (or even the starting point). Paul's primary reason for writing is spelled out in the opening verses of the letter. He reminds Timothy that he asked him to stay on at Ephesus so he could "command certain persons not to teach false doctrines any longer nor to devote themselves to myths and endless genealogies" (1 Tim. 1:3). So, "how people ought to conduct themselves in God's household" (1 Tim. 3:15) must be read in light of Paul's larger concern regarding false teaching.

That false teaching is Paul's overriding concern is evident from the fact that he bypasses the normal letter-writing conventions (like a thanksgiving section and closing greetings) and gets right down to business. This is also clear from how often the topic of false teaching surfaces in the letter. It consumes roughly 35 percent of Paul's direct attention and colors much of the rest.

A closer look shows that Paul's concern about false teaching even influences what he has to say about church order. If the primary concern were local church management, we would expect to see matters of a managerial sort surface in Paul's instructions to Timothy (as we find in the *Didache* or *Teaching of the Twelve*). Instead we find a concern for character, family life, and commitment to sound doctrine. This is per-

fectly understandable against a background of false teaching, especially
if (as Paul claims) the teachers are motivated by greed (1 Tim. 6:5), decry
the family ("forbid people to marry," 1 Tim. 4:3), and delight in controversy and arguments (1 Tim. 6:3–4).

False teaching also dominates what Paul has to say about elders. We
learn very little about what elders do, but we learn quite a bit about how
*not* to choose elders (1 Tim. 5:21–22) and what to do with those who
err (1 Tim. 5:19–20). This makes sense if we are dealing with a problematic situation at Ephesus. Persistent sin, the need for a public rebuke,
and the concern that others take warning point us particularly in this
direction (5:19–20).

Can we assume the presence of false teaching also influenced Paul's
comments about women? A quick survey of what Paul says about the
false teachers suggests women were at the very center of the storm.

The nature of the false teaching is not unlike what Paul encountered
at Colossae (a neighboring city) just a few years earlier. It has syncretis-
tic and Gnostic features but with distinctly Jewish overtones. There is a
similar emphasis on esoteric knowledge. Paul says some have professed
"what is falsely called knowledge . . . and in so doing have wandered from
the faith" (1 Tim. 6:20–21). "Endless genealogies" (1:4), "godless
myths" (4:7), "controversies" (1:4), and "meaningless talk" (1:6) all
point in this direction. "God our Savior, who wants *all* people . . . to
come to a knowledge of the truth" (1 Tim. 2:3–4 italics added) adds an
additional piece.

There is also a similar ascetic focus. The false teachers order people
to abstain from certain foods and forbid them to marry (1 Tim. 4:3). A
belief that the resurrection has already happened undoubtedly fueled their
commands (2 Tim. 2:17–18; cf. Luke 20:34–35). A cosmic dualism (spiritual is good/material is evil) that relegates Christ to an inferior place in
the redemptive scheme of things also seemed to be present. We can tell
this from Paul's corrective statements. "Everything God created is good"
(not evil) and should be "received with thanksgiving" (not avoided; 1 Tim.
4:4). "There is one God and one mediator [not many] between God and
humanity, Christ Jesus, himself human" (1 Tim. 2:5 AT).

The false teaching at Ephesus has a distinctly Jewish character. Those
who seek to propagate it come especially from the circumcision group
(Titus 1:10). They want to be teachers of the Mosaic law but do not know
what they are talking about (1 Tim. 1:7). They stimulate arguments and
quarrels about the law (Titus 3:9). They devote themselves to Jewish leg-
ends (Titus 1:14) and genealogies (1 Tim. 1:4; Titus 3:9). They command food restrictions that smack of Jewish ritualism (1 Tim. 4:3).

How influential this heretical teaching was can be judged from its impact on the leadership of the Ephesian church. It certainly reached to the highest level. Two leaders were expelled for promoting it (Alexander and Hymenaeus, 1 Tim. 1:20), and some of the elders needed to be rebuked publicly for it (1 Tim. 5:20).[32] Its impact on the congregation was devastating. In its wake it left "ruined households" (Titus 1:11 AT), "envy, strife, malicious talk, evil suspicions and constant friction" (1 Tim. 6:4–5).

Women seem to have been particularly attracted to this aberrant teaching. The false teachers, Paul states, "worm their way into homes and gain control over" them (2 Tim. 3:6). Younger widows especially seem to be ready evangelists for this false teaching, "going about from house to house, . . . saying things they ought not to" (1 Tim. 5:13). That something more than nosiness or gossiping is involved is evident from Paul's evaluation that "some have in fact already turned away to follow Satan" (1 Tim. 5:15).

Another thing to note is that it is only here in Paul's letters that we find him telling women to marry and raise a family (1 Tim. 5:14). He even goes so far as to say that "women will be saved [or perhaps *kept safe*] through childbearing" (1 Tim. 2:15)—a statement that has mystified theologians down through the centuries. Taken alongside 1 Corinthians 7, in which women are counseled *not* to marry, Paul comes across as terribly inconsistent. But if women were heeding the false teacher's command not to marry because sexual contact is unhealthy and polluting, the Pauline corrective is perfectly understandable. Paul says as much in 1 Timothy 4:3–4, when he states that "everything God created is good."

Some think wealthy widows were the primary target. It fits with the greedy motivation of the false teachers (1 Tim. 6:10; Titus 1:11). It also accounts for the amount of attention Paul gives to widows in this letter (17 out of 113 verses or 15 percent) and for Paul's seemingly harsh remarks toward those who do not provide for their elderly relatives (that person "has denied the faith and is worse than an unbeliever," 1 Tim. 5:8). If younger widows were being encouraged to redirect support of an elderly mother or grandmother into the coffers of these false teachers, much would be explained (1 Tim. 5:4, 16).

Were any of the false teachers women? Most assume they were men. But on what basis? "Going about from house to house, . . . saying things they ought not to" (1 Tim. 5:13) seems to suggest some sort of evangelistic role. "Always learning but never able to acknowledge the truth" (2 Tim. 3:7) sounds like a training relationship. While women may not have been the primary offenders, they may have proved to be eager followers who were encouraged to make more disciples (like Jehovah's Witnesses today). It may even be that these women got caught up in studying genealogies and mythologies (1 Tim. 1:4; Titus 3:9) and used this kind of esoteric knowledge to gain the upper hand over the men in the congregation. This would explain why women are the particular focus of Paul's prohibition in 1 Timothy 2:12–15. It would also account for the disproportionate attention they receive in the letter. No other New Testament book devotes such a high percentage of its content to women.

### CLEAR FEATURES

A second step in getting a handle on 1 Timothy 2:11–15 is to identify the clear aspects of the text so we have a framework for making decisions about matters that are not so clear. The first thing to note is that Paul is not giving routine instruction. He is responding to a situation that has gotten out of hand. False teachers need to be silenced (1 Tim. 1:3–7, 18–20; 4:1–8; 5:20–22; 6:3–10, 20–21). Elders need to be publicly rebuked (5:20). The men of the congregation are angry and quarrelsome (2:8). Women are dressing immodestly (2:9). Some younger widows have turned away from the faith to follow Satan (5:15). The rich have become arrogant and are putting their hope in wealth (6:17). Some in the church have turned to godless chatter and controversies and in so doing have wandered from the faith (6:20–21). Two leaders of the church have been expelled (1:20). Overall, it is not a positive picture (not to mention an immense pastoral challenge).

This is particularly the case in 1 Timothy 2. A command for peace (as opposed to disputing) is found four times in the space of fifteen verses. Prayers for governing authorities are urged "that we may live peaceful and quiet lives" (v. 2). The men of the church are told to lift up hands in prayer that are "free from anger or disputing" (v. 8 AT). The women are commanded to learn in a "peaceful" (not quarrelsome) fashion (v. 11 AT) and to behave "quietly" (v. 12 AT).

It is also clear that Paul intends his instruction in 1 Timothy 2 to be understood in light of the situation of false teaching at Ephesus. The opening "therefore *[oun]* I urge first of all" (v. 1 AT) ties what follows back to Paul's stated purpose for writing (1 Tim. 1:3–7) and to the shipwrecked faith of some Ephesian believers (1 Tim. 1:18–20). The subsequent "therefore *[oun]* I want" (1 Tim. 2:8 AT) does the same.

Another clear feature of the text is the concern for propriety. Women are told to dress and adorn themselves in a modest *(aidous)* and sensible *(sōphrosynēs)* way (twin virtues in Greco-Roman culture) as is proper *(prepei)* for those who profess faith in God (1 Tim. 2:9–10). Holiness with propriety *(hagiasmō meta sōphrosynēs)* is a necessary feminine virtue

(1 Tim. 2:15). Children are to be respectful and well behaved (1 Tim. 3:4). Proper conduct *(anastrephesthai)* in God's household is of utmost importance (1 Tim. 3:15).

The commands for peaceful behavior and the concern for propriety are with a view to preserving the witness of the church. "So that no-one will malign the word of God" (Titus 2:5) is the bottom line for Paul. Prayers are to be offered for governing authorities so that all may "be saved and come to a knowledge of the truth" (1 Tim. 2:2–4). One qualification for an overseer is to have a good reputation with outsiders (1 Tim. 3:7). Younger widows are to live in such a way as "to give the enemy no opportunity for slander" (1 Tim. 5:14). Slaves are to respect their masters so that God's name and the church's teaching may not be slandered (1 Tim. 6:1). It is reasonable therefore to think Paul's prohibition about women teachers is equally motivated by a concern for the church's witness.

An additional clear feature is Paul's affirmation of a woman's right to learn and to be instructed. This is easily overlooked in the heat of debate. "Let a woman learn" (1 Tim. 2:11 NRSV) is the way the passage begins. *How* they are to learn is the issue at hand, not their right to do so. We can also be fairly certain that women were functioning as teachers in the Ephesian community; otherwise, Paul would have no need for a corrective.

Some think the descriptions in 1 Timothy 2:9–10 fit women who were wealthy and married. The wealthy, to be sure, were the ones who could most readily afford the luxuries described here (hair braided with gold ribbon, pearls, expensive clothes). Yet we also know that women aped the latest fashions in hairstyles and dress regardless of their social standing (see chapter 2, pp. 128–29). So Paul's descriptions could easily be aimed at a broader audience.

Were these married women? Some translate verse 12 with *wife* and *husband.* For example, the NRSV margin has, "I permit no wife to teach or to have authority over her husband; she is to keep silent." But the vast majority do not, and for good reasons. Although Paul does refer to Adam and Eve (v. 13), he does so as the prototypical male and female, not as the first married couple. *Wives* and *husbands* would also be out of keeping with the context, which has to do with congregational worship. "I want the men to pray" *(boulomai proseuchesthai tous andras,* v. 8), and "I also want women" (vv. 9–10 AT) simply cannot be limited to husbands and wives. Nor can the references to women and men be read in this way in the verses that immediately follow. Paul gives no clue whatsoever that he is shifting at verse 11 from women in general to married women in specific.

There is one final matter. Do we know whether Paul is articulating a general dictum in this passage, or is he giving a local opinion? A close look shows that his instructions are quite specific to the Ephesian situation. There is no "as in all the churches" (see 1 Cor. 7:17; 11:16), no "this is what I teach everywhere in every church" (1 Cor. 4:17), and no "I received from the Lord what I also passed on to you" (1 Cor. 11:23; 15:3; cf. 1 Cor. 11:2; Phil. 4:9; 2 Thess. 2:15; 3:6; 2 Tim. 2:2). There are no phrases of apostolic authority, such as "by the word of the Lord" (1 Thess. 4:15 NRSV; cf. 1 Cor. 7:10) or "in the name of [or, through] our Lord Jesus Christ" (1 Cor. 1:10; 5:4; 2 Thess. 3:6; cf. 1 Thess. 4:2; 2 Thess. 3:12). There is no "I want you to know" or "I do not want you to be ignorant"— the way Paul introduces new information of an abiding sort (e.g., Rom. 11:25; 1 Cor. 10:1; 11:3; 12:1; 15:1; Gal. 1:11; 1 Thess. 4:13).

There are also a number of features that simply cannot be taken as universal church practice. Men praying with raised hands is a cultural phenomenon. Gold-braided hairstyles for women is also cultural. Some have sought to normalize these practices, but where sober judgment prevails, there is wide recognition that these are cultural (not universal) customs.

Yet, for many, cultural custom in 1 Timothy 2:8–10 suddenly becomes normative behavior in verses 11–12. On what basis though? Few today would think of forbidding women to braid their hair or to wear a string of pearls (1 Tim. 2:9). Why can't "let a woman learn in quietness and in full submission" and "a woman is not to teach . . . a man" (1 Tim. 2:11–12 AT) be equally cultural? What, if anything, warrants the sudden change of hermeneutics in moving from verses 8–10 to verses 11–12?

Some would say Paul's appeal to the creation and fall order in 1 Timothy 2:13–14 warrants it. Yet is this really what Paul is doing in these verses? It is true that he appeals to two historical facts: Adam was, indeed, created before Eve, and Eve was, in fact, deceived and did transgress as a result. But historical facts and normative ordering are very different things. The simple fact is that this is the lone New Testament reference to Adam's seniority. If it defines the pecking order of men and women, why does it surface only here? Also, what do we do with the principle of mutual submission found elsewhere in the New Testament (Eph. 5:21; 1 Peter 2:13–17)? Male rule and mutual submission are not easily reconciled.[33]

An even bigger problem is created by normalizing what Paul has to say about Eve. If we take as universally applicable Paul's statement that it was Eve, and not Adam, who was deceived and became a transgressor (1 Tim. 2:14), then we are faced with a theological conundrum. For elsewhere in Paul's writings, he is quite clear that it was Adam's transgression (not Eve's) that brought sin, death, and condemnation to all (e.g., Rom. 5:12–19). It is a theologically crucial point: For "just as *one* man's [Adam's] trespass led to condemnation for all," so it is that "*one* man's [Christ's] act of righteousness leads to justification and life for all" (Rom. 5:18 NRSV).

### KEY INTERPRETIVE ISSUES

There are still a number of interpretive issues with which we have to deal. The major one is: If Paul is targeting a behavioral problem on the part of women, what is it? Is it women teaching in a domineering fashion (NEB)? Or is it women teaching in an authoritative manner (NIV)?

Our first clue is Paul's command that women learn "quietly" (*en hēsychia*, v. 11) and be "quiet" (*einai en hēsychia*, v. 12; *Phillips,* NEB, REB, NLT, NASB). This suggests the women (like the men) were doing just the opposite. The men were praying in an angry and contentious way; the women were learning (and teaching?) in a less than calm and peaceful manner. Since Paul targets women who teach men (v. 12) and uses the example of Adam and Eve as a corrective, it would be a fair assumption that there was something of a battle of the sexes going on in the congregation.

Some have opted to translate the Greek term *(hēsychia)* as "silent," in which case Paul would be prohibiting women from speaking in a congregational setting. Women are to learn "in silence" and "be silent" (KJV, NKJV, RSV, NRSV, TEV, CEV, NIV, JB; cf. "keep quiet" TEV). This is problematic on a number of grounds. For one, it makes no sense. Learning and silence are not very compatible ideas in the Greek educational arena (or American, for that matter). To learn *quietly* and to speak *calmly,* on the other hand, fit well first-century standards of propriety for women.

Also, Paul does not use the Greek term in this way elsewhere. When he has absence of speech in mind, the word he chooses is *sigaō* (Rom. 16:25; 1 Cor. 14:28, 30, 34). When he means "at rest" or "at peace," he uses *hēsychia* (and its cognate forms; 1 Thess. 4:11; 2 Thess. 3:12; 1 Tim. 2:2). In fact, the adjective *hēsychion* appears nine verses earlier with this very sense: "I urge . . . that requests, prayers, intercession and thanksgiving be made . . . for kings and all those in authority, that we may live peaceful and *quiet* lives in all godliness and holiness" (1 Tim. 2:2 italics added).[34] This makes any other usage in verses 11–12 doubly problematic.

Women are not merely to learn quietly but also to learn "in full submission" (1 Tim. 2:11). What does this mean? The verb *to submit* *(hypotassō)* is one we have encountered a number of times in the New Testament (Eph. 5:21–22; Col. 3:18; Titus 2:4–5; 1 Peter 3:1). It is to be distinguished from the verb *to obey.* Submission is a voluntary act of deferring to the wishes of an equal. Obedience is following the wishes of a superior (see chapter 2, p. 118). We should also note that just as "in quiet" *(en hēsychia)* is another way of saying "quietly," so "in submission" *(en hypotagē)* is another way of saying "submissively." Both phrases describe *how* women are to learn.

To what or to whom are women called to submit? Some take submission to a husband as a given, but on what grounds? "Let a woman learn" (1 Tim. 2:11 NRSV) does not suggest anything of the sort, yet it is so often assumed to be the case. (Perhaps that says more about us than about Paul.) Better possibilities include submission to: (1) the teachers of the church, (2) church rules, (3) those in leadership, (4) oneself, and (5) the gospel. Of these five, submission to a teacher suits a learning context quite well. An even better option is that of self-control. We ran across this use in 1 Corinthians 14:32 (and perhaps in 14:34). It also fits with the calm, submissive spirit that was a necessary prerequisite for learning back then.[35]

If Paul had ended at this point, it is doubtful many feathers would have been ruffled down through the centuries. Yet move on he does—and perhaps it is more of a leap (or so it appears in many of our English translations). It is one thing to command that women learn in a quiet and self-controlled fashion and quite another not to permit women to teach when men are present in the congregation. Or is there another meaning to be found?

Whatever meaning we give to 1 Timothy 2:12, it is important to note that Paul introduces verse 12 as a point of contrast with verse 11. The initial *de* ("but") makes this quite clear. "Let a woman learn in a quiet and submissive fashion *but* do not let her teach."

There are a number of decisions to make in unpacking verse 12. The first one is whether Paul is presenting a temporary restriction ("I am not permitting at this time") or a universal prohibition ("I do not permit at any time"). For the record it must be said that when Paul does give a universal dictum, he does not do it in this way. A present tense indicative verb is simply not suited for this purpose. The future indicative ("I shall not permit"), the present imperative ("stop permitting"), or the aorist subjunctive ("do not start permitting") are the ways to express a prohibition in Greek.

The verb itself would be a rather surprising choice for a decree. One expects "I command," rather than "I permit not." Also problematic is the fact that the verb *to permit* is not used this way in biblical Greek (e.g., "And he [the king] permitted it to be so done," Esther 9:14; cf. Job

32:14; 1 Macc. 15:6; 4 Macc. 4:17–18; 5:26). All in all, "I am not permitting [at this time]" fits Greek and Pauline usage the best.

The exact wording of Paul's restriction needs to be looked at carefully. In some translations there are actually two prohibitions (instead of
one). A woman is not permitted to teach, and she is not permitted to
have authority over (or to dominate) a man. This, however, does not
accurately render the *neither (ouk)/nor (oude)* construction (a single coherent idea in Greek). It also does not fit with Paul's instruction that the
older women are to teach and train the younger women of the congregation in Crete (Titus 2:3–5). Perhaps a better rendering would be, "I
am not permitting a woman to teach-or-tell a man what to do."

What kind of teaching is Paul prohibiting at this point? Although some
are quick to think in terms of a teaching office or a position of authority in the church hierarchy, we must resist reading our way of doing things
back into the practice of the early church. Teaching in the New Testament era was an activity, not an office (Matt. 28:19–20). It was a gift,
not a position of authority (Rom. 12:7; 1 Cor. 12:28; 14:26; Eph. 4:11;
see pp. 39–40). We must also resist reading early church practice in light
of second-century developments. Teaching in the New Testament period
was something every believer was called to do (not merely church leaders; Col. 3:16; Heb. 5:12).

Also to be avoided is the idea that authority resides in the act of teaching or in the person who teaches. Authority resides in the deposit of
truth—the "truths of the faith" (1 Tim. 3:9; 4:6), "the faith" (1 Tim.
4:1; 5:8; 6:10, 12, 21), "the trust" (1 Tim. 6:20 AT)—that Jesus passed
along to his disciples and that they in turn passed on to their disciples
(2 Tim. 2:2). The Greek term for *authority (exousia)* is simply not used
of either local church leadership or the activity of teaching (see pp.
134–38). The prerogative to exercise authority is Christ's. Our job is to
make disciples, through baptizing and teaching (Matt. 28:18–20).

Then too, teaching is subject to evaluation just like any other ministry of the church. This is why Paul instructs Timothy to publicly rebuke
(1 Tim. 5:20) any and all who depart from "the sound instruction of
our Lord Jesus Christ" (1 Tim. 6:3).

Some have argued that the term *teaching* takes on the more official
sense of *doctrine* in 1 Timothy and that teaching doctrine is something
women cannot do. Once again, though, we want to be careful not to
read more into the text than is permissible. *Doctrine* as a system of thought
is alien to 1 Timothy. While Paul urges Timothy to "command and teach
these things" (1 Tim. 4:11; see also 6:2), the "things" are not doctrines;
they include matters like avoiding "godless myths and old wives' tales"

(4:7), godly training (4:7–8), God as "the Savior of all" (4:9–10), and slaves treating their masters with full respect (6:1–2)—hardly what we would call *doctrine* today. But then perhaps that is where we have gotten off the track. Although some translations have "sound doctrine," the phrase is actually "sound teaching" (*hygiainousē didaskalia,* 1:10; 4:6 NRSV; "sound instruction," 6:3; "our teaching," 6:1; cf. 2 Tim. 4:3; Titus 1:9; 2:1). This puts a different spin on it for the modern ear.

So, is Paul forbidding women to teach in a congregational setting (i.e., where men would be present)? Putting it this way has its difficulties, for women are most certainly affirmed elsewhere as teachers. Teaching was part of what a prophet did. To prophesy is to speak "words to instruct" (*katēchēsō;* 1 Cor. 14:19). "You can all prophesy in turn," Paul says to the Corinthians, "so that everyone may be instructed and encouraged" (1 Cor. 14:31). Since there were women prophets in the Corinthian church (1 Cor. 11:5), instruction was most definitely part of what these women did.

Could these women have prophesied only in private settings (e.g., a small group Bible study)? Not according to Paul. Prophecy was a gift that was appropriately exercised in a congregational setting. "If the whole church comes together and everyone . . . is prophesying," an outsider will be convicted of sin and "fall down and worship God" (1 Cor. 14:23–25). Paul also assumes that when believers gather corporately, "everyone has a hymn, *a teaching,* a revelation, a tongue, or an interpretation" (1 Cor. 14:26 AT italics added). There is no gender distinction here. Women can bring "a teaching" to the congregation just as readily as men.

It is sometimes said that the prophetic role was not an authoritative one, whereas teaching was, but if any distinction is to be made, it would be prophecy that is authoritative. *Prophet* always precedes *teacher* in the New Testament lists of gifts and leadership roles. The leadership at the church of Antioch consisted of prophets and teachers (Acts 13:1–3). Prophecy is second only to apostleship in Paul's three lists of gifts (Rom. 12:6–8; 1 Cor. 12:28; Eph. 4:11), and it is on the foundation of the apostles and the prophets (not the teachers) that Christ's church is built (Eph. 2:20).[36]

It has long been recognized that the key phrase in 1 Timothy 2:12 is *oude authentein andros* (variously translated "nor to dominate a man" or "not to have authority over a man"). To unpack its meaning, two questions must be answered. First, what is the sense of *authentein?* Does it have the positive meaning that many translators give it ("to exercise authority")? Or is it basically a negative term ("to domineer," "to hold sway") as an increasing number of New Testament scholars say? A second, equally important question is the function of the *neither/nor (ouk/oude)* construction. In general, it serves to define a single, coherent idea, but the relationship of the two main verbal ideas still needs to be clarified.

So what about *authentein?* It cannot be emphasized enough that Paul picks a term that is found nowhere else in the New Testament and only twice in the entire Greek Bible. Even then, it is not the verb (as in 1 Tim. 2:12) but the noun that appears—and the meaning of the noun does not even come close to something reasonable for our passage (Wisdom of Solomon 12:6, "parents who *murder [authentas]* helpless lives"; 3 Macc. 2:29, "former limited *status [authentia]*"). This alone should give us pause. As Philip Payne rightly notes, it is precarious to deny anything to women on the basis of the uncertain meaning of a verb that occurs nowhere else in the Bible.[37] It is even more precarious to assume the meaning is "to have authority." If Paul had wanted to speak of the ordinary exercise of authority, he could have picked any number of words—the most common one being *exousia/exousiazō.*[38] Since he did not, we must ask why he did not. There has to be something about the term *authentein* that particularly fits the Ephesian situation.

It is important to be very clear on what the verb *authentein* can and cannot mean (i.e., to determine its lexical range). In the second century B.C. to A.D. first century, occurrences of the noun are common enough but the verb is quite rare. The predominant usage up to the second century A.D. is to commit a crime or act of violence (e.g., murder, suicide, sacrilege). For example, in the first century B.C. historians Diodorus (robbing a sacred shrine, 16.61.1) and Polybius (the massacre at Maronea, 22.14.2–3) used it of those who perpetrate a foul deed. Beyond this, uses include: (1) to take matters into one's own hands, (2) to exercise mastery over, and (3) to hold absolute sway or full power over someone or something (LSJ 275).[39] For instance, one of the Berlin papyri has, "I *had my way* with him and he agreed to provide Calatytis the boatman with the full payment within the hour" (BGU 1208 italics added). The first century B.C. rhetorician Philodemus speaks of certain orators "who fight with *powerful* rulers" (*Rhetorica* II Fragmenta Libri [V] fr. IV line 14 italics added), and second-century astronomists talk about the "*dominance* of Saturn over Mercury and the moon" (e.g., Ptolemy *Tetrabiblos* 3.13 [#157] italics added).[40]

The one meaning that does not seem to be in evidence during this period is the simple exercise of authority.[41] So that even if we opt for the meaning "to have authority over," it must be taken in the sense of holding sway or mastery over another (compare "autocrat," "master" in Moulton-Milligan's *The Vocabulary of the Greek New Testament* 91). This is supported by the grammar of the verse. If Paul had the exercise of authority in mind, he would have put it first, followed by *teaching* as a specific example ("I am permitting a woman neither to exercise authority over nor to teach a man"). The word order "to teach" *(authentein)* makes the latter word dependent on the former, as does the *neither/nor* construction (see below).

So what does *authentein* mean in 1 Timothy 2:12? This is difficult to determine with certainty. Suggestions include: (1) "to originate or initiate an action," (2) "to instigate violence," (3) "to wield influence," and (4) "to hold sway over or be dominant." Option 2 is the most widely found meaning of this word group, but it does not fit the context terribly well ("I am not permitting a woman to teach with murderous intent"). Option 1 has the same difficulty ("women who seek to be first in everything"). Options 3 and 4 are fairly close. Of the two, "to dominate" or "to have one's way" seems to provide the better fit. The Vulgate *(dominari in virum* "to dominate over a man") and early Latin versions seemed to think so too.

Where do we go from here? In my opinion, not enough attention has been paid to the *neither/nor (ouk/oude)* construction of this verse. What many have overlooked is that we are dealing with a poetic device. In biblical Greek (and Hebrew) *neither/nor* sets in parallel two or more natural groupings of words, phrases, or clauses. "He [the Lord] who watches over Israel will neither slumber nor sleep" (Ps. 121:4) is a familiar example.

The *neither/nor* construction is so frequently found in Scripture that it is easy to overlook its significance. This has been the case especially with 1 Timothy 2:12. In part, this is because we tend to use *neither/nor* differently today. In English *neither* and *nor* are coordinating conjunctions that connect sentence elements of equal *grammatical* rank. For example, if I want to be grammatically proper in punishing my daughter, I will say, "You can neither play with a friend nor watch television." Two unrelated activities are thereby prohibited. In biblical Greek, however, *neither/nor* connects similar or related ideas—like *slumber* and *sleep* in Psalm 121.[42]

A study of *neither/nor* constructions in the New Testament shows it serves to pair or group in one of the following ways:

| | |
|---|---|
| to pair synonyms | neither despised nor scorned (Gal. 4:14) |
| to pair antonyms | neither Jew nor Greek, neither slave nor free (Gal. 3:28) |
| to pair closely related ideas | neither of the night nor of the dark (1 Thess. 5:5) |

| | |
|---|---|
| to define a related purpose or a goal | where thieves neither break in nor steal (i.e., break in to steal, Matt. 6:20) |
| to move from the general to the particular | wisdom neither of this age nor of the rulers of this age (1 Cor. 2:6) |
| to define a natural progression of related ideas | they neither sow, nor reap, nor gather into barns (Matt. 6:26)[43] |

Of the options listed above, it is obvious that *teach* and *dominate* are not synonyms or antonyms. Nor do they form a natural progression of related ideas ("first teach, then dominate"). If *authentein* did mean "to exercise authority," we might have closely related ideas, but the word order would need to be "to exercise authority" (general) followed by "to teach" (particular). Using the pair to define a purpose or goal actually provides an admirable fit: "I do not permit a woman to teach in order to gain mastery over a man," or "I do not permit a woman to teach with a view to dominating a man."[44] It also results in a good point of contrast with the second half of verse 12: "I do not permit a woman to teach a man in a dominating way but to have a quiet demeanor" (literally, "to be in calmness").

Paul would then be restricting not teaching per se but teaching that tries to get the upper hand. The women at Ephesus (perhaps encouraged by the false teachers) were trying to gain the advantage over the men in the congregation by teaching in a dictatorial fashion. The men in response became angry and disputed what they were doing. This interpretation fits well the broader context of 1 Timothy 2:8–15, where Paul aims to correct inappropriate behavior on the part of both men and women. The men are not forbidden to pray but are commanded to pray in a noncontentious way (v. 8). The women are not forbidden to learn but commanded to learn in a noncontentious way (i.e., in a quiet and submissive fashion, v. 11) and to teach in a nondictatorial way (i.e., in a gentle fashion).

While this is a reasonable reconstruction, it still leaves us with an important question: Why were the Ephesian women doing this? One explanation is that they were influenced by the cult of Artemis, where the female was exalted and considered superior to the male. The importance of this cult to the citizens of Ephesus in Paul's day is evident in their two-hour-long chant "Great is Artemis of the Ephesians" (Acts 19:34). Artemis, it was believed, was the child of Zeus and Leto. Because of the severity of her mother's labor, she herself never married. Instead she turned to a male consort for company. This made Artemis and all her female adherents superior to men.[45] Today, we might liken her to the queen bee with her male attendants.

An Artemis influence would certainly explain Paul's correctives in 1 Timothy 2:13–14. While some may have believed Artemis appeared first and then her male consort, the true story was just the opposite. Adam was formed first, then Eve (v. 13), and on top of that, Eve was deceived (v. 14)—hardly a basis on which to claim superiority.

It would also explain Paul's statement that "women will be kept safe through childbirth" (1 Tim. 2:15 AT), for Artemis was the protector of women. Women turned to her for safe travel through the childbearing process.[46] Verse 15 refocuses this belief in the proper Christian direction. Yes, women can be confident of divine protection, but only "if they remain in faith, love and holiness with propriety" (AT).

Alternately, some think Paul's comments are best understood against the background of a heresy that became full-blown in the second century (usually called incipient- or proto-Gnosticism). In this system of thought, women were elevated as the favored instruments of revelation. The Genesis 2 narrative was reread in light of female superiority. Eve (not Adam) was the one who was created first and then sent as an instructor to raise up Adam in whom there was no soul. Her progeny, in turn, became the source of special revelation to men from that point on.[47]

Can we get any more clarity on verses 13–14 of 1 Timothy 2? The opening *for* (*gar*) signals that Paul at last is going to provide some explanation for his previous instructions. But how much is included? Some see verses 13–14 as Paul's explanation for the prohibition regarding women teachers in the immediately preceding verse. We would be better helped, however, by going back to verse 8, for it is here that Paul begins to tackle male-female problems at Ephesus: "I want *men* to pray without anger and disputing. . . . Likewise [I want] *women* [to pray] without ostentation . . . to learn in a calm fashion and to teach *men* in a non-dictatorial manner. For *Adam* was created first, then *Eve*" (1 Tim. 2:8–15 AT italics added).

Some take *for* as causal (rather than as explanatory) and see it as introducing a creation order dictum. Women must not teach men *because* men in the created order are first and women by nature are prone to deception. This is problematic on a number of grounds. For one, the principal causal conjunction is *hoti,* not *gar* (Blass, Debrunner, Funk, *A Greek Grammar of the New Testament,* §456). Paul could be using *gar* in this way, but there is nothing in the context that would support it. In fact, verse 15 is against it. (It is nonsense to say women must not teach men *because* Eve was deceived but will be saved through childbearing.) Second, although some are quick to assume a creation and fall ordering in verses 13–14, virtually all stop short of including "women will be saved [or kept safe] through childbearing" (v. 15). To do so, though, is to lack hermeneutical integrity. Either all three statements are normative or all three are not. Finally, to see verses 13–14 as normative is to fly in the face of clear biblical teaching elsewhere in Scripture (see below).

Yet, by noting that Adam was first in the process of creation, is Paul not saying something about male superiority or leadership? We want to be careful not to import assumptions about Ephesians 5:23–24 (the husband as "head" of the wife; see chapter 2, pp. 121–26), and we especially do not want to read our culture back into the text. Today we tend to think of *first* as the best or the winner. Being first is having the advantage, the edge. To Jesus' way of thinking, however, to be first is to be last and the servant of all (Matt. 19:30; 20:27). This, ultimately, is what must form our thinking—not our competitive Western mind-set.

Also, the animals preceded Adam in creation, yet we hardly give them the advantage or the lead. John the Baptist came before Jesus, yet we scarcely think of him as Jesus' superior. Paul himself uses *first (prōtos)/then (eita)* language without any idea of superiority or personal advantage. One of the clearest examples is 1 Thessalonians 4:16–17. "The dead," Paul states, "will rise first *[prōton]* and then *[epeita]* we who are still alive will be caught up with them in the clouds" (AT). Here, *first/then* defines temporal advantage without any implication of superiority or authority. A passage that is closer to home is 1 Timothy 3:10, in which Paul states that deacons must be tested "first" *(prōton)* and "then" *(eita)* let them serve. So *first/then* language need do no more than define a sequence of events or ideas. In fact, nowhere in the New Testament does it mean anything more than this.[48]

What about Eve's seniority in transgression? "And Adam was not the one deceived; it was the woman who was deceived and became a transgressor" (1 Tim. 2:14 AT). Do we have something of a universal truth stated in verse 14? Is Paul affirming that women by nature incline toward deception?[49] Although some have said so, this conflicts with scriptural teaching elsewhere. If women were so inclined, Paul would not instruct older women to teach and train the younger ones (Titus 2:3–4). Also, while Paul does assert that all human beings without exception sin, at no time does he suggest women are more susceptible to sin's deceiving activity than men (e.g., Rom. 3:9–20). In fact, it was two men (not women) who were expelled from the Ephesian community for false teaching that stemmed from personal deception (1 Tim. 1:19–20).

Could it be, though, that Paul is using Eve as an example of what can go wrong when women usurp the leadership role of men?[50] To say this, however, is to discount the facts. Eve was not deceived by the serpent into taking the lead in the marital relationship. She was deceived into disobeying a command of God (not to eat the fruit from the tree of the knowledge of good and evil). She listened to the voice of false teaching and was deceived by it.

The language of deception calls to mind the activities of the false teachers at Ephesus. If the women were being encouraged to assume the role of teacher over men as the superior sex, this would go a long way toward explaining verses 13–14. The relationship between the sexes was not intended to be one of female domination and male subordination, but neither was it intended to be one of male domination and female subordination. Such thinking is endemic to a fallen creation order (Gen. 3:16). It is not how God originally intended the sexes to relate ("corresponding to him in every way," Gen. 2:18 [AT]; "bone of my bones," Gen. 2:23–24).

The trap is the deceptive allure of false teaching—a trap Paul places squarely on Satan's shoulders. What happened to Eve is the warning; gender has nothing to do with it. Paul used a similar warning with the Corinthian congregation. "I am afraid," he warned, "that just as Eve was deceived by the serpent's cunning, your minds may somehow be led astray from your sincere and pure devotion to Christ" (2 Cor. 11:3). In Corinth's case, the false teaching involved preaching a Jesus, Spirit, and gospel different from that which Paul had preached (2 Cor. 11:4–5). In Ephesus's case, the false teaching encouraged women to abandon their marital and domestic roles (1 Tim. 4:3; 5:14; cf. 2:15) and to spurn a collegial relationship with their sexual counterparts (1 Tim. 2:11–14). Some, in fact, had "already turned away to follow Satan" (1 Tim. 5:15).

One can surmise from the situation at both Corinth and Ephesus that women had difficulty handling their newly found freedom in Christ and sometimes expressed this freedom in inappropriate ways. At Corinth their eagerness to learn resulted in a disruption of the orderly flow of worship. At Ephesus their freedom to learn and to teach led them to do so in a contentious and dictatorial fashion. Both abuses are understandable given the primarily domestic and lifelong subordinate roles women played in the culture of that day, but both need correcting, whether it be in Paul's day or in ours. The relationship of the sexes is to be one of mutual submission. Paul's command, "Submit to one another out of reverence for Christ" (Eph. 5:21), makes this abundantly clear.

# *Epilogue*

T hree biblical truths can be gleaned from our study. The first truth is that God gifts women in exactly the same ways he gifts men. Nowhere in the New Testament are gifts restricted to a particular gender. Women are affirmed as prophets, teachers, deacons, and worship leaders. They are commended for their faithfulness and excellence as apostles, evangelists, and patrons. They are praised as *co*workers, *co*prisoners, and *co*laborers in the gospel.

The second truth is that God intended the male-female relationship to be equal and mutual. "Bone of my bones," "flesh of my flesh," "woman," "in correspondence to" *(kĕnegdô)* are phrases that drive this truth home (Gen. 2:18, 23). The creation order of male and female is egalitarian. This comes through loud and clear in the accounts of Genesis 1–2. Equality is the key note—an equal task in society *(dominion),* an equal role with regard to family *(fruitful),* equally created in God's image, and spiritual equals in God's sight.

The third truth is that in the church "there is not . . . male and female" (Gal. 3:28 AT). Church roles in the New Testament are nowhere defined on the basis of gender. This is because the concept of the local church in the New Testament is an organic one, not a hierarchical one. As Paul says, it is only as each one does his or her part that "the whole body, joined and held together by every supporting ligament, grows and builds itself up in love" (Eph. 4:16). The governing principle of relationships in the local church is one of mutual submission (not top-down management). We are called to submit ourselves to one another out of reverence for Christ (Eph. 5:21). Indeed, we are called to submit ourselves for the Lord's sake "to every human creature" ( *pasē anthrōpinē ktisei;* 1 Peter 2:13).

Why then has the evangelical church been so hesitant to affirm women in leadership positions? Some of it is sheer prejudice. It is prejudged that women cannot serve in these roles, and when a woman's name is found, every effort is made to explain it away. Phoebe was merely a "servant" (Rom. 16:1 KJV, NIV, TEV) not a "deacon" (*Phillips,* RSV; cf. "holds office" NEB). She was a "good friend" (Rom. 16:2 NEB, TEV), not a "benefactor" (NRSV). Syntyche and Euodia were a "help" (Phil. 4:2–3 JB) to Paul in the evangelistic labors, not colaborers in the gospel (cf. TEV, RSV). It was a man named *Junias,* not a woman named *Junia,* who was outstanding among the apostles (Rom. 16:7).

Some of it is a simple misconception regarding biblical leadership. As soon as one thinks of leadership in terms of being *first* and *in authority over,* this easily leads to notions of hierarchy and dominance (at least to our twenty-first-century mind-set). Yet this is truly the language of secular society and not that of the redeemed community. The New Testament language of local church leadership is the language of pastoral care—guide, shepherd, overseer, servant—and the way of leadership is by example and hard work.

Although *to govern* and *bear rule* may be a familiar (and even comfortable) model of leadership today, it is not biblical. One need only look at Jesus to see this. The disciples followed Jesus not because he ruled them well but because he pastored them well. He is the Good Shepherd who knows each sheep by name and willingly lays down his life for them (John 10:2–3, 11, 14–15; 1 Peter 2:25; 5:4). This model of leadership is echoed in both Peter and Paul. Leaders are those who "keep watch over the flock" and "shepherd God's church" (Acts 20:28–35 AT). Leaders are "eager to serve; not lording it over those entrusted to them by the Holy Spirit, but being examples to the flock" (1 Peter 5:2–3 AT).

Questions of authority and offices are far more complex now than they were in the A.D. first century because of the top-down way churches tend to structure themselves. The early church, by contrast, was a bottom-up, charismatic organization. There were no offices as we know them today. When the church gathered in worship it was for mutual edification through the sharing of spiritual gifts. "When you come together," Paul tells the Corinthian church, "everyone has a hymn, or a word of instruction, a revelation, a tongue or an interpretation. All of these must be done for the strengthening of the church" (1 Cor. 14:26). To *teach* in the congregational context, then, was to offer a *word of knowledge* (1 Cor. 12:8; 14:26), not to hold an office or exercise governing authority. Respect and submission were earned by hard work, tender loving care, and an exemplary life (1 Cor. 16:16; Heb. 13:17; cf. Rom. 16:6, 12). They were not mandated by the holding of an office but acquired through a job well done.

The title of Gretchen Gaebelein Hull's 1987 book sums it up well: *Equal to Serve.*[1] Ministry and leadership in the New Testament are a cooperative venture, whose success depends on the gifting and empowerment of women and men committed to serving Christ and his church. As we move into the twenty-first century, may we labor faithfully at providing men and women every possible avenue to function as the partners and coworkers God created them to be.

# Notes

**Chapter 1:** *In Which Ministries Can Women Be Involved?*

1. Some even believe that certain careers are not options for women. Any job that would require a woman to dictate to a man is problematic. Such jobs would include a school principal, college teacher, bus driver, bookstore manager, staff doctor, judge, lawyer, police officer, legislator, counselor, and television newscaster. See, for example, J. Piper and W. Grudem, eds., *Recovering Biblical Manhood and Womanhood* (Wheaton: Crossway Books, 1991), 50.

2. *Acts of Synod.* Grand Rapids: Christian Reformed Church in North America, 1994 and 1995.

3. One must be careful not to depend too heavily on the rabbis for information about women's roles. Rabbinic materials, on the whole, reflect a conservative theologian's outlook toward women rather than the actual practices of women. It is synagogue records, inscriptions, burial epitaphs, and art that bring us close to the real-life situation of Jewish women.

4. While it was the obligation of all to celebrate the three annual feasts (Exod. 23:14; Deut. 16:13–15), it was only the duty of males to appear before the Lord at the central sanctuary (Exod. 23:17; 34:23; Deut. 16:16). This was undoubtedly because domestic responsibilities made such a trip unrealistic for many women—especially those with young children. Even so, it was not uncommon for the entire family to make the trip (e.g., 1 Sam. 1:1–8; Luke 2:41–44).

5. There is no Mosaic law or any other Old Testament passage that excludes women as legal witnesses in a court of law. This suggests that the practice was a first-century development.

6. For example, *m. Ber.* 3.3 states, "women, slaves, and minors are exempt from reciting the Shema and from wearing phylacteries, but they are not exempt from saying the Tefillah, from the law of the Mezuzah or from saying the Benediction after meal."

7. For a discussion of the impact of the women's liberation movement on Judaism, see B. H. Nathanson, "Reflections on the Silent Woman of Ancient Judaism and Her Pagan Roman Counterpart," in *The Listening Heart: Essays in Wisdom and the Psalms in Honor of Roland E. Murphy,* ed. K. Hoglund et al. (Sheffield, England: JSOT Press, 1987), 259–60.

8. According to Rabbi Avira, it was as a reward to the righteous women of that generation that the Israelites were redeemed from Egypt (*b. Sota* 11b).

9. See, for example, Colin Brown, "Woman," in *New International Dictionary of New Testament Theology,* ed. Colin Brown, 3 vols. (Grand Rapids: Zondervan, 1975–1978), 3:1058; Albrecht Oepke, "γυνή," in *Theological Dictionary of the New Testament,* ed. Gerhard Kittel, Gerhard Friedrich, and Geoffrey W. Bromiley, trans. Geoffrey W. Bromiley, 10 vols. (Grand Rapids: Eerdmans, 1964–1976), 1:782.

10. Safrai, Cohen, and Brooten include helpful discussions. One must be careful not to read later liturgical practices back into the biblical time period. H. Safrai, "Women and the Ancient Synagogue," in *Daughters of the King,* ed. Grossmann (New York: Simon and Schuster, 1974), 41; S. J. D. Cohen, "The Women in the Synagogues of Antiquity," *Conservative Judaism* 34 (1980): 25; and Bernadette J. Brooten, *Women Leaders in the Ancient Synagogue,* Brown Judaic Studies 36 (Chico, Calif.: Scholars Press, 1982), 137–38.

11. The Beruriah tradition includes a number of what are probably late Babylonian elaborations. For example, it is unlikely that Beruriah was the wife of the renowned Rabbi Meir. It is also unlikely that she gained her knowledge of the Torah through a formal rabbinic education. For further discussion, see D. Goodblat, "The Beruriah Traditions," in *Persons and Institutions,* ed. W. S. Green (Missoula, Mont.: Scholars Press, 1977), 207–35.

12. Synagogue inscriptions dating from the first century B.C. through the A.D. sixth century show that donors throughout the Roman Empire included both women and men. The appendix in Brooten, *Women Leaders,* 157–65, cites the texts of these inscriptions.

13. For a more in-depth treatment, see D. Irvin, "The Ministry of Women in the Early Church: The Archaeological Evidence," *Duke Divinity School Review* 45 (1980): 78.

14. For a discussion of female heads of synagogues, see Brooten, *Women Leaders,* 35–39; Randall Chestnutt, "Jewish Women in the Greco-Roman Era," in *Essays on Women in Earliest Christianity,* vol. 1, ed. Carroll Osborne (Joplin, Miss.: College Press, 1993), 124; Cohen, "Women in the Synagogue," 25; Irvin, "Ministry of Women," 76–86.

15. For an overview of the responsibilities of the synagogue ruler, see Kevin Giles, *Patterns of Ministry among the First Christians* (Melbourne: Collin Dove, 1989), 76; and Emil Schrer, *The History of the Jewish People in the Age of Jesus Christ,* rev. English ed. (Edinburgh: T. & T. Clark, 1979), 2:433–39.

The synagogue ruler was assisted by an attendant *(hypēretēs)* who looked after the details of the service, such as bringing out the Scriptures, handing the scroll to the assigned reader, and replacing the Scriptures. It was this individual who handed Jesus the scroll of the prophet Isaiah in his hometown synagogue (Luke 4:20).

16. Compare "Tomb of Faustina the elder. Shalom" *(CII* 597); "Sophia of Gortyn, elder and head of the synagogue of Kisamos" *(CII* 731c); "Tomb of Rebeka, the elder, who has fallen asleep" *(CII* 692); "Tomb of Beronikene, elder and daughter of Ioses" *(CII* 581); "Tomb of Mannine, elder, daughter of Longinus, father, granddaughter of Faustinus, father, 38 years" *(CII* 590); "Tomb of Makaria (or 'the blessed') Mazauzala, elder" (SEG 27 [1977] #1201); "Here lies Sara Ura, elder (or perhaps 'aged woman')" *(CII* 400); "[. . .] gerousiarch, lover of the commandments, and Eulogia, the elder, his wife" (Antonio Ferrua, "Antichita cristiane: le catacombe di Malta," *La Civilta cattolica* [1949] 505–515).

17. See Giles, *Patterns of Ministry,* 74–76; Schürer, *History of the Jewish People,* 3:87–107.

18. The connection of the priestess Marin with Leontopolis, Egypt, is also intriguing. Leontopolis was the home of the high priestly family that went into exile during the time of the Maccabees in the second century B.C (the Oniads). While there, permission was gained from Ptolemy VI to build a temple. It was here that the legitimate Zakokite high priesthood carried out its priestly functions for 230 years. For discussion, see F. F. Bruce, *Israel and the Nations* (Grand Rapids: Eerdmans), 157.

19. For further discussion, see Brooten, *Women Leaders,* 83–90.

20. "The Jewish community living in the colony of Ostia . . . gave it [a plot of land] to him [Gaius Julius Justus] at the request of Livius Dionysius, *father,* of [. . . .] us, *gerusiarch,* and of Antonius [archon-for-life?]" (early second century; *CII* 533). See Brooten's helpful treatment, ibid., 72.

21. For a good overview of upper-class women in first-century society, see Riet Van Bremen, "Women and Wealth," in *Images of Women in Antiquity,* ed. A. Cameron and A. Kuhrt (Detroit: Wayne State University Press, 1987), 225–37.

22. For further statistics, see S. K. Heyob, *The Cult of Isis among Women in the Greco-Roman World* (Leiden: Brill, 1973), 81–86. Archeological remains, particularly those from Pompeii, suggest a somewhat higher degree of female participation than inscriptions indicate. Ibid., 110.

23. For further discussion, see John Stambaugh and David Balch, *The New Testament in Its Social Environment* (Philadelphia: Westminster Press, 1986), 134; and V. Abrahamsen, "Women at Philippi: The Pagan and Christian Evidence," *JFSR* 3 (1987): 21–22.

24. See Ross Kraemer's helpful overview in *Her Share of the Blessings* (Oxford: Oxford University Press), 81.

25. From Ephesus alone, R. A. Kearsley identifies fifteen women who served as imperial high priest from the first through the third centuries in "Asiarchs, Archiereis, and the Archiereiai of Asia," *Greek, Roman and Byzantine Studies* 27 (1986): 186–87.

26. See Van Bremen's helpful overview, "Women and Wealth," 225.

27. For further discussion, see Sue Blundell, *Women in Ancient Greece* (Cambridge: Harvard University Press, 1995), 161.

28. See Sarah Pomeroy's more detailed discussion, *Goddesses, Whores, Wives, and Slaves: Women in Classical Antiquity* (New York: Schocken, 1995), 210–14.

29. For further discussion, see Eva Cantarella, *Pandora's Daughters: The Role and Status of Women in Greek and Roman Antiquity,* trans. M. B. Fant (Baltimore: Johns Hopkins University Press, 1967), 151.

30. For more detail, see Pomeroy, *Goddesses,* 217–26; and Cantarella, *Pandora's Daughters,* 155–58.

31. Even in classical Athens, the position of priestess was the one public office that could be held by a woman.

32. See Pomeroy, *Goddesses,* 211–12.

33. *Kopiaō* literally refers to a striking or beating. It was used of labor that was rigorous and exhausting. In Paul's letters it describes both his trade as a worker of goats-hair cloth (1 Cor. 4:12; 1 Thess. 2:9; 2 Thess. 3:8) and his missionary labors (1 Cor. 15:10; 2 Cor. 6:5; 10:15; 11:27; Gal. 4:11; Col. 1:29; 1 Thess. 3:5; 1 Tim. 4:10)—although the two are connected, since he plied a trade so as not to be a financial burden on his churches (2 Thess. 3:8).

34. The only roles lacking female names are *overseer* and *elder,* but then specific men are not singled out in these capacities either.

35. See Wayne Meeks's section on women in the Greco-Roman city in *The First Urban Christians* (New Haven: Yale University Press, 1983), 23–25.

36. For the statistics, see Wendy Cotter's article, "Women's Authority Roles in Paul's Churches: Countercultural or Conventional," in *Novum Testamentum* 36 (1994): 364 n. 42.

37. For further discussion, see Meeks, *First Urban Christians,* 76.

38. See LSJ s.v.

39. See Everett Ferguson's concise treatment in *Backgrounds of Early Christianity* (Grand Rapids: Eerdmans, 1987), 45.

40. See note 42 below.

41. For discussion of the scope and function of the apostolate, see Rudolf Schnack-enburg, "Apostles Before and During Paul's Time," in *Apostolic History and the Gospel: Essays Presented to F .F. Bruce,* ed. W. W. Gasque and R. P. Martin (Grand Rapids: Eerd-mans, 1970), 287–303; C. K. Barrett, "*Shaliah* and Apostle," in *Donum Gentilicum,* ed. E. Bammel (Oxford: Clarendon, 1978), 88–102; Colin Brown, "Apostle," in *New International Dictionary,* ed. Brown, 1:126–37.

We do well to distinguish the gift of apostleship from the role of church delegate. The Greek term *apostolos* on occasion in the New Testament means "envoy" and is used of a local church representative. In 2 Corinthians 8:23, for example, Paul speaks of two "brothers" who represented their churches *(apostoloi ekklēsiōn)* in the delivery of the Jerusalem relief monies. And in Philippians 2:25 Paul talks about Epaphroditus as the Philippian church's representative *(hymōn apostolon)* in caring for Paul's needs. This is quite different from the absolute use of *apostle* to denote the gift and role of church planter (1 Cor. 12:28–29; Eph. 4:11).

42. The masculine accusative ending of *Iounias* is the same as the feminine accusative ending of *Iounia.* The sole difference is the accent. The contracted (or shortened) form would have a circumflex. The feminine form would have an acute accent. Ancient manuscripts typically did not contain accents, so the Greek technically can go either way. However, from the time accents were added to the text until the early decades of this century, Greek New Testaments printed the acute accent (feminine) and not the circumflex.

The reason for this is not hard to see. As John Thorley in a recent article states, the shortened form of *Junianus* would be *Junas,* not *Junias* ("Junia a Woman Apostle," *Novum Testamentum* 38 [1996]: 24–26). Moreover, while it is true that Greek nicknames were abbreviations of longer names, Latin nicknames were typically formed by lengthening the name, not shortening it—hence *Priscilla* for *Prisca* (Acts 18:2, 18, 26; cf. Rom. 16:3; 1 Cor. 16:19; 2 Tim. 4:19) or *Johnny* for *John* (to use a modern example).

It is only the United Bible Societies' (from 1966 on) and Nestle-Aland's (from 1960 on) editions of the Greek New Testament that have the circumflex. The explanation of the editors is revealing. The masculine circumflex was printed because some members of the UBS's editorial committee thought it unlikely that a woman would be among those called apostles. See Bruce Metzger, *A Textual Commentary on the Greek New Testament,* 2d ed. (Stuttgart: United Bible Societies, 1994), 475; Ray Schulz, "Romans 16:7: Junia or Junias?" *The Expositor Times* 89 (1987): 108–10.

Some concede the feminine gender of *Iounian* but read "esteemed *by* the apostles" or "outstanding *in* the sight of the apostles," instead of "among the apostles." Agency in Greek, however, is normally rendered by *hypo* plus the genitive, not *en* plus the dative. Then too, the notion of being considered outstanding by the apostles is one that is foreign to Paul's thinking.

In light of the overwhelming evidence for *Iounian* being feminine, J. D. G. Dunn's observation is worth noting: "The assumption that it *[Iounian]* must be male is a striking indictment of male presumption regarding the character and structure of earliest Christianity." J. D. G. Dunn, *Romans 9–16, Word Biblical Commentary* vol. 38B (Waco: Word, 1988), 894. See also S. Scott Bartchy, "Power, Submission, and Sexual Identity among the Early Christians," in *Essays on New Testament Christianity,* ed. R. C. Wetzel (Cincinnati: Standard, 1978, 50–53.

43. For a presentation and evaluation of the evidence, see R. Cervin, "A Note Regarding the Name 'Junia(s)' in Romans 16:7," *New Testament Studies* 40 (1994): 464–70; B. J. Brooten, "'Junia' . . . Outstanding among the Apostles (Romans 16:7)," in *Women Priests,* ed. L. Swidler and A. Swidler (New York: Paulist Press, 1977), 141–43; Lampe,

"*Iunia/Iunias: Sklavenherkunft im Kreise der vorpaulinischen Apostel (Röm* 16:7)," *Zeitschrift für die neutestamentliche Wissenschaft* 76 (1985): 132.

44. All the church fathers up to the twelfth century who quote Romans 16:7 have the name Junia (the majority) or Julia (a minority). See Schulz, "Junia or Junias?", 109.

45. Pastoring in the New Testament is inseparable from teaching. This is especially evident in Ephesians 4:11, where the two nouns *poimenas* and *didaskalous* have a single article and are conjoined by *kai.* This arrangement of the grammatical pieces serves to conceptually unite the two ideas and should be translated "pastor-teacher."

46. This is a point well made by Howard Marshall, "The Role of Women in the Church," in *The Role of Women,* ed. S. Lees (Downers Grove, Ill.: InterVarsity Press, 1984), 182.

47. For more details, see Walter Liefeld, "Women and Evangelism in the Early Church," *Missiology* 15 (1987): 297.

48. Although John's Gospel zeros in on Mary Magdalene, the larger group of women is clearly in the background. The plural *we* is to be noted: "They have taken the Lord out of the tomb, and we don't know where they have put him!" (John 20:2; cf. Matt. 28:8–10).

49. A word of explanation about letter carriers is needed here. There were no professional postal carriers in the first century. Letters got from one place to another by way of someone who was going in that direction or who was officially commissioned for the task. Paul's letter carriers were of the latter sort. One of the official letter carrier's responsibilities was to read the letter out loud and to answer any questions afterward that the listeners might have. Their credentials were hence vitally important. They meant the difference between the community's reception or rejection.

50. For further discussion, see A. Swidler, "Women Deacons: Some Historical Highlights," in *A New Phoebe: Perspectives on Roman Catholic Women and the Permanent Diaconate,* ed. Ratigan and A. Swidler (Kansas City: Sheed and Ward, 1990), 81; and E. S. Fitzgerald, "The Characteristics and Nature of the Order of the Deaconess," in *Women and the Priesthood,* ed. Hopko (Crestwood, N.Y.: St. Vladimir's Seminary Press, 1983), 78.

51. What the context does not support is a position like K. Romaniuk's, who thinks that 1 Timothy 3:11 is intended to show who a deacon should marry and what qualities a future wife should possess ("Was Phoebe in Romans 16:1 a Deaconess?" *Zeitschrift für die neutestament liche Wissenschaft* 81 [1990]: 132). For further discussion, see Daniel Arichea, "Who Was Phoebe? Translating *Diakonos* in Romans 16.1," *The Bible Translator* 39 (1988): 401–9.

52. Robert Lewis makes a somewhat similar suggestion in his article, "The 'Women' of 1 Timothy 3:11," *Bibliotheca Sacra* 136 (1979): 167–75.

53. There were women ordained to the diaconate in Italy and Gaul, but the numbers did not to match those in the Eastern churches. For further discussion, see P. Hünermann, "Conclusions Regarding the Female Deaconate," *Theological Studies* 36 (1975): 329.

54. We also possess fourth- through sixth-century inscriptions that name women deacons from a range of geographical locations. Two are from Jerusalem, two others are from Italy and Dalmatia, one is from the island of Melos, one is from Athens, and ten are from the Asia provinces of Phrygia, Cilicia, Caria, and Nevinne. See R. Gryson, *The Ministry of Women in the Early Church* (Collegeville, Minn.: Liturgical Press, 1976), 90–91; and D. R. MacDonald, "Virgins, Widows and Paul in Second Century Asia Minor," *Society of Biblical Literature Seminar Paper* 16 (Atlanta: Scholars Press, 1979): 181, n. 11.

55. Wendy Cotter accurately notes that women in the early centuries were able to take advantage of the greater social mobility to visit friends and set up networks for evangelism (Cotter, "Women's Authority Roles," 369).

56. There is a fair range of opinion on what these "broken pledges" constituted. Opinions include: (1) a vow of celibacy, (2) a pledge of faithfulness to their first husband, (3) a pledge not to marry a nonbeliever, and (4) a pledge to serve Christ as an "enrolled" widow. The first is by far the best fit in the context.

57. Paul includes a final qualification. The "enrolled" widow must also be at least sixty years of age. This was the age when sexual attraction was no longer considered to be a distraction and the pressure to marry no longer existed.

58. For further discussion, see B. Thurston, *The Widows: A Women's Ministry in the Early Church* (Minneapolis: Fortress Press, 1954).

59. The church's philanthropic work on behalf of widows was a natural outgrowth of Judaism. One of the ministries of the local synagogue was meeting the basic needs of the sojourner and the poor in their midst. The latter group would have included widows. See Bruce Winter, "Providentia for the Widows of 1 Tim. 5:3–16," *Tyndale Bulletin* 39 (1988): 31–32.

60. See Canon 59 of the *Canons of Hippolytus,* the *Didascalia Apostolorum,* and the *Apostolic Constitutions* 2.35, 3.3.

61. See F. Gillman's helpful article "The Ministry of Women in the Early Church," *New Theology Review* 6 (1993): 90.

62. While the variation could be stylistic, the key thing to note is that Luke is very precise throughout Acts about the order of names in ministry teams. For instance, when the missionary team is formed, commissioned, and sent off by the church at Antioch, the order of names is "Barnabas and Saul" (Acts 11:30; 12:25; 13:2–7). When Saul takes the lead in Cyprus's capital city, however, the order from that point on becomes "Paul and Barnabas" (Acts 13:9–12, 43; 14:11–12, 20; 15:2, 22, 35).

## Chapter 2: *What Roles Can Women Play in Society?*

1. For discussion, see Pat Gundry, "Why We're Here," in *Women, Authority and the Bible,* ed. Alvera Mickelsen (Downers Grove, Ill.: InterVarsity Press, 1986), 20–21.

2. Some state it even more strongly. For example, Robert Culver in his essay "A Traditional View" believes that women by nature (and not just as a result of the fall) are prone to deception (in *Women in Ministry: Four Views,* ed. Bonnidell Clouse and Robert Clouse [Downers Grove, Ill.: InterVarsity Press, 1989], 36). This would imply that God's creation of humankind as male and female was not, in fact, "very good" (Gen. 1:31).

3. See, for example, Wayne Grudem and John Piper, eds., *Recovering Biblical Manhood and Womanhood* (Wheaton: Crossway Books, 1991), 35–36.

4. See, for example, the affirmations of the "Danvers Statement" of the Council on Biblical Manhood and Womanhood (Wheaton, Ill.), n.d.

5. See the document "Men, Women and Biblical Equality" of Christians for Biblical Equality (St. Paul, Minn.), n.d.

6. Compare Josephus, who says women are inferior in every respect (*Against Apion* 2.24 §201).

7. For further discussion about Jewish attitudes toward women, see Lellia Cracco Ruggini, "Intolerance: Equal and Less in the Roman World," *Classical Philology* 82 (1987): 188; Mary Evans, *Women in the Bible* (Downers Grove, Ill.: InterVarsity Press, 1983), 33–38; J. Baskin, "The Separation of Women in Rabbinic Judaism," in *Women, Religion,*

*and Social Change,* ed. Y. Haddad and E. Findly (Albany, N.Y.: State University of New York, 1985), 6.

8. See Nathanson, "Reflections on the Silent Woman," 260, and Baskin, "Separation of Women," 10.

9. See, for example, Colin Brown, "Woman," *NIDNTT* 3:1057.

10. This was because they spoke authoritatively to men. In Deborah's case it was to Barak, her general. In Huldah's case it was to the king of Judah.

11. For further discussion, see Joachim Jeremias, *Jerusalem in the Time of Jesus* (Philadelphia: Fortress Press, 1969), 363; and J. Neuffer, "First Century Cultural Backgrounds in the Greco Roman Empire," in *Symposium on the Role of Women in the Church,* ed. J. Neuffer (Plainfield, N.J.: General Council of the Seventh Day Adventist Church, 1984), 62.

12. Josephus states that Jewish law did not admit women as legal witnesses in courts of justice because it couldn't be guaranteed that they would tell the truth ( *Jewish Antiquities* 4.8.15 §219). No such stipulation, however, can be found in Israel's law code. It also appears to be in conflict with a number of Mishnaic rulings regarding the testimony and vows of single women (see p. 77). It may, however, have been a scribal ruling during Josephus's time and would explain why female witnesses to the resurrection of Christ do not appear in church tradition (see, for example, 1 Cor. 15:1–11).

13. The precedent for a daughter to inherit is already found in Mosaic times. The daughters of Zelophehad claimed the right to inherit their father's property and won their case (Num. 27:1–11). Numbers 27:8 states: "If a man dies and leaves no son, turn his inheritance over to his daughter." The only condition was that the girl marry someone from her father's tribe (Num. 36:1–12).

14. As Randall Chesnutt observes, with the advent of these first-century documents no self-respecting scholar can picture the Israelite woman as mere chattel ("Jewish Women," 127–30).

15. On the education of Jewish children, see Ferguson, *Backgrounds,* 84–85.

16. For further discussion about Jewish women and divorce, see L. Swidler, *Women in Judaism: The Status of Women in Formative Judaism* (Metuchen, N.J.: Scarecrow Press, n.d.), 157–62; Nathanson, "Reflections on the Silent Woman," 264; Ben Witherington, *Women in the Ministry of Jesus* (Cambridge: Harvard University Press, 1984), 5; Neuffer, "Cultural Backgrounds," 65.

17. For Jewish legislation regarding divorce, see Jacob Neusner, "From Scripture to Mishnah," *Journal of Jewish Studies* 30 (1979): 147.

18. For further information on the public roles of Jewish women, see Jeremias, *Jerusalem in the Time of Jesus,* 362; Ross Kraemer, "Hellenistic Jewish Women: The Epigraphical Evidence," in the 1986 *Society of Biblical Literature Seminar Papers,* 194–95; Chestnutt, "Jewish Women," 127; and Nathanson, "Reflections on the Silent Woman," 263–64.

19. See, for example, Ross Kraemer, "Ecstasy and Possession: The Attraction of Women to the Cult of Dionysos," *Harvard Theological Review* 72 (1979): 74.

20. For further discussion, see Blundell, *Women in Ancient Greece,* 54.

21. In Diogenes Laertius's *Antisthenes* 6.12.

22. See the helpful overview by L. Swidler, "Greco-Roman Feminism and Reception of the Gospel," in *Traditio-Krisis-Renovatio aus Theologischer Sicht,* ed. B. Jaspert (Marburg: N.G. Elwert, 1976), 42; and Neuffer, "Cultural Backgrounds," 67.

23. See Cantrella, *Pandora's Daughters,* 74.

24. For the primary materials, see Mary R. Lefkowitz and Maureen Fant, *Women's Life in Greece and Rome: A Source Book in Translation,* 1st ed. (Baltimore: Johns Hopkins University Press, 1982), 27–31; compare Pomeroy, *Goddesses,* 73.

25. For discussion, see L. Swidler, "Greco-Roman Feminism," 46.

26. For the evidence, see Van Bremen, "Women and Wealth," 231–33.

27. The presence of women politarchs in Macedonian cities bears testimony to this development (*CIG* 2.5.2–3; *IG* 9.2). For further discussion, see Ferguson, *Backgrounds,* 61.

28. For further discussion, see Neuffer, "Cultural Backgrounds," 69.

29. For more about the educational advances of women, see Pomeroy, *Goddesses,* 136; and L. Swidler, "Greco-Roman Feminism," 41–55.

30. See Dyfri Williams, "Women on Athenian Vases: Problems of Interpretation," Cameron and Kuhrt, eds., *Images of Women,* 94; and Ferguson, *Backgrounds,* 57–58.

31. Only Jewish law continued to maintain that the right of divorce belonged solely to the husband. See ibid., 56–57.

32. Ben Witherington, *Women in the Earliest Churches* (Cambridge: Harvard University Press, 1988), 12. For a general overview, see Pomeroy, *Goddesses,* 125.

33. For further information, see Pomeroy, *Goddesses,* 134–36; and Van Bremen, "Women and Wealth," 228.

34. For the primary sources, see Lefkowitz and Fant, *Women's Life in Greece and Rome,* 23–24.

35. For a treatment of the public roles of women, see Van Bremen, "Women and Wealth," 229; Pomeroy, *Goddesses,* 127; Ferguson, *Backgrounds,* 58; and L. Swidler "Greco-Roman Feminism," 46.

36. For an overview of Roman women, see L. Swidler, "Greco-Roman Feminism," 53; Nathanson, "Reflections on the Silent Woman," 278; Witherington, *Women in the Earliest Churches,* 17–18; Neuffer, "Cultural Backgrounds," 71–76; Pomeroy, *Goddesses,* 159; and Ferguson, *Backgrounds,* 58.

37. Pomeroy, *Goddesses,* 175–76.

38. For further discussion, see Pomeroy, *Goddesses,* 170; and Neuffer, "Cultural Backgrounds," 72.

39. For further information about the legal status of Roman women, see Gregory Sterling, "Women in the Hellenistic and Roman Worlds (323 B.C.E.–138 C.E.)," in *Essays on Women in Earliest Christianity,* ed. Carroll Osborne, vol. 1 (Joplin, Miss.: College Press, 1993), 69–70; Pomeroy, *Goddesses,* 177, 209; Nathanson, "Reflections on the Silent Woman," 270; R. MacMullen, "Women in Public in the Roman Empire," *Historia* 29 (1980): 210–11; and John Stambaugh and David Balch, *The New Testament in Its Social Environment* (Philadelphia: Westminster Press), 112.

40. At first, widows were allowed only one year after the death of their spouse before they were required to remarry (which caused an uproar). This was later changed to three years.

41. For further details about Roman marriages, see L. Swidler, "Greco-Roman Feminism," 53; JoAnn McNamara, "Wives and Widows in Early Christian Thought," *International Journal of Women's Studies* 2 (1979): 576–78; Neuffer, "Cultural Backgrounds," 73; Pomeroy, *Goddesses,* 209; Sterling, "Women in the Hellenistic and Roman Worlds," 64; and Stambaugh and Balch, *Social Environment,* 112. On *univira,* see M. Lightman and W. Ziesel's article, "Univira: An Example of Continuity and Change in Roman Society," *Church History* 46 (1977): 21–25.

42. The trend during Roman times was to shift greater and greater administrative responsibilities on the shoulders of the mistress (e.g., managing the estates and businesses). A common thought is that this shift was due to Roman men being away from their homes for long periods of time to serve in the army or in some governmental capacity.

43. For further discussion on the Roman mistress, see Lightman and Ziesel, "Univira," 21–24; and Cotter, "Women's Authority Roles," 358–59.

44. On the public roles of women, see Pomeroy, *Goddesses,* 200; Meeks, *First Urban Christians,* 24; and Macmullen, "Women in Public," 210.

45. *Update: Newsletter of the Evangelical Women's Caucus* 10, no. 3 (fall 1986), 4.

46. For a typical statement of this position, see Raymond Ortlund, "Male-Female Equality and Male Headship," in Grudem and Piper, *Recovering,* 95–112.

47. The three parallel clauses are as follows:
> So God created humankind in his image.
> in the image of God he created them;
> Male and female he created them (Gen. 1:27 NRSV).

48. For further discussion, see John Oswalt, *"Bāśār,"* in *Theological Wordbook of the Old Testament,* ed. R. L. Harris, G. L. Archer, and B. K. Waltke, 2 vols. (Chicago: Moody Press, 1980), 1:136; and Claus Westermann, *Genesis 1–11,* trans. John J. Scullion (Minneapolis: Augsburg, 1981), 233. In some places in the Old Testament the term *flesh* means *clan* or *kindred* (e.g., Lev. 18:6; 25:49). Becoming "one flesh" would then be the equivalent of becoming a blood relative (although this seems less likely in the context).

49. For a more detailed treatment of Genesis 2:23–24, see Walter Brueggemann, "Of the Same Flesh and Bone (GN 2, 23a)," *Catholic Biblical Quarterly* 32 (1970): 532–42; Marsha M. Wilfong, "Genesis 2.18–24," *Interpretation* 42 (1988): 58–63; Victor Hamilton, *The Book of Genesis: Chapters 1–17* (Grand Rapids: Eerdmans, 1990), 181; and Gordon Wenham, *Genesis 1–15,* Word Biblical Commentary, vol. 1 (Waco, Tex.: Word, 1987), 71.

50. See John Oswalt, *"Kābaš,"* in *Theological Workbook,* ed. Harris, Archer, and Waltke, 1:430.

51. Some find a divinely prescribed distinction of roles in Genesis 3:16–19, where mention is made of the woman's pain in childbearing and the man's toil in working the ground. To do so, however, is to overlook the nonprescriptive character of Genesis 3. Roles are prescribed in Genesis 1:28 ("God blessed them and said to them, 'Be fruitful and increase in number. . . . Rule over the fish of the sea. . . . '"). The facts regarding sin's impact is what one finds in Genesis 3, and these facts do not include role distinctions. Nor is the impact prescriptive. The marital norm throughout Scripture is Genesis 2:24, not Genesis 3:16 (for discussion, see pp. 103–8).

Why then the pairings of the woman and childbearing and the man and toiling the land in Genesis 3:16–19? They certainly do make sense. Only women can bear children, and certain physical tasks are more readily accomplished by men. Yet this is a far cry from saying that the woman's divinely ordained role is inside (i.e., the domestic sphere) and the man's divinely ordained role is outside (i.e., the public sphere). Nothing in Genesis 1–3 explicitly supports this.

52. For a more detailed treatment, see Thomas McComiskey, *"Iš,"* in *Theological Workbook,* ed. Harris, Archer, and Waltke, 1:38.

53. See, for example, Ortlund, "Male-Female Equality," 98.

54. For discussion, see George Ramsey, "Is Name-Giving an Act of Domination in Genesis 2:23 and Elsewhere?" *Catholic Biblical Quarterly* 50 (1988): 33; and Anthony Thiselton, "The Supposed Power of Words in the Biblical Writings," *Journal of Theological Studies* 25 (1974): 283–99.

55. Paul is the sole biblical writer to appeal to the priority of Adam over Eve. Although some have maintained that "Adam was formed first, then Eve" in 1 Timothy 2:13 denotes personal superiority (and so the male's headship), *first/then* usage elsewhere in the New Testament is clearly temporal in nature (see, for example, Mark 4:28; 1 Cor. 15:46;

1 Thess. 4:16–17; 1 Tim. 3:10; and James 3:17; the one exception is Heb. 7:2 where *prōton . . . epeita* means "first, . . . then also"). In fact, Paul uses it in this very way just ten verses later. Deacons, he states, must be tested "first" *(prōton)* and "then" *(eita)* let them serve (1 Tim. 3:10). For further discussion, see p. 179.

A reasonable backdrop for Paul's appeal is the Ephesian cult of Artemis and its teaching that Artemis was created first and then her male consort. See page 178.

56. "Genesis 1–3 and the Male/Female Role Relationship," *Grace Theological Journal* 2 (1981): 21–33.

57. "Traditional View," 40–41.

58. "A Male Leadership View," in *Women in Ministry: Four Views,* ed. B. Clouse and R. G. Clouse (Downers Grove, Ill.: InterVarsity Press, 1989), 75.

59. Some would translate the first part of verse 16 as two separate pronouncements: "I will greatly increase your toil [i.e., the woman's efforts in farming the land] and your childbearing." See, for example, Richard Hess, "The Roles of the Woman and the Man in Genesis 3," *Themelios* 18 (1993): 16; Carol Meyers, *Discovering Eve* (New York: Oxford University Press, 1988), 105; and Richard Davidson, "The Theology of Sexuality in the Beginning: Genesis 3," *Andrews University Seminary Studies* 26 (1988): 124. Since the second clause seems to restate the first clause ("with pain you will give birth to children"), the first clause is more likely a hendiadys (two phrases expressing one idea): "I will greatly increase your toil in childbearing." For further discussion, see Westermann, *Genesis 1–11,* 262.

60. For this position, see Ortlund, "Male-Female Equality," 107–9; Foh, "Male Leadership View," 75; Evans, *Women in the Bible,* 19; and Hamilton, *Book of Genesis,* 202.

61. See, for example, Adrien Bledstein, "Are Women Cursed in Genesis 3.6?", in *A Feminist Companion to Genesis,* ed. A. Brenner (Sheffield: JSOT Press, 1993), 145.

62. For further discussion, see Irvin Busenitz, "Woman's Desire for Man: Genesis 3:16 Reconsidered," *Grace Theological Journal* 7 (1986): 208; and Joy Elasky Fleming, *Man and Woman in Biblical Unity: Theology From Genesis 2–3* (St. Paul: Christians for Biblical Equality, 1993), 40.

63. See, for example, Wenham, *Genesis 1–15,* 81.

64. This is the position of Foh, "Male Leadership View," 75–76; and Ortlund, "Male-Female Equality," 107.

65. For this position, see Robert Vasholz, "'He (?) will rule over you': A Thought on Genesis 3:16," *Presbyterion* 20 (1994): 51.

66. See LSJ, s.v.

67. For further discussion, see Karl Rengstorf's study of οἰκοδεσπότης in the *Theological Dictionary of New Testament Theology,* 2:49.

68. For more details, see William Lillie, "The Pauline House-Tables," *Expository Times* 86 (1975): 182.

69. See, for example, Wayne Grudem who argues that *kephalē* never means "source," "The Meaning of *Kephalē* ('Head'): A Response to Recent Studies," in *Recovering Biblical Manhood and Womanhood,* ed. W. Grudem and J. Piper (Wheaton: Crossway Books, 1991, 425–68).

70. See, for example, Gilbert Bilezikian who argues that *kephalē* as "ruler" was foreign to the Greeks in New Testament times (*Beyond Sex Roles* [Grand Rapids: Baker, 1985], 215–52). Compare Stephen Bedale, "The Meaning of κεφαλή in the Pauline Epistles," *Journal of Theological Studies* 5 (1954): 211–12.

71. There is no evidence in early Greek writings that *kephalē* was used in the sense of "ruler." Neither Liddell-Scott-Jones's *Greek-English Lexicon* nor Moulton and Milligan's *The Vocabulary of the Greek Testament Illustrated from the Papyri and Other Non-Literary*

*Sources* (Grand Rapids: Eerdmans, reprint edition 1982) give examples of *kephalē* with this meaning. The first time *kephalē* appears with the meaning of "ruler" is in the late B.C. and early A.D. period. See Joseph Fitzmyer, "*Kephalē* in I Corinthians 11:3," *Interpretation* 47 (1993): 54.

72. The nominative case of both phrases makes it clear that *kephalē tēs ekklēsias* and *autos sōtēr tou sōmatos* are in apposition and, hence, parallel ideas.

73. See Ceslas Spicq, *Theological Lexicon of the New Testament,* trans. James D. Ernest (Peabody, Mass.: Hendrickson, 1994), 2:184.

74. Ephesians 5:30 in the Western and Byzantine families of manuscripts, versions, and Fathers from the second century on reads, "For we are members of his body, of his flesh and of his bones."

75. The NRSV (revision of the RSV)and the NLT (revision of the Living Bible) retain the "husband-wife" language. The CEV (revision of the TEV) in line with most modern translations says "a man is the head over a woman."

76. Louw and Nida's *Greek-English Lexicon of the New Testament* (based on semantic domains) helps us see the social overtones of Paul's language. *Aischros* ("shameful") means to act in defiance of social and moral standards with resulting disgrace, embarrassment, and shame (88.149–150). *Atimia* ("disgraceful") pertains to not having honor or respect because of low status (87.71–72). *Prepon* ("proper") concerns what is fitting or right, with the implication of possible moral judgment involved (66.1).

77. Jerome Murphy-O'Connor, "Sex and Logic in 1 Corinthians 11:2–16," *Catholic Biblical Quarterly* 42 (1980): 485–86, may not be far off the mark when he supposes Paul is concerned that the Corinthians' actions would be read by outsiders in a homosexual light.

78. For an overview of current hairstyles, see Cynthia Thompson, "Hairstyles, Head-coverings and St. Paul: Portraits from Roman Corinth," *Biblical Archeologist* 51 (1988): 99–115.

79. *Anti* plus the genitive in 1 Corinthians 11:15 most likely denotes equivalency. Long hair is given "in place of" or "for" a covering. See BAGD s.v. *Peribolaion* is anything that covers around—like clothing, a bedcover, a chariot cover, a covering for the feet, and a dressing gown. See LSJ s.v.

80. It is wrong to say that *epi* plus the genitive demands a hairdo piled up on the head, as opposed to a veil that covers the head (e.g., Jerome Murphy-O'Connor, "Sex and Logic," 265–74). The preposition *epi* is the opposite of *hypo* ("under") and differs from *hyper* ("above") in implying actual rest upon some object. This would fit either hair piled "upon" the head or a veil "over" the head. See Murray Harris, "Prepositions and Theology in the Greek New Testament," in *New International Dictionary,* ed. Colin Brown, 3:1193.

81. See Plutarch *Moralia* 200F, where the language is virtually identical to that of Paul's: "He was walking with his toga covering his head" *(kata tēs kephalēs echōn to himation)*.

82. For a discussion of first-century customs regarding head coverings, see Richard Oster, "When Men Wore Veils to Worship: The Historical Context of 1 Corinthians 11.4," *New Testament Studies* 34 (1988): 495; Mark Black, "1 Cor. 11:2–16—A Re-investigation," in *Essays on Women,* ed. Osborne, 1:201–2; Cynthia Thompson, "Portraits from Roman Corinth,"112; and David Gill, "The Importance of Roman Portraiture for Head-Coverings in 1 Corinthians 11:2–16," *Tyndale Bulletin* 41 (1990): 251.

## Chapter 3: *Can Women Hold Positions of Authority?*

1. Whether women can be ordained is also a hotly debated question today. Unfortunately, both the term and the concept are lacking in the pages of the New Testament. Commissioning for a particular ministry is more what we find. The church at Antioch commissioned Saul and Barnabas as missionaries (Acts 13:1–3). Elders were commissioned at Ephesus (1 Tim. 5:17–22); Timothy was commissioned as an evangelist (1 Tim. 4:14; 2 Tim. 1:6); and Paul was commissioned as an apostle to the Gentiles (Acts 9:17–19; 22:12–16; Rom. 15:15–16). Yet this is a far cry from how churches use the term *ordain* today. In my denomination, for example, ordination authorizes a person to preach the Word, administer the sacraments, and bear rule in the church (*The Covenant Book of Worship,* The Evangelical Covenant Church [Chicago, Ill.: Covenant Press, 1981], 298).

2. For an overview of the concept of authority in Paul's letters, see L. Belleville, "Authority," in *Dictionary of Paul and His Letters,* ed. G. Hawthorne, R. Martin, and D. Reid (Downers Grove, Ill.: InterVarsity Press, 1993).

3. The only possible exception is found in 1 Corinthians 11. In verse 10 Paul states, "For this reason a woman [who prays and prophesies] ought to have *authority* [perhaps *power* or even *freedom*] on her head because of the angels" (AT italics added). While the translation is fairly straightforward, the meaning of the verse is not. Interpretations are wide-ranging. Ones that have been largely rejected because they are extraneous to the context include the following: A woman's head covering is: (1) a shield from the prying eyes of angels, visitors, or other men in the congregation, (2) a charm or phylactery to ward off evil spirits or jealous angels, and (3) a sign of the woman's subjection to her husband (a grammatical and lexical impossibility).

The following provide a better contextual fit. A woman's head covering is: (1) a badge of her own dignity and power (to move about in public); or (2) a sign of her God-given authority (to pray and prophesy in worship).

If (as some argue) this verse has nothing to do with head covering, then we can add: (1) A woman should have prophetic authority over her metaphorical head (i.e., men); and (2) a woman exercises control over her literal head by covering it.

Yet, in spite of the plethora of interpretations, two things are clear. First, verse 10 in its plain, grammatical sense speaks of an authority that a woman herself possesses (unless we resort to textual emendation, as some are inclined to do). Second, Paul's basic concern in the passage is with the proper attire of women when they pray or prophesy in public. This makes head covering as a sign of a woman's authority to engage in ministry activities the better option by far. It also fits with "on account of the angels." The presence of angels during worship was a common enough Jewish belief, especially in the role of upholders of order and propriety (e.g., *Rule of the Congregation* 2.3–9).

See the more detailed treatment of 1 Corinthians 11 in the previous chapter (pp. 126–31).

4. See J. P. Louw and E. A. Nida, *Greek-English Lexicon* (New York: United Bible Society, 1989), s.v.; BAGD, s.v.; LSJ, s.v.

5. The Greek word *epimelēsetai* ("care for") stresses a person's ability to guide and nurture the community of believers.

6. The Greek word for *example (typos)* means literally to strike a blow or to leave an imprint (Louw and Nida, *Greek-English Lexicon,* s.v.). Today we might say that to be an example is to make a distinct impression on those around us.

7. See Louw and Nida, *Greek-English Lexicon,* s.v.; H. W. Beyer, ἐπισκέπτομαι, *Theological Dictionary of the New Testament,* 2:604.

8. *Episkopountes* ("serving as overseers") is missing from א* B and *cop^sa*. However, 𝔓72, A, and other manuscripts contain it. The omission could have been prompted by a perceived redundancy after *poimanate* ("Be shepherds") and would further support the fact that these two terms are virtual synonyms.

9. See Louw and Nida, *Greek-English Lexicon,* s.v.; L. Coenen, "πρεσβύτερος" in *New International Dictionary,* ed. Brown, 1:192–200.

10. This is suggested as well by references in the apostolic fathers to the elders standing in the place of the council of the apostles. See, for example, Ignatius *Trallians* 2.2 and *Smyrnaeans* 8.1.

11. As Walter Liefeld notes, the Greek term for *ministry* (which has to do with giving service or assistance) has become *the ministry,* that is, a class of professionals. ("Women and the Nature of Ministry," *Journal of the Evangelical Theological Society* 30 [1987]: 54).

12. See, for example, Kevin Giles's treatment of house-church leadership in *Patterns of Ministry,* 27–35.

13. For this position, see James I. Packer, "Let's Stop Making Women Presbyters," *Christianity Today* 35 (Feb. 1991): 20; and James A. Borland, "Women in the Life and Teachings of Jesus," in *Biblical Manhood and Womanhood,* ed. Piper and Grudem, 120.

14. For this position, see F. W. Grosheide, *The First Epistle to the Corinthians* (Grand Rapids: Eerdmans, 1953), 341–43. "Women," he says, "are allowed to prophesy but not when the congregation officially meets."

15. For this position, see Michael Stitziner, "Cultural Confusion and the Role of Women in the Church: A Study of 1 Timothy 2:8–14," *Calvary Baptist Theological Journal* 4 (1988): 32–33.

16. It is not clear who "the others" are. They could be the other prophets, in which case verse 29 would read: "Two or three prophets should speak, and the other [prophets] should weigh carefully what is said" (1 Cor. 14:29). "The others" could also be the rest of the congregation. In 1 Thessalonians 5:21 Paul urges the Thessalonian congregation to test prophecies (with the intent to prove their genuineness). They could even be those who have the gift of discernment. In Paul's list of spiritual gifts (two chapters earlier), the gift of prophecy is paired with the ability to discern spirits (1 Cor. 12:10).

This last option seems the likely one. In the immediately preceding verses, it is Paul's expectation that speaking in tongues will be followed by interpretation (1 Cor. 14:27–28). It is natural then to think that prophecy would be subjected to the scrutiny of those gifted to determine whether the speaking is from God.

17. The United Bible Societies' and Nestle-Aland's current Greek text editions paragraph at verse 33b and then again at verse 37. This is highly misleading. The fact that some early manuscripts and versions place verses 34–35 after verse 40 means that verses 33b–36 were not seen as a unit. Add to this the fact that 𝔓46, א, A, D, and 33 have a breaking mark at the beginning of verse 34 and at the end of verse 35.

18. For a detailed discussion of codex Fuldensis, see Philip Payne, "Fuldensis, Sigla For Variants in Vaticanus, and 1 Cor. 14.34-5," *New Testament Studies* 41 (1995): 240–62. To this evidence should be added the fact that there is a bar-umlaut text-critical siglum in codex Vaticanus indicating awareness of a textual problem at the end of verse 33 (ibid., 250–60).

19. The fact that verses 34–35 are found in two places in the text tradition casts suspicion on their originality. A marginal note is a reasonable way to account for the dislocation of these verses. For further discussion (and supporters), see Gordon Fee, *The First Epistle to the Corinthians* (Grand Rapids: Eerdmans, 1987), 699–705; Payne, "Fuldensis," 240–62; Peter Lockwood, "Does 1 Corinthians 14:34–35 Exclude Women from the Pastoral Office?" *Lutheran Theological Journal* 30 (1996): 30–37; Jacobus Petzer,

"Reconsidering the Silent Women of Corinth—A Note on 1 Corinthians 14:34–35," *Theologia Evangelica* 26 (1993): 132–38.

20. See, for example, Petzer, "Reconsidering the Silent Women," 133–37.

21. See, for example, Earle Ellis, who thinks that Paul (or his amanuensis at his bidding) added verses 34–35 in the margin of the manuscript before sending it on its way to Corinth ("The Silenced Wives of Corinth [1 Cor. 14:34–5]," in *New Testament Textual Criticism,* ed. E. J. Epp and Gordon Fee [Oxford: Clarendon Press, 1981], 213–20).

22. As Scott Bartchy wisely notes, since no Old Testament submission text can be found, the word *law* (1 Cor. 14:34) should not be capitalized as it has been in the NASB, NIV, and others ("Power, Submission and Sexual Identity among the Early Christians," in *Essays on New Testament Christianity,* ed. W. C. Robert [Cincinnati: Standard, 1978], 69–70).

23. For a discussion of Jewish and Greek marriage contracts, see pages 79–81 and 88–89. Other suggestions include submission to the elders of the church, submission to those who weigh prophecies, and submission to one's prophetic spirit.

24. Women in both native and imported cults were far from silent, and there simply is no Mishnaic ruling excluding women from speaking in the Jewish worship service. There were some who thought it was disgraceful for a woman to make a public speech. Cato (195 B.C.), for instance, thought a public demonstration by women protesting new legislation that limited their use of luxury items was shameful. "What kind of behavior is this?" he asked. "Running around in public, blocking streets and speaking to other women's husbands! Could you [the women] not have asked your own husbands the same thing at home?" (Livy *History of Rome* 34). Yet, Cato was merely expressing an opinion, not quoting Roman law.

25. For a good example of this position, see Richard and Catherine Kroeger, "Pandemonium and Silence at Corinth," in *Women and the Ministries of Christ,* ed. R. Hestenes and L. Curley (Pasadena, Calif.: Fuller Theological Seminary, 1979), 49–55; and Catherine Kroeger, "Strange Tongues or Plain Talk," *Daughters of Sarah* 12 (1986): 10–13. "As the law says" would then be Roman law. As the Kroegers point out, there were a number of Greek and Roman legislative attempts to regulate religious frenzy (connected with the cults of Dionysus and Bacchus).

26. Joseph Dillow, *Speaking in Tongues: Seven Crucial Questions* (Grand Rapids: Zondervan, 1975), 170, believes that Paul is forbidding women to exercise the gift of tongues in the church. There is nothing, however, in the context to support such a position.

27. For this position, see James Hurley, "Did Paul Require Veils or the Silence of Women? A Consideration of 1 Cor. 11:2–16 and 1 Cor. 14:33b–36," *Westminster Theological Journal* 35 (1973): 190–220; Ellis, "Silenced Wives," 216–18; and Wayne Grudem, *The Gift of Prophecy in 1 Corinthians* (Lanham, Md.: University Press of America, 1982), 249–55.

28. For this position, see W. F. Orr and J. A. Walther, *I Corinthians,* Anchor Bible (Garden City, N.Y.: Doubleday, 1976), 312–13; C. K. Barrett (if 1 Cor. 14:34–35 is authentic), *A Commentary on the First Epistle to the Corinthians,* 2d ed., Harper's New Testament Commentaries (New York: Harper & Row, 1971; reprint Peabody, Mass.: Hendrickson, 1987), 332. Compare Ann Jervis, "1 Corinthians 14:34–35: A Reconsideration of Paul's Limitation of the Free Speech of Some Corinthian Women," *Journal for the Study of the New Testament* 58 (1995): 60–73.

29. See, for example, G. Engel, "Let the Woman Learn in Silence, II," *Expository Times* 16 (1904–05): 189–90; Bartchy, "Power, Submission and Sexual Identity," 68–70.

30. For this position, see Neal Flanagan and Edwina Snyder, "Did Paul Put Down Women in 1 Cor. 14:34–36?", *Biblical Theology Bulletin* 11 (1981): 10–12; Chris

Ukachukwu Manus, "The Subordination of the Women in the Church: 1 Cor. 14:33b–36 Reconsidered," *Revue Africaine de Theologie* 8 (1984): 183–95; David Odell-Scott, "Let the Women Speak in Church: An Egalitarian Interpretation of 1 Cor. 13:33b–36," *Biblical Theology Bulletin* 13 (1983): 90–93; compare 17 (1987): 100–3; Linda McKinnish Bridges, "Silencing the Corinthian Men, Not the Women," in *The New Has Come,* ed. A. T. Neil and V. G. Neely (Washington, D.C.: Southern Baptist Alliance, 1989); Charles Talbert, "Biblical Criticism's Role: The Pauline View of Women as a Case in Point," in *Unfettered Word,* ed. R. B. James (Waco: Word Books, 1987), 62–71.

Verse 36 begins with the particle ἤ (translated "What!" in the KJV and RSV), which supporters of this position say is used to reject or refute what has come before. See Daniel Arichea, "The Silence of Women in the Church," *Bible Translator* 46 (1995): 101–12. The difficulty, though, is that there is no indication that verses 34–35 are a quotation such as one finds elsewhere in 1 Corinthians (e.g., 1 Cor. 6:12, 13; 7:1; 8:1; 10:23). In addition, while ἤ can denote an exclamation expressing disapproval, Liddell and Scott's *Greek-English Lexicon* lists only two instances, and in both cases there is a double ἤ ἤ and not the single ἤ we have in 1 Corinthians 11:36 (which is surely why the revisions of the KJV and the RSV drop the "What!").

31. Some have resolved the difficulty by arguing for the non-Pauline authorship of these verses (and of the entire letter, for that matter). It is proposed that a second-century churchman penned these words in Paul's name to deal more effectively with women (spurred on by false teachers) who sought to challenge the structure of male leadership in the church and in the family. A major difficulty, though, is that the external evidence unanimously supports Pauline authorship of the passage, and in terms of the letter itself, only Romans and 1 Corinthians are more strongly attested. The first explicit Pauline attribution occurs around A.D. 175 (Irenaeus *Against Heresies* 3.3.3). By A.D. 200 it was accepted and used in such diverse geographical locations as Rome (Muratorian Canon), Carthage (Tertullian), France (Irenaeus), and Alexandria (Clement). Pauline authorship was not seriously questioned by anyone until the nineteenth century.

32. The NIV translation of 1 Timothy 5:20, "Those who sin are to be rebuked publicly, so that the others may take warning," is misleading. The tense and mood are present indicative. Paul is not treating a hypothetical possibility but a present reality. He did not use the subjunctive: "Should any sin, they are to be rebuked." "Those who are continuing to sin" is a more accurate rendering of the Greek. In the broader context, this sinning is undoubtedly of a heretical sort.

33. Some would say that 1 Corinthians 11:8–9 is another passage that appeals to Adam's seniority. Yet, the language of the text is biological, not hierarchical (or even sequential). Created "from *(ek)* man" is a reference to the creation of woman from the first man's rib. This bespeaks sameness, not hierarchy (Gen. 2:18, "I will make a counterpart" [AT] and Gen. 2:23, "bone of my bones and flesh of my flesh"). The woman, Paul states, was also created "for man" (*dia* plus the accusative), recalling the woman's raison d'etre, namely, to be a partner or helpmate (and not the hired help, as some would maintain; Gen. 2:18, 20). For discussion, see pages 97–103.

34. This is also the case for the rest of the New Testament. See *sigaō* in Luke 9:36; 18:39; 20:26; Acts 12:17; 15:12, 13) and *sigē* (the noun) in Acts 21:40 and Revelation 8:1. For *hēsychia* (and related forms) meaning "calm" or "restful," see Luke 23:56; Acts 11:18; 21:14; 1 Thess. 4:11; 2 Thess. 3:12; 1 Peter 3:4. For the sense "not speak," see Luke 14:4 and, perhaps, Acts 22:2.

Stitziner, "Cultural Confusion," 31, mistakenly states that "three of the four uses of the term *esuchia* [sic] in the NT (Acts 22:2; 1 Tim. 2:11–12; 2 Thess. 3:12) are translated *silence* by the major lexicons." The standard New Testament Greek lexicon (Arndt-

Gingrich-Bauer-Danker's *A Greek-English Lexicon of the New Testament*) gives "quietness, rest" for 2 Thessalonians 3:12 and "quiet down" for Acts 22:2. First Timothy 2:11–12 is not listed. The standard biblical and extra-biblical Greek lexicon (Liddell and Scott's *A Greek-English Lexicon*) does not include any of these passages.

35. For further discussion, see Kevin Giles, "Response," in *The Bible and Women's Ministry: An Australian Dialogue,* ed. A. Nichols (Canberra, Australia: Acorn Press, 1990), 73.

36. We also need to look carefully at the public character of convicting (1 Cor. 14:24), instructing (vv. 19, 31), and exhorting (v. 31) the congregation.

37. See Phil Payne, "Libertarian Women in Ephesus: A Response to Douglas J. Moo's Article, '1 Timothy 2:11–15: Meaning and Significance,'" *Trinity Journal* 2 NS (1981): 175.

38. There are many words in the New Testament that mean "to rule over" or "to exercise authority over" in a positive sense. The most common are *exousiazō, krinō, kyrieuō, katakyrieuō, archō,* and *hēgeomai.* Yet, Paul picks none of these.

39. For an extended treatment, see Leland Wilshire, "The TLG Computer and Further Reference to ΑΥΘΕΝΤΕΩ in 1 Timothy 2.12," *New Testament Studies* 34 (1988): 120–34; and his more recent article, "1 Timothy 2:12 Revisited: A Reply to Paul W. Barnett and Timothy J. Harris," *The Evangelical Quarterly* 65 (1993): 43–55.

40. George Knight III has argued that *authentein* in *BGU* 1208 and Philodemus has the positive sense "to exercise authority over" ("ΑΥΘΕΝΤΕΩ in Reference to Women in 1 Timothy 2.12," *New Testament Studies* 30 [1984]: 143–54). The Greek texts themselves, however, do not suggest such a meaning.

The Berlin papyrus recounts a disagreement between the author and another individual regarding the fare that should be paid to the boatman. "I exercised authority over him" hardly fits the context. Nor can the preposition *pros* be construed as "over" *(kamou authentēkotos pros auton).* It must mean something like "I had my way *with* him"—or perhaps as Preisigke *(Wordbook of the Greek Papyri)* translates: "I stood firm *(fest auftreten)."*

The Philodemus text is too fragmented to be certain about the exact wording. What we have is: *hoi hrētores . . . diamachontai kai syn authent[ ]sin an[ ].* The editor's guess is *authent[ou]sin an[axin].* The text would then read: "These orators . . . even fight with powerful lords [or possibly, gods]." But this, in any event, is merely a guess. In neither case, however, is the sense "to exercise authority over" an appropriate one.

41. One first begins to see a positive usage of the noun *authentēs* in the writings of the church fathers. See, for example, Hermas *Parables* 9.5.6, "Let us go to the tower, for the owner of the tower is coming to inspect it."

42. Philip Payne highlighted the importance of the *neither/nor* construction in a paper he presented to the Evangelical Theological Society's annual meeting on November 21, 1986. His own position is that *neither/nor* in this verse joins two closely associated couplets (e.g., "hit n'run," "teach n'domineer").

43. Other examples include:

| | |
|---|---|
| to pair synonyms | neither labors nor spins (Matt. 6:28) |
| | neither quarreled nor cried out (Matt. 12:19) |
| | neither abandoned nor given up (Acts 2:27) |
| | neither leave nor forsake (Heb. 13:5) |
| | neither run in vain nor labor in vain (Phil. 2:16) |
| to pair antonyms | neither a good tree nor a bad tree (Matt. 7:18) |
| | neither the one who did harm nor the one who was harmed (2 Cor. 7:12) |
| to pair closely related ideas | neither the desire nor the effort (Rom. 9:16) |
| | neither the sun nor the moon (Rev. 21:23) |

| to define a related purpose or goal | neither hears nor understands (i.e., hearing with the intent to understand, Matt. 13:13) neither dwells in temples made with human hands nor is served by human hands (i.e., dwells with a view to being served, Acts 17:24) |
| to move from the general to the particular | you know neither the day nor the hour (Matt. 25:13) I neither consulted with flesh and blood nor went up to Jerusalem to consult with those who were apostles before me (Gal. 1:16–17) |
| to define a natural progression of closely related ideas | born neither of blood, nor of the human will, nor of the will of man (John 1:13) neither the Christ, nor Elijah, nor the prophet (John 1:25) neither from man nor through man (Gal. 1:1) |

44. Along somewhat similar lines, Donald Kushke maintains that *oude* introduces an explanation: "to teach in an authoritative fashion" ("An Exegetical Brief on 1 Timothy 2:12," *Lutheran Quarterly* 88 [1991]: 64).

45. For further discussion of the cult of Artemis, see Sharon Gritz, *Paul, Women Teachers, and the Mother Goddess at Ephesus: A Study of 1 Timothy 2:9–15 in Light of the Religious and Cultural Milieu of the First Century* (Lanham, Md.: University Press of America, 1991), 31–41. See also the *Encyclopaedia Britannica*, 1997 CD, s.v. "Artemis."

46. Artemis was seen as the Mother Goddess. She was the mother of life, the nourisher of all creatures, and the power of fertility in nature. Maidens turned to her as the protector of their virginity; barren women sought her aid, and women in labor turned to her for help. Gritz, *Mother Goddess,* 31–34.

47. For a more detailed presentation, see Catherine Kroeger, "May Women Teach? Heresy in the Pastoral Epistles," *Reformed Journal* 30 (1980): 14–18; Steve Motyer, "Expounding 1 Timothy 2:8–15," *Vox Evangelica* 24 (1994): 100; Timothy Harris, "Why Did Paul Mention Eve's Deception? A Critique of Paul Barnett's Interpretation of 1 Timothy 2," *Evangelical Quarterly* 62 (1990): 345–47.

48. Compare: "All by itself the soil produces grain—first *[prōton]* the stalk, then *[eita]* the head, then *[eita]* the full kernel in the head" (Mark 4:28); "The spiritual did not come first *[prōton],* but the natural and then *[epeita]* the spiritual" (1 Cor. 15:46 AT); "But the wisdom that comes from heaven is first *[prōton]* of all pure; then *[epeita]* peace-loving, considerate . . ." (James 3:17).

49. For this position, see Culver, "Traditional View," 36.

50. For this position, see Michael Stitziner, "Cultural Confusion," 34; and James Hurley, *Man and Woman in Biblical Perspective* (Leicester, England: Inter-Varsity Press, 1981), 216.

## Epilogue

1. Gretchen Gaebelein Hull, *Equal to Serve: Women and Men in the Church and Home* (Old Tappan, N.J.: Fleming H. Revell, 1987).

# Selected Bibliography

Brooten, Bernadette J. *Women Leaders in the Ancient Synagogue.* Brown Judaic Studies 36. Chico, Calif.: Scholars Press, 1982. A groundbreaking work that carefully documents the religious and societal roles of Jewish women.

Cantrella, Eva. *Pandora's Daughters: The Role and Status of Women in Greek and Roman Antiquity.* Translated by M. B. Fant. Baltimore: Johns Hopkins University Press, 1967. An insightful study of the role and status of women in Greek and Roman antiquity.

Clouse, Bonnidell, and Robert Clouse. *Women in Ministry: Four Views.* Downers Grove, Ill.: InterVarsity Press, 1989. This volume includes traditionalist, male leadership, plural ministry, and egalitarian positions on the topic of women in ministry. The introduction presents a concise history of women in ministry. There are three respondents to each position.

Evans, Mary. *Women in the Bible.* Downers Grove, Ill.: InterVarsity Press, 1983. A concise and very readable overview of the topic.

France, R. T. *Women in the Church's Ministry.* Grand Rapids: Eerdmans, 1997. This brief volume (only ninety-six pages) is one of the most balanced and understandable treatments of the hermeneutical issues involved in dealing with biblical texts such as 1 Corinthians 11:3, 14:34–35, and 1 Timothy 2:11–15.

Giles, Kevin. *Patterns of Ministry among the First Christians.* Melbourne, Australia: Collin Dove, 1989. A helpful study of the major leadership roles in the early church.

———. "Response." In *The Bible and Women's Ministry: An Australian Dialogue,* edited by A. Nichols. Canberra, Australia: Acorn Press, 1990. One of the best treatments of the tough New Testament passages.

Grudem, Wayne, and John Piper, eds. *Recovering Biblical Manhood and Womanhood.* Wheaton: Crossway Books, 1991. This volume includes an extensive collection of essays from a traditionalist perspective.

Kraemer, Ross. *Her Share of the Blessings.* Oxford: Oxford University Press, 1992. One of the most readable works on the religious roles of women in Greco-Roman and Christian times.

———. "Hellenistic Jewish Women: The Epigraphical Evidence." In *Society of Biblical Literature Seminar Papers,* edited by Kent H. Richards, 183–200. Atlanta: Scholars Press, 1986. An insightful essay that raises the appropriate cautions in dealing with Jewish sources. The author takes Bernadette Brooten's work a step further.

———. *Maenads, Martyrs, Matrons, Monastics.* Philadelphia: Fortress Press, 1988. An important sourcebook on women's religions in the Greco-Roman world.

Kroeger, Catherine, and Richard Kroeger. *I Suffer Not a Woman.* Grand Rapids: Baker, 1992. An exhaustive and able treatment of 1 Timothy 2:11–15 by someone with expertise in classical languages.

Lefkowitz, Mary R., and Maureen Fant. *Women's Life in Greece and Rome: A Source Book in Translation.* 2d ed. Baltimore: Johns Hopkins University Press, 1992. A comprehensive, annotated compilation of primary sources dating from Homeric through Roman times.

Liefeld, Walter. "Women and the Nature of Ministry." *Journal of the Evangelical Theological Society* 30 (1987): 49–61. One of the most balanced and helpful treatments of women in leadership.

Mickelsen, Alvera, ed. *Women, Authority and the Bible.* Downers Grove, Ill.: InterVarsity Press, 1986. These essays were presented at the Evangelical Colloquium on Women and the Bible held October 9–11, 1984, in Oak Brook, Illinois.

Osborne, Carroll, ed. *Essays on Women in Earliest Christianity.* Vol. 1. Joplin, Miss.: College Press, 1993. This collection of essays is one of the most helpful and balanced studies of the roles of women in biblical times. No stone is left unturned in terms of the biblical materials.

Pomeroy, Sarah. *Goddesses, Whores, Wives, and Slaves: Women in Classical Antiquity.* New York: Schocken, 1995. A careful study of the lives of Greek and Roman women from classical through Roman times.

Van Bremen, Riet. "Women and Wealth." In *Images of Women in Antiquity.* Edited by A. Cameron and A. Kuhrt. Detroit: Wayne State University Press, 1987. A concise overview of the roles of wealthy women in the Greco-Roman world.


The egalitarian position on women is ably and understandably presented in the following volumes: Aída Spencer, *Beyond the Curse*, Peabody, Mass.: Hendrickson, 1985. Gilbert Bilezikian, *Beyond Sex Roles,* 2d ed., Grand Rapids: Baker, 1985. Ruth Tucker and Walter Liefeld, *Daughters of the Church,* Grand Rapids: Zondervan, 1987.

A readable presentation of the traditionalist position can be found in Susan Foh's *Women and the Word of God: A Response to Biblical Feminism*, Phillipsburg, N.J.: Presbyterian and Reformed Publishing Co., 1980, and Wayne House's *The Role of Women in Ministry Today,* Nashville: Thomas Nelson, 1990.

# Subject Index

# Scripture Index

Linda L. Belleville is professor of biblical literature at North Park Theological Seminary.